Fishing for Growth

**Export-led Development
in Peru, 1950-1967**

Fishing for Growth

Export-led Development
in Peru, 1950–1967

Michael Roemer

Harvard University Press
Cambridge, Massachusetts
1970

To Linda

Preface

I undertook this study as a doctoral dissertation in economics at the Massachusetts Institute of Technology. Two years in Nairobi as a planning officer for the Government of Kenya had convinced me that many, if not most, less developed countries could ill afford to indulge themselves in skepticism about the role of primary product exports in economic development: they had no viable alternatives. My aim was not only to complete a case study that would put export-led development in a favorable light, but also to draw some practical conclusions for other developing countries which must depend on primary exports to propel development. The reader will be able to judge the extent to which these goals have been accomplished by this investigation of export-led development in Peru.

All the research, except for some more recent updating of readily available data, was completed in 1966 and 1967. I spent five months in Lima during the first half of 1967, collecting data and conducting interviews on all aspects of fishmeal industry development and its impact on the Peruvian economy. Peruvian economic policy has taken a new, sharply different turn since 1967. The shift was in part a natural consequence of events during the export-led growth period, but was primarily due to autonomous policy decisions. I have refrained from any analysis or evaluation of the new policy, both because it is too early for any assessment and because I have no first-hand knowledge of the situation since 1967. It can be said that this is a study of an era that has ended, although of course its influence will be felt whatever the resolution of Peru's current situation.

My first thanks are due to Charles P. Kindleberger, whose remark during a class lecture gave me the idea for a study of Peru and whose enthusiastic support kept me going for the better part of two years. Shane Hunt and Wilson Brown gave support and encouragement in the formative stages of my work.

A National Science Foundation grant made possible my stay in Peru. Lima and environs are filled with businessmen and officials in whose debt I remain, but the large majority of them will consider their promised anonymity thanks enough. It would have been impossible to reach all these people without the sustenance of the *Banco Central de Reserva,* whose Sr. Ysidoro Korngold gave me a desk and invited me to use all the facilities of the bank for my research. The list of his colleagues who offered their help is too long to include here. Sr. Juan Lora Cortinez of the *Oficina Sectorial de Planificación Pesquera* and Sr. Ulises Robles Freyre of the Sociedad Nacional de Pesquería were generous with both time and data throughout my visit.

The observations of John R. Harris on the first draft led to significant improvements in later versions. I am grateful to Richard S. Eckaus for his guidance and to Gordon R. Sparks for his advice on the econometrics of Chapter 6.

My wife, Linda, has served at various times as typist, editor, and guardian of the sanctity of my study. Her forbearance made it possible to finish this book.

Michael Roemer

Washington, D.C.
August 1970

Contents

Figures

Tables

Fishing for Growth

**Export-led Development
in Peru, 1950-1967**

1

Introduction

From 1950 to 1967, Peru achieved one of the outstanding growth records among the less developed countries. Gross national product grew at a compound annual rate of 5.5% over the 17 years ending in 1967, rising to $5.7 billion in current prices. Per capita income grew at 2.9% a year, reaching $459 in 1967. The most notable feature of this growth was the key, if not dominant, role played by primary product exports through most of the period. Exports, in 1963 prices, grew at 7.0% a year over those 17 years and accounted for one-fifth of GNP in 1967, while export earnings expanded at 8.4% a year and provided $757 million of foreign exchange in 1967. During the boom years, 1958–1964, when GNP grew at 6.8% a year, export volume expanded by 10.7% a year.[1]

Export earnings came from a diversified and changing list of primary products. In 1950, cotton, sugar, and petroleum accounted for 63% of export value; in 1967, fish products, copper, iron ore, and cotton provided 69% of export earnings. Copper production underwent a major expansion with the opening of a new mine in 1960, and copper exports quadrupled in volume.[2] But the most spectacular growth was in the production and export of fishmeal, a high-protein additive to livestock feeds, which is manufactured in Peru from anchovy:[3] in the ten years from 1956 to 1965, fishmeal output increased at a *compound* rate of 42% a year, while export earnings multiplied by a factor of 111. The gross value of the industry's production amounted to only 0.1% of the real gross national product in 1955, but ten years later was the equivalent of 4.3% of GNP. Peru's ability to supply a large fraction of the growing demand for high-protein animal feed enabled it to leap from twentieth to first place among the fishing nations of the world by landing 8.9 million tons of raw fish in 1964.

Not only was the industry's expansion statistically impressive, it was also colorful. Fishmeal in Peru is a story of neophytes and adventurers, as well as experienced fish processors, scrambling to build highly profitable reduction plants to process the anchovy, which is found in great abundance along the Peruvian coast. In 1956, there were 27 plants producing fishmeal in Peru; but, by 1964, 157 factories were in production with a capacity over 50 times greater than eight years earlier. For those who felt unable to meet the technical or financial demands of an industrial operation, an alternative route of entry was available: fishing boats. All sorts of unqualified people, seeking a share of the lucrative business, bought purse seiners and sent them out under hired captains to catch anchovies for sale to the new reduction plants. Whatever the means of entry into the fishmeal industry, the equity capital involved was dwarfed by debt-financing, offered at short and medium term by banks, which liked the high interest rates that the new entrepreneurs were able and willing to pay, and by equipment suppliers, for obvious motives.

To supply the mushrooming demand for capital equipment, new industries were established in Peru. Ships were constructed, with or without qualified labor, and certainly without much capital, in empty lots and in the streets of Callao, Peru's major port. Three of these yards have survived to become major producers of fishing boats. Metal fabricators and construction firms built fish reduction equipment and plants, while the manufacturing of pumps, motors, nets, and other equipment was begun in Peru for the first time. Coastal towns were transformed by the new activity in fishmeal. Chimbote, the most notable example, experienced a three-year surge in which its population may have tripled to 85,000 in 1962.[4]

Although the dynamic effects of growth in the copper export sector were perhaps largely contained within the kind of enclave familiar to development economists, the stimuli from fishmeal expansion were successfully transmitted to the rest of the Peruvian economy. Fishmeal exports not only earned considerable foreign exchange, but also contributed substantially to industrial growth in Peru. Here is a case of a less developed country, a textbook example of an export-oriented economy, that has succeeded in promoting diversification and industrialization, not in spite of, but because of its primary product exports. Raw material exports have formed the leading sector in Peru's economic development, much as they did during the nineteenth and early twentieth centuries in North America, Argentina, Australia, New Zealand, and South Africa.

Peru's experience runs counter to the expectations of many economists who have focused attention on the shortcomings of export-led growth as a viable development strategy. Since the end of the forties, there has been a continuing debate in the literature about the role of foreign trade in the process of economic development. To simplify considerably, the line has been drawn between economists who uphold the traditional role of primary product exports as a leading sector in development and those who deprecate the dynamic potential of exports and espouse policies of import substitution and balanced growth. There is probably no "correct" position in this debate. The countries in the process of development are numerous and diverse. For some, a heavy dose of planned import substitution and forced industrialization will be an effective development strategy, while others should place greater reliance on an expanding primary export sector. The returns from further debate on a general or theoretical level are rapidly diminishing. There is far more to be gained from the provision of new data, aimed at delineating the conditions under which primary exports, import substitutes, or manufactured exports are more likely to lead to high and sustained growth rates.

There is, in fact, a growing literature of case studies relating the successes and failures of trade-centered growth strategies as they have been applied in recent years. Growth, at least partly through import substitution, in Mexico and Pakistan; the rapid growth in Taiwan and Korea led by manufactured exports; and the dominant role of expanding primary product exports in countries like Venezuela, Thailand, the Philippines, and Zambia are becoming familiar stories. This study of Peruvian fishmeal delves into the rather different case of a primary product export industry which not only provided foreign exchange to fuel development, but itself created strong backward linkages directly stimulating Peruvian industry. This contradicts the normal expectations that associate primary product exports either with foreign, technologically advanced enclaves or with traditional agriculture. However, the Peruvian experience with fishmeal is more than a curious exception. The major purpose in studying the industry is to extract the characteristics that were responsible for consequent growth in the domestic economy. When the description of fishmeal growth is reduced to fundamentals, it seems possible to apply the lessons of Peruvian fishmeal to other primary product export industries in other countries. This case may demonstrate that the nineteenth century strategy of primary export-led growth could be applicable on a larger scale in mid-twentieth century.

The best analytical tool for this purpose is the staple theory of economic development, which concentrates on the production function of the leading export sector as an explanation for the growth path of an economy. The next chapter discusses this concept, and the third chapter examines the arguments of those skeptics who hold that primary commodity exports are unlikely to be an effective vehicle for economic development in the twentieth century. Peru's growth record is analyzed in Chapter 4, and the focus is narrowed to the nature and history of the fishmeal industry in Chapter 5. The sixth chapter offers quantitative estimates of the production function for Peruvian fishmeal; Chapters 7, 8, and 9 deal with the linkages from fishmeal to other Peruvian industry and the impact of fishmeal demand on Peruvian factor markets. Conclusions and implications are presented in Chapter 10.

2
The Staple Theory of Export-led Growth

In order to place the Peruvian case in historical and theoretical perspective and to obtain tools of analysis, it is essential to review the literature on the relation between exports and economic development. Because this literature is so extensive, considerable selectivity must be exercised to move the discussion from general considerations to the specific case of Peruvian fishmeal in a tolerable number of pages. The major criterion used in selecting material for inclusion has been to further the investigation of the Peruvian case itself, although I interpreted this standard broadly enough to incorporate some peripheral material for the sake of completeness. The literature of formal mathematical or geometrical growth models has not been emphasized, because these are unable to handle conveniently the number of variables required to explain the complex phenomenon of export-led growth. Instead, the emphasis is on more general, descriptive models, which are essentially inductive, attempting to reach broad conclusions from the data of economic history. Finally, the following discussion, as well as the study of Peru, deals primarily with the impact of technology and the response of the economy to it. That is, the nature of the production function is emphasized as the critical consideration in determining if and how growth can be transmitted to the domestic economy. The role of exchange rate and commercial policy, although important, is kept in the background.

The Production Function Approach

The production function, rather more broadly defined than in neoclassical theory, provides both the point of departure and the unifying feature for this discussion of export-led development. Over 30 years ago, H. A. Innis implicitly used the notion of a production function in his "staple theory" of Canadian economic development.[1] Since then, R. E. Baldwin[2] and D. C. North[3] have explicitly employed the production function as a tool for analyzing the growth process in a way that reinforces and extends the work of Innis. A staple is a primary product that faces a large and growing demand in world markets, does not require elaborate processing, and has a high enough value-to-weight (or volume) ratio to bear transportation costs. In other words, it is a profitable primary commodity export. Such an export industry may be established as a consequence of recent discovery, increased demand, cost-reducing technological change, or any combination of these. Staple production is necessarily intensive in natural resources and probably also in capital. In the Canadian case, highly skilled labor was not required.[4] For present purposes, however, the specification of capital and labor intensity should be left open to allow a wider application of staple theory than is usually envisaged by Canadian historians.

The focus of analysis is not so much on the export industry itself as on the effects of staple production on the rest of the economy.[5] Secondary and tertiary industry is likely to develop around the export base through the external effects of inputs demanded, outputs supplied, consumer markets created, and education provided or stimulated by the export industry. Inputs to the export production process, for example, may include processed materials or equipment that can be produced within the economy, so that a growing export industry could then stimulate investment in such supply industries. Also, an existing supply industry operating in the range of increasing returns may have its market widened sufficiently by demand from the export industry to provide its output at significantly reduced prices, which could in turn stimulate production from other potential users of its output. A particularly important input is likely to be transportation, especially railroads or roads, or other social overheads such as electric power or water supply. These facilities, once in place to serve the staple industry, will lower costs to other potential industries and may well stimulate further investment on that account. Such pecuniary external economies, are, of course, precisely what Hirschman calls backward linkages.[6]

Forward linkages may also be mechanisms of development, the most obvious one being the further processing of the staple commodity itself before export. If the staple is a key input to a different industry, such as nitrates to farming, less direct forward linkages are possible, but are unlikely to provide a very strong stimulus for subsequent investment by themselves.[7] Baldwin, writing with reference to the underdeveloped economies of Africa, provides a caveat on the operation of both forward and backward linkages. If the production of capital goods or material inputs demanded by the export industry is subject to significant returns to scale, the demand generated by staple production may be insufficient to justify the establishment of a supply industry and the inputs will be imported instead. Also, if either supply or processing industries require scarce factors, such as skilled labor, they may not be able to compete for, or import, the needed factors and still remain competitive with imports.[8]

As the primary export industry develops, it creates new consumer goods markets through its payments to local factors of production. If these markets are sufficiently large, they will be served eventually by local firms, or "residentiary industry" in North's term.[9] The size of the market is also dependent on the production function. A highly capital-intensive process such as mining, perhaps employing only a few well-paid, skilled workers, provides a narrower market than a labor-intensive process like plantation agriculture.[10] On the other hand, plantation agriculture yields a skewed income distribution, with many low-paid workers whose demand is largely for dietary staples and minimal clothing and shelter, and a very few owners and managers whose demand is for luxury goods. This sort of demand pattern does not provide a large enough market for mass-produced consumer goods and therefore is unlikely to stimulate domestic industry. Instead, most nonsubsistence consumer goods and some foodstuffs are imported, while the subsistence goods supplied locally are grown on small-scale farms and garden plots or produced by handicraft industry. By contrast, staples produced on family farms are likely to result in a more egalitarian income distribution, which in turn leads to a much broader demand for mass-produced consumer goods and is more likely to stimulate investment in such industry locally. Hence the economies of scale inherent in plantation crops tend to work against subsequent development through residentiary industry, while the diseconomies of other crops favor it.[11]

The transportation system constructed to serve the export industry will also have its effect on residentiary industry, but the outcome is not clear. On the one hand, a rail or road system makes distribution cheaper within the region or country, broadening the market geographically and encouraging exploitation by local industry. However, that same network allows foreign producers to reach the market more cheaply. The latter effect will be particularly strong in cases where the system was developed to transport bulky cargo for export, thus creating excess capacity on the return journey, allowing cheaper backhaul rates and reducing the natural protection of distance enjoyed by local industry.[12]

Staple production has two different kinds of contributions to make through education. First and more obviously, if skilled labor is necessary to the export industry, it may have to undertake training; the incidental "output" of trained workers, managers, and perhaps even entrepreneurs may represent a substantial external economy to other industry. Mining, for example, is capital intensive and also requires skilled labor to operate equipment. If unskilled labor is hired and trained for this work, then the export industry, by providing the economy with an output of skilled labor, may encourage the establishment of other industry. Plantations, however, provide only unskilled tasks for their labor and do not offer this important external economy.[13]

The second relation between export production and education also derives from the skill mix demanded by the production function, but is more subtle. In a society whose economic base requires skilled labor, great value is likely to be placed on education, which alone can provide the skills needed in quantity. Consequently, substantial portions of public expenditure will likely be devoted to education. However, in societies dependent on activities that require few skills, like plantation agriculture, mass education is not only inessential, it can actually be detrimental to the extent that educated labor may emigrate in search of more highly skilled jobs. It is probable that fewer resources will be devoted to general education.[14] In such plantation economies, then, the possibilities of establishing subsidiary industries requiring skilled labor are considerably reduced, because the costs of training a work force will be correspondingly greater. So production functions that lead to egalitarian income distributions and mass markets may also tend to provide a better-educated work force, and this will further stimulate local producer and consumer goods industries requiring labor skills.

Applications

The staple theory of growth was developed as an interpretation of economic history; its significance is best understood through historical example. Several cases of development led by a primary export sector will illustrate the theory: Canada at the turn of the century, the United States before the Civil War, Denmark in the last 20 years of the nineteenth century, Zambia (Northern Rhodesia) since World War II, and South Africa after its mineral discoveries in the late nineteenth century. In the course of these examples, some extensions of, and qualifications to, the theory will be noted.

Understandably, the most straightforward and instructive example is that of Canadian development, since the staple theory was originated to explain it. Caves and Holton have given an excellent summary of Innis's analyses of that case.[15] Canada has had a series of staples, beginning with cod and furs; followed by timber and wheat during the nineteenth century, and minerals and newsprint in the twentieth. Of all Canada's staples, wheat probably had the most decisive and durable effects. Rising European demand for grains at the end of the nineteenth century, reduced ocean freight costs, and cost-handling technological changes in wheat production all combined to create a boom in Canadian wheat exports from the middle of the 1890s until the First World War. From 1895 to 1914, the volume index of exports from Canada of all food products other than livestock grew at a compound rate of 10.7% a year, while the index for all exports grew at 6.8% a year.[16] Wheat production trebled from 1900 to 1910.

The production function of wheat had several important consequences for the Canadian economy, all operating through backward linkages. First, it was land- and capital-intensive, and thus required new farm construction, an extensive rail network of both trunk and feeder lines, agricultural machinery, and motor vehicles. From 1896 to 1914, railroad mileage was almost doubled (to 41,000 miles), with over half the additional track laid in the prairie provinces.[17] The construction of railroads and farm buildings stimulated a doubling of the value of sawmill products from 1901 to 1911. Railway rolling stock and agricultural equipment were both produced in Canada, and their output grew by four times and two times, respectively, over the first ten years of the century.

Wheat is one of those crops grown economically on farms manageable by single families operating considerable capital equipment, so its production created the kind of relatively egalitarian income distribution that can form the basis for a mass consumer goods market. Furthermore, railroad construction significantly reduced the costs of exploiting that market or, looked at another way, broadened it considerably. Consequently, the industries of eastern Canada experienced an expansion in which almost all major classes of manufacturing at least doubled their net output, while the value of manufacturing production grew at the rate of 11.1% a year, over the period 1900 to 1910.[18] During those years, real gross national product sustained a growth rate of 5.3% and income per capita grew at 2.5% a year.[19]

Canada's fortunate history of succeeding staples does not end with wheat, but goes on to include metals and newsprint during and after the First World War. As general economic development proceeds, stimulated by a series of primary export products, the effect of any single new one on the entire economy is lessened. The required inputs are more likely to represent only a marginal increase in output for the supplying sector and less likely to create whole new industries within the country; the new staple may be able to use existing transportation facilities easily or require only slight expansion. As the economy develops, it employs an immensely wider range of production processes and acquires the capacity to switch among them (transform) smoothly as market conditions change.

In fact, the capacity to transform is itself one of the most important by-products of development. The Canadian economy displayed this capacity in considerable measure as it moved through its series of staples over the last two centuries. Canadian economic history has been characterized as a succession of varying motive forces (staples) propelling steady growth in sectors producing for the home market.[20] The demand for exports of individual commodities is determined by exogenous factors, which tend to produce irregular patterns of demand. Thus export booms are usually not sustained over long periods (say more than 10 or 15 years) and the economy that is flexible enough to transform its output to take advantage of these market irregularities is better able to sustain a high growth rate. Furthermore, each period of growing output of a given staple may, depending on the nature of the production function, bring into the economy new factor supplies that will add to the capacity to transform. The extensive rail system constructed for the wheat economy in Canada is a prime example. It is clear, then, that with a shifting base of primary exports, the capacity to transform plays a critical role in long-run economic development.

Early in their discussion of Canadian development, Caves and Holton issue a warning that one critical set of factors, the character of Canadians and their social institutions, is not explained but assumed by staple theory.[21] Non-French Canadians, like Americans, inherited British institutions that, while reasonably stable, were also capable of accommodating considerable change. Societal values encouraged acquisitiveness and innovation, and hence productive investment. Thus the stimulus provided by foreign demand for Canadian primary products found a positive response in a society favorably predisposed toward development. The potential for technological linkages inherent in a given primary production function offers a set of necessary, but not sufficient, conditions for economic development to take place. To ensure that development does ensue, the social milieu must be receptive to the technological and economic stimuli of an export industry. This condition cannot be assumed for the more traditional societies of underdeveloped countries, which are the focus of this study. Hence, what will be called "societal responses" will be discussed more fully in Chapter 3. Meanwhile, it is well to keep in mind that staple theory cannot tell the whole story of development without some consideration of the societal conditions surrounding its operation.

Chambers and Gordon have attacked the whole concept of staple theory by using a simple, two-sector general equilibrium model to show that the wheat economy cannot be given much credit for Canada's growth from 1901 to 1911. They assume that, in the absence of the staple industry, all resources used other than land would have been employed in other industry at constant returns to scale. Hence the contribution of prairie agriculture to increased income is measured by the increase in actual land rent in 1911 over a hypothetical figure based on labor productivities prevailing in 1901 in agriculture, and in 1911 in other industry. The conclusion is that a maximum of only 8.4% of increased income per capita can be attributed directly to prairie agriculture.[22]

Staple theory is vulnerable to the charge that, in determining the contribution of exports to development, it ignores alternative uses of resources employed in the export sector. However, a case can be made that staple theory comes closer to describing that contribution than do Chambers and Gordon. To justify their supposition that Canadian industry could have provided close to the same growth rates, it is necessary to suppose that a whole set of less productive industries would have been able to grow in balanced fashion, creating their own domestic markets in the probable absence of foreign markets in which these industries could have competed. Such development would have required many different technologies and the greater risks of investment in unproved markets, both of which would have demanded a high degree of entrepreneurship. By comparison, production of wheat for export required only a few pioneers whom the many farmers could imitate. Foreign markets provided clear signals for profitable investment in production for export, and the technologies were comparatively simple. Moreover, foreign capital showed a far greater propensity to enter primary export and related sectors during the nineteenth century. Finally, subsidiary industry, which perhaps did require sophisticated technology, at least had a large domestic market in existence before investments were necessary.

The burden of these points is not that Canada would have stagnated without staple exports, but rather that it seems a dubious proposition that growth would have been so rapid or certain. For presently underdeveloped countries, about which this study centers, these arguments have far greater validity. Labor and capital immobility and a lack of entrepreneurs make it highly unlikely that rapid, balanced growth can be initiated or sustained. In fact, the problem is whether conditions are favorable enough to allow even minimal response to the clear and obvious signals of vigorous primary export growth. A second point is that staple theory is better history than the Chambers and Gordon approach. It is intended primarily to describe a growth path and provide some explanation for the emergence of that particular path, which it does rather well.

North has applied the apparatus of the production function, as developed by himself and Baldwin, to the economic development of the United States before the Civil War.[23] The case for export-led growth in the United States is not as clear-cut as for Canada, if only because United States exports were so much smaller a fraction of gross national product: less than 7.5% during the 30 years before the Civil War, compared to roughly 15% in Canada during the wheat boom.[24] The argument that United States growth was led by exports can perhaps be made on two grounds. First, the volume index of exports did grow rapidly during two ten-year periods before the Civil War: by 6.6% a year from 1830 to 1840 and by 9.2% a year from 1850 to 1860.[25] The available data show that the growth rate of real national income over the 30 years before the war was a slower but substantial 5.2% annually, a rate that was, however, sustained even during the period of sluggish export growth during the 1840s; income per capita grew at 2.2% a year over the entire period.[26]

Second, and more important for present purposes, North really treats the United States not as one country but as three regions: the Northeast, the South, and the West. When interregional commodity flows are considered as "exports," the dependence of national product on "exports," as measured by the ratio of the latter to the former, becomes more marked. Furthermore, in the cases of the South and the West, the primary commodity exported overseas was also the major commodity in interregional trade, increasing the degree of dependence on one or two crops in each case. To a certain extent, this treatment of United States economic history begs the question, since it is always possible to break a country into smaller regions and show an increased relative dependence on interregional trade. Nevertheless, North's treatment is instructive because of his insightful use of the production function technique.

The South experienced two decades of rapid expansion of its economic base before the Civil War, one during the 1830s and a second in the 1850s, when the value of cotton exports grew at annual rates of 8.0% and 10.3%, respectively; the volume growth rates were somewhat higher. Over the 30-year period, cotton exports grew at 6.5%

a year.[27] In spite of these favorable conditions, the South did not industrialize about its export base. Urbanization proceeded extremely slowly, so that only New Orleans of all southern cities ranked in the first 15 in the United States by 1860. In that year, less than 10% of the population of the South lived in urban areas, compared with over 35% in the Northeast and over 13% in the rapidly urbanizing Middle West. Very little residentiary industry was developed and even retail trade was rudimentary, compared with that in other regions. North finds the explanation for this lack of growth transmittal in the production function of cotton. Unlike wheat, it is a crop subject to increasing returns to scale, which was grown on plantations. The slave economy, with its extremely skewed income distribution, could not generate the broad market essential to the establishment of consumer goods industry or even support an extensive retail trade. Another consequence of its social structure was the neglect of education: in 1840 there were fewer than 6 pupils per 100 of white population in the South, while the corresponding figure in nonslave states was over 18. And it may be imagined that plantation production did not impart whatever skills may have been needed by industry.

That cotton production did not entail social overhead construction was due less to the technology of cotton than to the South's generous endowment of navigable waterways, which eliminated the need for an extensive rail system. This should have been a net benefit to the economy. However, given the South's social structure, such savings were undoubtedly captured by landowners whose expenditure patterns largely encouraged imports, rather than stimulate demand for local industry. Had railroad construction been required, more effective linkages might have been realized. Transportation played a further retarding role in that eastward and northward flows of cotton produced excess capacity and lower rates on return voyages, further encouraging the few consumers to import their purchases. Finally, because this fairly simple trade was financed largely by northern banks, financial institutions did not develop beyond the trading firms that acted as factors.[28]

The development of the West stands in marked contrast to that of the South. The growth process in this region, based on exports of wheat and corn, resembled that of Canada at the turn of the century, not too surprisingly since both the production functions and the societal responses were similar. As an index of the vigor of the export sector, the volume of flour and grain shipped from Chicago grew at the rate of 6.8% a year from 1830 to 1860.[29] The production of wheat and corn in Illinois doubled over the decade, 1850 to 1860, as did the population. Industrialization of the region actually took place after the Civil War.

The war itself would be sufficient to explain why development succeeded in the West and not in the South. However, the South had a long period of export growth before the war and showed no signs of advancing toward a major industrial sector, so the contrasting production functions probably hold much of the explanation for the different behavior of the two regions. Unlike the South, the West enjoyed a broad range of production possibilities, which included several metals in addition to grains. These carried important linkages, both forward (the iron industry and flour milling, for example) and backward (agricultural equipment). The rail network constructed for the export of wheat and corn yielded significant external economies in the form of lower costs for manufacturing industries.[30] The family farm system, with its comparatively equal income distribution, provided mass consumer goods markets and led to a social structure that encouraged education with its external economies.[31]

Denmark, during the last 20 years of the nineteenth century, provides an interesting case of primary export-led growth in a settled country, in which technological and organizational change played key roles.[32] The exports were dairy and meat products, which became profitable as demand in Britain and Europe switched toward them and away from grains during the last quarter of the century. The development, during the late 1870s, of a more efficient cream separator that could handle agitated milk made it possible to process milk transported from widely scattered areas and hence introduced small farmers to the cream and butter market. A by-product of the creameries, skim milk, was fed to hogs and led to the development of the bacon industry. A new organization, the producers' cooperative, was organized originally to ensure the transportation of milk from farm to creamery; cooperatives also owned the creameries. Danish farmers, social equals and relatively well educated, found the cooperative form to their liking; when the bacon industry began growing, it, too, was organized on a cooperative basis. Here, then, is a clear-cut example of the kind of favorable societal response that not only allows but encourages the effective operation of linkages.

From roughly 1880 to 1900, a major change took place in the composition of Danish exports. Denmark, formerly an exporter of grain, began to import grain as more resources were devoted to dairy and pork production. Volume exports of butter and eggs grew almost fivefold, and, while the value of exports of whole hogs shrank to less than one-tenth of the 1880 level, that of pork and bacon exports grew by ten times. The annual growth rate of all exports was a modest 4.0% from 1885 to 1900,[33] but the changed composition had important effects on the economy. The new agriculture was more capital-intensive than grain farming, requiring creameries and elaborate transportation and handling facilities. Most important, the substitution of capital for labor at the margin enabled agricultural incomes to grow, providing a larger market for industry, while agriculture demanded a decreasing fraction of the work force. Backward linkages included the production of separators and freezing equipment by Danish machine shops, while cheap backhaul rates worked to the advantage of industry, which used imported iron, cotton, and coal.

The reorganization of the agricultural sector thus worked major changes in the economy, but the total export volume did not expand rapidly enough to produce dramatic growth in national income: net domestic product only increased at 3.5% a year from 1885 to 1900. However, with the population growing at 1% a year over the last half of the nineteenth century, there was substantial growth in per capita income.[34] The Danish case is instructive because growth required a change in the production function and a reallocation of resources internally. It could not proceed, as in the lands of recent settlement, primarily by means of increased factor inputs (although technological change was important in Canadian and American growth as well). The need for intensive, rather than extensive, exploitation of natural resources and the requirement that Denmark's primary exports be processed before shipping are departures from the pure staple theory as Canadian historians have developed it. These relaxations of the definition of a staple are essential if the theory is to be useful in explaining development in the twentieth century. In one important respect, the Danish situation just 100 years ago resembles that of most developing countries today: faced with limited land, increased income per capita depends on capital formation and technological change. As the Danish example shows, development led by primary commodity exports is feasible under these conditions.

Baldwin's recent study of Northern Rhodesia (now Zambia) extends the staple theory of growth to mining and to a country developing in mid-twentieth century.[35] The macroeconomic case for export-led growth is clear enough: from 1945 to 1961, monetary gross domestic product grew at 9.5% a year, led by a copper mining sector which grew by 8.7% a year from 1946 to 1960. Copper output was valued at about 50% of gross domestic product during the period and accounted for over 80% of export earnings.[36] However, mining apparently did not lead to the sort of spread effects noted by Innis and North in North American development. In fact, had residentiary industries grown markedly about the copper export base, copper output would have represented considerably less than the 44% of monetary gross domestic product that it did in 1961.

The reasons for these incompletely developed linkages have been indicated earlier. Copper extraction is highly capital intensive. A high fraction of the workers must be skilled and until recently labor skills were imported from Europe. Hence, although the skill mix kept wages high, the number of laborers was limited and the wage bill consequently small, so that the market for nonsubsistence goods was insufficient to support local manufacturing on a large scale. High wages in the mining sector also effectively raised wages in other sectors, mainly through the intervention of government and trades unions, discouraging the establishment of labor-intensive industry in a manner typical of dual economies.[37] On the other hand, the external economy of labor training was important. The mining companies encouraged the establishment of local independent supply companies, and the skills learned by both European and African miners were often the basis for starting such industries. However, there was a limit to this kind of development, because the skilled labor was available much more cheaply in Southern Rhodesia and especially in South Africa. Furthermore, the larger market in South Africa tended to keep production of mining equipment out of Northern Rhodesia.

Rhodesian copper mines cannot claim credit for the country's rail network, which was constructed to serve Rhodesian lead and Katangan copper mines and happened to be well situated to serve

Rhodesian copper when it became a factor. However, the industry's demand for electric power did lead to the construction of the Kariba Dam, which now provides ample cheap power for future industrialization. The dam in turn stimulated a tripling of the country's cement-producing capacity and this should encourage the construction industry in the future.[38] However, low-cost power and construction probably cannot by themselves stimulate new industry; they are good examples of what Hirschman means when he says that forward linkages (other than further processing) do not work alone, but require some backward linkage, or demand pressure, to become effective.[39] In fact, Baldwin concludes his study on the mildly pessimistic note that the linkages between copper mining and the rest of the economy are too weak to transmit growth and that the only potentially strong linkage is the one between the government's copper revenues (which account for 40 to 60% of total revenues) and the development expenditures made possible by them.[40] It is a conclusion corroborated by Reynolds in his study of Chilean development, also based on copper.[41]

The Rhodesian experience can undoubtedly be used to explain the lack of induced growth in other mineral-exporting countries today. However, mineral sectors have been known to lead development in the past: gold and diamonds in South Africa are one notable example. South Africa's development was set in motion by the discovery of the Kimberley diamond mine in 1870 and the Rand gold deposits in 1886. Apparently, mining in South Africa before World War I was more labor-intensive than in Northern Rhodesia after World War II, probably due partly to capital-using technological change in mining since the First World War. In any case, the mines attracted sufficient labor from the subsistence sector to stimulate cash crop production and, after a time, a consumer goods industry. In 1919, it was reported that the gold mines alone employed about 250,000 workers, over 90% of them Africans.[42]

In addition to creating a broad consumer goods market, mining in South Africa also offered strong backward linkages. Supply industries, especially in explosives and iron and steel, were established at an early stage. In the 1930s, the forward linkage industries of metal refining, minting, and diamond cutting began to operate in South Africa. In this instance, the mines were directly responsible for the country's rail system, which was substantially completed by 1895. And the fiscal linkage was effective, as mining taxes were used to subsidize secondary industry, agriculture, and the railroad.[43]

Staple theory can offer at least two tentative explanations for the different responses of Northern Rhodesia and South Africa to their mineral sectors. South Africa began its rapid growth at a time when mining technology was relatively simple and labor-intensive. This meant that, first, backward linkages were more readily developed in South Africa, since the products demanded by the mines were easily produced locally. Second, for any given scale, South Africa's mining sector would employ more local labor than Rhodesia's and thus provide a potentially broader consumer goods market, in the sense that more workers had incomes high enough to be demanders of other than subsistence goods. If these explanations hold, technological change in mining may make it difficult to follow the South African example today. Thus the case against development led by mineral sectors looks formidable on production function grounds alone. However, Zambia is certainly one of those countries for which it is not valid to assume societal responses conducive to growth transmission, even if technological linkages may exist. More will be said in the next chapter on the possible role of societal responses in preventing the functioning of linkages in such cases.

Relation to Other Growth Theories

These illustrations make it somewhat easier to visualize the relation between staple theory and other growth theories. The essence of staple theory is the increasing exploitation of natural resources, which may involve additional inputs of these resources, technological change to allow more intensive utilization of them, and often both. In any case, discovery of either new resources or new processes is a prerequisite for growth, and discovery is, by its very nature, a discontinuous process. Hence growth is expected to be irregular. Neoclassical growth theories are also supply-oriented, working with aggregate production functions, either one for the whole economy or one for each of two sectors. Attention is centered on the growth of factor inputs and the effects of technological change. However, in contrast to staple theory, neoclassical treatments usually either ignore inputs of the factor "land," which includes natural resources, or takes its growth to be nil, producing decreasing returns. The factor inputs normally considered are capital and labor, and constant rates of growth are assumed for their supply. The other element of growth, technological change, is also assumed to take place at a steady rate; in steady-state growth it is the only means of increasing per capita income. Since homogeneous (single-product) outputs are assumed, at least for each sector, growth in national income or in the output of each sector takes place at a constant rate as a consequence of steady increases in factor supplies and productivity.[44]

Practical applications of neoclassical growth theory attempt to measure the contributions to national income growth from increased factor supplies, and hence to isolate the residual or unexplained differences between these contributions and income growth. The residual can be smaller the more willing the investigator is to assume that capital formation embodies technological progress or that labor productivity increases systematically due to education.[45] There is arbitrariness in any assignation of the residual, however. It can only be said for certain that it includes all contributions to growth other than increased factor supplies, which may include technological progress (advance of knowledge), education (improved labor quality), improved management or organization, economies of scale, more efficient resource allocation, and so forth.[46]

One role of staple theory is to show how the particular choice of production functions may affect all these sources of growth, including factor supplies, education, management, and the other residual items. Thus the staple and applied neoclassical approaches to growth are complementary.

The neoclassical tradition in trade theory, which is synonymous with the Heckscher-Ohlin theory, has been extended to problems of factor growth and technological change by writers such as Johnson, Findlay and Grubert, Bhagwati, and others.[47] However, their models have dealt entirely with the effects of growth on trade and do not seem equipped to analyze the impact of trade on growth. Oniki and Uzawa, and Bardhan have approached the problems of trade and growth from the other direction, extending the neoclassical growth theory of two factors and two sectors into a two-country world.[48]

Although these models seem able to say more about the influence of trade on growth, they, like other neoclassical models, are severely limited in their ability to handle conveniently several factors and sectors. Thus the important detail contained in the production function approach is lost. Because neoclassical models depend on aggregate production functions, they are more suitable for explaining growth in developed countries, which have a wide range of production possibilities and can switch readily among them.[49]

Investigations of the role of foreign aid in development have produced the familiar "two-gap" models of growth, which take a different view of the role of export growth.[50] In these linear models, factors are not substitutable and growth rates may be constrained by a shortage of labor skills, savings, or foreign exchange. If foreign exchange, required to purchase essential producers goods that cannot be produced domestically, is the operative constraint on growth, then a growing export sector contributes to development primarily by increasing the capacity to import. However, if the economy is constrained by either savings or skills, then export growth does not contribute directly to income growth. In this schema, sustained, rapid export growth is likely to lead into a savings-limited regime, emasculating the role of the export sector in development. Although certainly very different in spirit, the two-gap model can be reconciled with staple theory. The latter recognizes that a vigorous export sector can, and probably will, contribute importantly to increasing supplies of factors, including not only foreign exchange, but also savings and skilled labor. Thus, whatever the binding constraint, a leading export sector can probably help to relieve it and stimulate growth.[51]

Myint has invoked the "vent for surplus" theory of Adam Smith to explain the great growth in exports from both the newly settled areas and the newly opened colonial areas in the nineteenth century. His model is one of idle land and labor, in the sense that more of one or both was available than was necessary to produce for the inhabitants' needs. Once the area was opened to trade, these excess resources could be used to produce goods for export. Myint has in mind primarily the peasant export economies of Asia when he speaks of surplus labor. He implies that production was not capital-intensive, but he credits the railroad with opening up surplus land.[52] As Caves points out, Myint's theory is very close to that of Innis, except that the former puts emphasis on labor inputs rather than capital as the factor complementary with natural resources.[53]

In a recent study, Hicks and McNicoll have applied essentially the Myint model to postwar Philippine growth. They picture an export sector that is expanding primarily by extending the margin of cultivated land at constant or slightly falling productivity. Export earnings fuel the growth of an import-dependent, highly protected industrial sector, and the export sectors' wage payments contribute importantly to the demand for domestically produced goods. Because Philippine industry is uncompetitive in world markets, export expansion is being limited by the availability of land and other natural resources, and productivity is not rising in either sector, growth cannot be sustained.[54]

Rostow's theory of take-off into sustained economic growth, depending as it does on a leading sector, bears some resemblance to staple theory. However, he stipulates that a sector producing raw materials can lead only if it involves the application of modern processing, as occurred in Danish dairy production. This stipulation would exclude North American wheat, which for the most part was not processed before export, and places Rostow in direct conflict with Innis and his followers. Rostow does date take-off in the American and Canadian cases during the years when wheat exports led growth according to the staple theorists. However, Rostow places the burden of development on the railroad which, he says, was a prerequisite to the development of a major export industry and also led to the establishment of modern coal, iron, and engineering industries.[55]

The strategic importance of the railroad in American development is subject to dispute. It has been skillfully challenged by Fogel, who casts serious doubt on the importance of the railroad's stimulus to production and technological change in manufacturing, and holds that almost as much new land could have been brought into cultivation (that is, brought within the margin of zero rent) by a feasible extension of the canal system.[56] Fishlow gives a more optimistic assessment of the backward linkages and social savings due to railroads, but also doubts that railroads actually made western agricultural growth possible; railroad construction typically responded to an existing demand for transportation.[57] It is unnecessary to argue whether the railroad was a permissive factor in the development of a primary export sector or if, instead, the staple industry forced the construction of rail networks. The fact is that, in the American West before the Civil War and on the Canadian prairies at the turn of this century, wheat exports would have been less profitable without the railroads and the railroads less profitable without wheat. But even if railroads are seen as the leading sector, the strategic role of primary exports should not be underemphasized, as Rostow tends to do.

Rostow is vulnerable on one other point, at least in respect to Canadian growth. Bertram's presentation of the staple theory, which was in fact done to refute Rostow's approach, shows that growth took place gradually in Canada as one staple after another generated steady growth in the rest of the economy over the entire period from 1870 to 1930. There was no clearly identifiable take-off. Furthermore, Bertram emphasizes the dependence of Canadian growth on international markets, in distinction to Rostow, whose theory emphasizes internal factors on both the demand and supply side.[58]

On the whole, then, staple theory is reasonably consistent with all the growth theories mentioned so far, at least in broad outline. It differs either in emphasis, as with the Rostow and Myint models, or in the degree of aggregation, as with the neoclassical models.

3
Barriers to
Export-led Growth

Staple theory, extended along the lines indicated in Chapter 2, can be applied to selected countries going through the process of development today. However, there is a well-known body of literature which holds that countries developing about a primary export base have found, and will continue to find, it extremely difficult to follow the successful examples set by the United States, Canada, Denmark, South Africa, and others during the nineteenth and early twentieth centuries. The skeptics have several reasons for their doubts, but they fall roughly into three categories: inadequate growth of export markets for primary producers; unfavorable market structure, including monopoly elements that work against primary producers; and ineffective or non-existent linkages to transmit growth from the export sector to the rest of the economy.

Export Market Growth

The principal spokesman for the position that export markets for primary products no longer grow fast enough to induce domestic growth was Ragnar Nurkse.[1] He did not deprecate the mechanism of export-led growth for primary producers. On the contrary, he held that any opportunities that present themselves for such growth should be fully exploited. But Nurkse doubted that such opportunities would arise for very many commodities (petroleum being the major exception), and this for five reasons:

1. Industrial countries are shifting from light to heavy industry, the raw material content of which is lower.

2. The rising share of services in national incomes of developed countries tends to lower their import coefficients.
3. Income elasticity of demand for agricultural commodities is low.
4. Western Europe has increased its protection against agricultural products.
5. Technological change has led to economies in the use of raw materials, by using synthetic substitutes and more efficient processes.

As a consequence of these developments, imports of all products by the industrial countries from primary producers, except petroleum, fell from 3.5% to 2.5% of the gross national product of the industrial countries between the late 1920s and the late 1950s. The import coefficient of the United States, the leading market for tropical exporters at mid-century, fell from 5.7% before the First World War to under 3%.[2] Since growth in the industrial countries is transmitted to the primary product suppliers after being scaled down by falling import coefficients, the growth of primary product exports is unlikely to match the rates of growth prevailing during the nineteenth century. The primary export market's "engine of growth" has been slowing down.

To appraise Nurkse's thesis, evidence of the growth of world trade in the nineteenth century from Imlah's work on British trade[3] has been used, from which the growth rates shown in Table 3.1 were

TABLE 3.1. Growth of world trade, 1820–1913

For the period	Compound annual growth rates in percent		
	Volume British imports	Exporters' capacity to import[a]	Value of world imports
1820–1860	4.1	5.5	3.7
1840–1872	4.5	4.2	5.2
1860–1897	3.3	2.8	2.7
1897–1913	2.4	1.9	4.8

Source: Calculated from Imlah, Pax Britannica, pp. 94–98, 189–190.

[a] Index of British import volume divided by British terms of trade index.

calculated. British import growth rates are presented because deflated series are available and because they are sometimes cited as being indicative of the behavior of primary commodity exports in the nineteenth century. In general, the annual growth rates for each decade are similar to the annual rates shown for longer periods and the growth rates of imports in value terms are slightly lower. "Exporters' capacity to import" is an index of the income terms of trade for British suppliers who also bought British goods; its greatest growth was 5.5%, from 1820 to 1860. World imports grew at 5.2% from 1840 to 1872, while the highest growth rate observable over a shorter period was 5.9%, for the interval from 1860 to 1872.

Corresponding figures for trade between the industrial and underdeveloped countries for the past 30 years compare favorably. In value terms, exports from the less developed countries to the developed countries have grown by 7.0% a year from 1938 to 1966, and by 4.7% a year from 1948 to 1964; the volume of exports grew at 4.9% a year over the latter period. During the 1948–1966 period, the terms of trade of the underdeveloped countries improved by about 5%, so their capacity to import increased by about 5.2% a year.[4] The superiority of the nineteenth century "engine of growth" over the primary export mechanism of the twentieth is not borne out by the data at hand.

The statistical defense of the twentieth century is supported by some cursory observations on the raw materials that have been important in twentieth-century trade. The increased consumption of rubber (undaunted by synthetics), petroleum, and newsprint, all of which figure importantly in world trade, is a phenomenon of this century, stimulated by mass use of the internal combustion engine and the growth of mass communications. Various oils, soybeans, aluminum, and even iron ore qualify as commodities with good growth records since World War I.[5] Even if the growth rate of primary commodity trade taken as a whole were not satisfactory, it is likely that individual commodities will experience growth sufficient to lead the development of selected countries. Also, certain countries will be well situated to take advantage of such growth if other conditions for domestic development are met.[6]

It is probably too much to expect the entire underdeveloped world to grow together, yet arguments like those of Nurkse and Raul Prebisch, which use two-country models of world trade, imply that such growth is expected. It is an unhappy fact, but one we must live with, that some countries will be near stagnation while others develop using export-led or other growth strategies. However, the countries developing at present will eventually provide additional markets for primary products, which in turn will make it easier for the others to escape from stagnation by means of growing primary exports.

There is indicative evidence that exports have stimulated growth in several less developed countries during recent years. Table 3.2 lists 11 countries that have experienced rapid export and GNP growth from 1958 to 1968. Of these, Spain, Portugal, Israel, Pakistan, Taiwan, and Korea depended chiefly on manufactured exports for

TABLE 3.2. Growth of exports and gross national product, selected countries, 1958–1968

	Compound annual growth rates (percent per year)	
Country	Export volume (1963 prices)	GNP (1967 prices)
Nicaragua	6.0[a]	6.0
Panama	10.8	7.8
Peru	8.0	5.8
Spain	13.0	5.7
Portugal	9.8[b]	6.2
Greece	7.3	6.6
Israel	15.1	8.6
Pakistan	9.1[b]	5.8
South Korea	16.0[c]	7.4
Taiwan	10.4	9.4
Thailand	8.3[d]	8.0

Sources: Export growth calculated from International Monetary Fund, *International Financial Statistics*, 22 (June 1969) and Supplement 1967/1968. The GNP growth is calculated from the United States Agency for International Development, *Gross National Product: Growth and Trend Data* (Washington, April 25, 1969).

[a] 1958–1966.
[b] Growth rate of export value.
[c] 1963–1968.
[d] 1958–1967.

expansion, although in most of these countries primary products and processed materials also played an important role. Also, foreign capital was a critical element in Greece, Israel, Pakistan, Taiwan, and Korea. Finally, these associations of export growth with the growth of output do not reveal the mechanisms that may be operating between the export sector and the rest of the economy. Indeed, they do not necessarily imply that causation runs from exports to GNP, rather than the other way around. Nevertheless, the experience of these 11 developing countries raises a presumption that vigorous export growth remains an important part of development strategy, even for primary producers in the twentieth century.

Market Imperfections

Although basing his pessimism on market imperfections, Raul Prebisch would agree with most of Nurkse's analysis; in fact, his familiar argument that the terms of trade of primary producers has deteriorated secularly and will continue to do so is based partly on the observation that the demand of industrial countries for primary products is growing more slowly than the demand of developing countries for manufactures. But Prebisch goes further, alleging that monopoly elements play a role in world markets detrimental to the position of developing countries. In the latter, productivity gains in the export sector are taken in the form of lower prices, while in the industrial countries, unions and oligopolistic industry are able to maintain or even raise prices in the face of increased productivity, taking the gains in the form of higher incomes. Thus productivity increases do not benefit the developing countries, which predominantly import manufactured goods, but do benefit the industrial countries, which are large importers of foodstuffs and raw materials.

A related point is that prices of primary products tend to fall as much in downswings as they rise in booms, while the prices of manufactured goods tend to rise more on the upswing than they fall during recessions. This ratchet effect is blamed on the same combination of monopoly elements: unions capture a share of increased prices in booms and do not relinquish them during slack periods. In other words, wages are rigid downward, a familiar Keynesian argument. Actually, it is the cyclical behavior that Prebisch sees as the mechanism which permits the secular rise in prices in industrial countries in spite of technical progress. As a consequence of these market imperfections and the income elasticity effects noted by Nurkse, the terms of trade of primary producing exporters has declined over the long run, as evidenced primarily by the improved United Kingdom terms of trade of about 36% from the late 1870s to the late 1930s. Moreover, they are likely to continue falling in the absence of effective world commodity agreements. Thus, part of the benefits of growth will be lost to the primary producers, which are taken to be synonymous with the underdeveloped countries, and transferred to the industrial world by price movements.[7]

The important qualifications to these arguments are almost as familiar as Prebisch's original case. The latter's use of British terms of trade is only indicative and hardly conclusive. In his work on European terms of trade, Kindleberger presents a more decisive index, that of the net barter terms of trade for all of industrial Europe vis-à-vis the rest of the world, excluding the lands of recent settlement. This index (1913 = 100), improved from 123 in 1872, to 176 in 1938, and 155 in 1952, thus supporting Prebisch's argument rather strongly.[8] It must be cautioned, however, that such indices cannot allow for improved quality or new products entering trade. As these factors undoubtedly figure far more importantly in the manufactured exports of Europe than in the primary exports of the underdeveloped world, the figures given probably overstate the deterioration in the latter's terms of trade: some value was received for the higher prices paid. Also, the common use of cost, insurance, and freight (cif) values for imports in constructing terms of trade indices means that, since freight costs fell by about 50% over the entire period used by Prebisch, the net prices received by primary product exporters, and therefore their terms of trade, were relatively higher during the 1930s than indicated by the measures available. It was the maritime nations, rather than the primary exporters, whose terms of trade bore the brunt of declining freight rates.[9]

Similar comments apply to the service of capital items in the current account: to some extent primary export prices include allowances for profits and interest remitted abroad, and price declines due to decreasing returns on capital do not hurt the exporting country. There is evidence of a secular decline in the rate of return of over 10%

from the 1870s to the 1930s, another factor adding to the overstatement of declining terms of trade for less developed primary producers.[10] Finally, it is far from clear that the net barter terms of trade are the proper ones to use. Both the income terms of trade, which give the capacity to import, and the single-factoral terms of trade are more appropriate measures of welfare. It is entirely possible, and in fact likely, that while the net barter terms have fallen, the income and single-factoral terms have improved for the less developed countries.[11]

Even if the statistical case for deteriorating terms of trade is granted, the explanation based on monopoly elements in the industrial countries is mistaken. In order to demonstrate the existence of monopoly prices in international markets, the existence of monopoly power over goods in international trade must be shown. National monopoly power, over either factors or goods, is insufficient to enforce monopoly prices in trade, because nations are in competition for foreign markets.

Kindleberger has a better explanation for the terms of trade moving against underdeveloped countries, which is based on domestic conditions within those countries, rather than on conditions in the developed areas. An important factor in maintaining favorable terms of trade is the ability to transfer resources away from export- and import-competing industries facing sluggish demand and toward those in more favorable circumstances. World demand is not static, but shifts among products in response to changes in tastes, technologies, and endowments. The country with sufficiently elastic supplies of goods will be able to maintain its export prices, while avoiding higher import prices. However, the very nature of underdevelopment precludes this capacity to transform from one resource allocation to another: labor skills, entrepreneurship, and capital are scarce; infrastructure is incomplete; unskilled labor is immobile; information is poorly disseminated; and so forth. So underdeveloped countries fare poorly in shifting international markets, regardless of the particular products they export, and only development can alleviate this situation.[12]

Linkage Problems

A third group of criticisms of export-led development ignores the arguments about slow export growth and deteriorating terms of trade.

Granted that the export sector may be vigorous and expansive, it is argued that it cannot transmit growth to the rest of the economy because the necessary linkages are missing. This argument hits directly at the major theme of this study, and in fact the analysis in Chapter 2 (pp. 17–18) of the impact of copper mining on the Northern Rhodesian economy tends to support it.[13] The typical case cited is that of extractive industry or plantation crops, dominated by foreign capital and skilled labor (including management), and producing almost entirely for the export market. A classic analysis of the foreign enclave was made by Jonathan Levin on the nineteenth-century Peruvian guano fertilizer industry.[14] Levin's example of the inability of an economy to grow about a primary export base is of special interest, because it deals with the same country and the same basic resource (anchovy, the fish eaten by "guano birds") as does this study of the fishmeal industry.

Levin's analysis centers on his observation that foreign factors of production dominated the guano industry. Contrary to the assumption of the Heckscher-Ohlin theory of trade, factors were far more mobile internationally than domestically. The industry was largely financed by foreign capital and managed by foreign contractors, while the guano deposits were mined mostly by Chinese coolies. The coolies lived at subsistence level and provided no market for consumer durables, while the other foreign factors remitted much of their income abroad and consumed imported luxuries. The Peruvian contractors and traders who benefited from the guano trade were also luxury importers. Hence the absence of a domestic market for nonsubsistence consumer goods, noted by Baldwin in Northern Rhodesia, was a major factor in Peru's inability to develop in response to its guano industry. Savings generated by exports tended to be channeled back into the export sector, especially sugar production, but not into domestic industry. Located at the coast and on off-shore islands, the guano industry did not require overhead capital that could serve other industry very well, and in particular had no effect on the interior of Peru. The fiscal linkage was used in the last years of the guano boom as the government channeled its proceeds from guano exports into railroad construction. The railroad was of long-run importance, but its immediate effect was choked off by the disastrous War of the Pacific with Chile from 1879 to 1884.[15]

Levin's description of Peru in the nineteenth century can, with minor alterations, be made to fit many primary producers today. Petroleum extraction is typical. Several countries have enjoyed growing exports of petroleum over an extended period, yet domestic development fails to follow, unless government taxes the petroleum industry in order to finance development programs. The dominance of foreign factors and the almost total absence of overhead capital useful to other industry may be blamed. Such export economies are one form of the dual economy, and an important one empirically. Capital-intensive to begin with and run by western managers who do not think in terms of labor-substituting methods, these export industries are unable to absorb the surplus labor of their host countries, yet they pay high wages commensurate with the high productivity of a technologically advanced, capital-intensive industry. Government and labor unions then act to secure uniformly high wages through the rest of the industrial sector of the economy. Other industries, more labor-intensive and with lower labor productivity, cannot hire labor at the price and substitute capital for labor wherever possible. In either case, unemployment persists and development is retarded.[16]

The pessimistic theses centering around "engine of growth" and market imperfections arguments are very much questions of one's point of view. With a different angle on the data or with a somewhat less demanding model of world trade and development, it is possible to temper their pessimism without ignoring the hard grain of truth they contain. Primary commodity exports do have the potential of leading the development process, Nurkse and Prebisch to the contrary, if the production function includes the technological linkages necessary to transmit growth from the export sector to the rest of the economy and societal responses allow these linkages to operate. However, skepticism about the availability of these linkages is probably more justified from experience and more difficult to refute summarily than the other two lines of skeptical reasoning. Moreover, Nurkse's doubts about export-led growth in this century loom larger when combined with the conclusions of Levin and Baldwin. It might be contended that those primary products now in demand offer few linkages and have become extremely capital-intensive. Petroleum is the prime example, while the contrast between Zambian and early South African mining indicates that shifts in technology may be working against primary export-led growth.

Still, although it is easy to cite individual cases of enclave economies, it should also be possible to demonstrate examples of successful growth transmission. Each case must be taken on its merits, until general principles can be induced from the data of specific cases. Then considerably more can be said about the extent to which primary export-led growth is feasible in the less developed world. The device of analyzing the production function of an export industry to determine the effects on development is probably the best one available for this task of organizing data.

Societal Responses

But there is a danger of trying to explain too much through the technological requirements of the production function while ignoring the requirements of favorable societal responses. It is frequently necessary to look at the characteristics of the society itself in order to explain the failure of the domestic economy to develop in response to growing exports. Levin approached the guano industry primarily from the point of view of factor supplies, rather than using the production function, and some of the effects he notes are rather hard to explain as technologically necessary. It may be possible to invoke increasing returns to scale and the need for assured means of transportation to export markets to explain why large amounts of capital were required to exploit guano (or copper in Rhodesia), but these cannot explain why the capital could not be found domestically. Part, but not all, of the answer may be in the overworked concepts of low levels of per capita income and the vicious circle of poverty. However, to complete the explanation something must be said of the propensity to save and invest productively in the society, the organization of capital markets, the willingness to use corporate organizational forms, and so forth. These in turn are rooted in the determinants of culture, being functions of class and family structure, traditional attitudes toward work, fundamental concepts of man and the universe, personality formation, and other factors beyond the professional ken of an economist. Similarly, Levin documents the importation of coolie labor to mine guano, and this cannot be explained solely by reference to the technological demands of the production function. The economist would probably be satisfied with a reference to domestic labor immobility, but ultimate causes lie in the same determinants of culture. Technology may limit the way a society can react to any given production function, but that limit almost always leaves considerable room for the operation of cultural factors, or what have been called societal responses, which may retard or enhance growth transmission.

A complete, although necessarily very lengthy, study of export-led growth would treat these societal responses in some detail on a cultural or psychological level to determine the extent to which a staple sector, rather than work within a predetermined social environment, can itself generate social change conducive to growth transmission. Although this study will not cover that ground, it is useful to outline the psychological and sociological setting for what follows.

The psychological approach is represented predominantly by McClelland and Hagen (who happens to be an economist).[17] Briefly, they hold that entrepreneurship is the key to development; its presence is determined by personality traits that are in turn formed by childhood reaction to parental behavior. While Hagen speaks in terms of innovational (as opposed to authoritarian) personalities, McClelland centers on an individual's need for achievement as the critical factor in entrepreneurial behavior. The prevailing conclusion from this approach is that psychological (and thus cultural) conditions conducive to development cannot be achieved within a generation; if they do not exist, it requires at least two and probably more generations to develop them, since the process assumes changes first in parents' and only then in children's personalities.[18]

Sociologists take a more aggregated and more optimistic view of societal responses. Kunkel has questioned the psychological approach to cultural change, holding that constructs such as personality are not directly measurable but can only be inferred from observed behavior. Observed behavior, however, is open to influence by group or societal norms and expectations, which encourage and reinforce certain actions and discourage others. He cites experience in the Peruvian Andes that demonstrates the possibility of inducing changes in the behavior of individuals in small societies favorable to economic development. In this view, the wait of several generations is not required; innovational or achieving behavior can be stimulated through education and physical organizational changes that encourage societies to reward such behavior.[19]

The economist, in a poor position to judge the relative merits of the two positions outlined, can at least note the dispute and point out the interpretation more favorable to the role of economics in development.[20] To bring the discussion to more familiar ground, Harris works in terms of a supply of entrepreneurs, which may be dependent on the psychological and sociological considerations discussed above, and a demand for them that depends on the level of economic activity. Thus, even if economic activity has no effect on the supply function of entrepreneurs, an improved economic climate may shift the demand curve for entrepreneurs to the right and, with any elasticity at all in the supply curve, increase the numbers of entrepreneurs actually supplied.[21] In fact, McClelland himself adopts something very much like this viewpoint when he describes the success of foreign firms in encouraging potential entrepreneurs by awarding subcontracts to local suppliers. He then speaks of the need for achievement as a scarce resource and the full utilization of this resource as a major policy goal.[22]

However, if the sociologists are correct, it may be possible to go further and suggest that certain economic activities could directly affect the supply schedule of entrepreneurs by influencing society to change its attitudes toward achieving behavior. Hoselitz, for example, draws from Turner's frontier theory of American history the proposition that societies expanding geographically, with high land-labor ratios, will promote the kind of social mobility (and, one might add, individualism) that encourages entrepreneurial activity; on the other hand, if economic expansion is intensive, taking place within established areas, traditional social structures are more likely to prevail.[23] Thus the American and Canadian wheat economies probably had a positive feedback effect on societal responses, which were favorable to begin with, while the Danish meat and dairy industry may be credited with a smaller influence on societal values, depending largely on societal responses that were fortunately supportive. North's discussion of the comparative effects of the plantation system and the family farm economy on education (Chapter 2, pp. 8–9) offers a further possible feedback effect from economic activity to societal responses. Finally, there are the more direct effects of a staple industry that broadens horizons, trains labor, and provides a demonstration of successful economic behavior, all of which may develop a society's capacity to respond.

In dealing with societal responses as a variable, the present study will have to observe two practical limitations. First, even if the potential effects of the export industry on societal responses be granted, such feedback is unlikely to have any major observable consequences for a number of years. An export sector that has been important for somewhat less than ten years can have only marginal impact on a large society's attitudes and values. Second, because the observer is trained as an economist, only certain economic manifestations of societal responses will be treated, such as labor mobility, the supply of entrepreneurs, propensities to save and import, the adequacy of the economic institutional framework, and the adequacy of the educational system in providing the skills necessary for modern economic activity.

Import Substitution and Balanced Growth

The pessimistic view of export-led development represented by Nurkse, Prebisch, and Levin all support balanced growth with a heavy emphasis on import substitution as preferred development policy. It is not expected that developing countries will diminish their total imports from industrial countries; on the contrary, imports are expected to grow, but their composition should shift away from consumer goods and toward producer goods, both raw materials and industrial machinery. Exports still have a role, but not the dynamic one of inducing growth. Instead, they fulfill the more permissive function of determining a country's capacity to import the investment goods needed for growth.[24] Just as the analysis that led to these conclusions is vulnerable, so can the efficacy of the recommended policies be doubted. Import substitution can be an effective means of development if selectively used. Hirschman has pointed to the role of imports as indicators of the size of domestic markets and thus as signals of the next step in industrialization, which is to produce domestically those goods imported in greatest quantities, using protection precisely and discriminately.[25] And import substitution has been given a major share of the credit for propelling both Japan and Mexico into industrialization.[26] However, those are not typical examples; in most less developed countries the path of import substitution has usually been a dead end.

The typical characteristics of growth strategies based on import substitution have been investigated in depth at the Center for Development Economics of Williams College. In a recent survey of that research, Henry Bruton emphasizes several interrelated, self-defeating features of import substitution as it is usually practiced. As is commonly recognized, most countries substitute for consumer goods imports first, since these include the simplest production techniques and face the broadest markets. Because domestic production of these goods requires imported capital and intermediate goods, the costs of imported producer goods is kept low, through low tariffs and overvalued exchange rates. Such price distortions have several debilitating effects. They discourage exports and encourage import-using production processes, thus exacerbating long-run, balance of payments difficulties. And they lead to the adoption of capital-intensive techniques in economies with surpluses of labor, limiting employment creation and creating unnecessarily high-cost industries. The distortions associated with import substitution also seem to limit productivity growth. Moreover, once domestic production of consumer goods is firmly established, there is pressure to encourage consumption at the expense of savings in order to keep the existing capacity utilized and avoid unemployment. Finally, this growth-limiting characteristic is reinforced by the difficulty of moving toward substitution for producer goods imports.[27] Not only are the technologies of producer goods industries usually more complex, but their introduction would markedly increase the costs of the already-established consumer goods industries, which have been favored by inexpensive imports of capital and intermediate goods.[28] The Williams investigators do not conclude that import substitution cannot work. On the contrary, they believe the strategy has potential if the distorting policies that typically accompany it can be avoided. But it is clearly no panacea and is probably no less demanding a path to development than export-led growth.

The argument for balanced growth is usually made on grounds other than those being considered here; this extensive literature will not be discussed in this book. Nurkse did propose balanced growth as a substitute for the growth mechanism of primary exports,[29] but the inevitable need for such a substitute has been questioned above. Although balanced growth requires substitution both for present imports and for those potentially induced by rising incomes, import substitution does not necessarily imply balanced growth, as Hirschman's espousal of it should demonstrate. It is sufficient for present purposes to say that export-led growth is necessarily unbalanced growth, at least over periods of, say, ten or fewer years. The historical examples of growth stimulated by primary export sectors are therefore examples of unbalanced growth, which has dominated the history of economic development. To the extent that the present study helps to establish the case for primary export-led growth in the modern world, it will also be a further indication that unbalanced development is still possible and effective.

4
Export-led
Growth in Peru

The vigorous performance of the Peruvian economy over the years from 1950 to 1967 has become familiar to development economists in the United States, at least in broad outline. This chapter has nothing fundamental to add to what has been written on the macroeconomics of Peruvian development. However, a reasonably brief description of the economy and its growth path since 1950 will serve to place the development of the fishmeal industry in perspective. Because of its strategic importance, the export sector will receive special attention. The year 1950 is taken as the point of departure for two reasons. First, it marks a major change in the policy of the Peruvian government toward the export sector and, perhaps consequently, the beginning of dynamic export growth. Second, the national accounts for Peru have been revised and published by the Central Reserve Bank for the years 1950 to 1967, providing a ready source for description and comparison. The latter factor is admittedly more compelling than the former.

The Peruvian Economy from 1950 to 1967

A review of the growth rates of national product and its principal components reveals an impressive 17-year performance (Table 4.1). Gross national product in 1963 prices increased at a rate of 5.5% a year to a level of $3.63 billion in 1967 ($5.7 billion in current prices).[1] With population rising at 2.6% to an estimated 12.49 million in 1967, income per capita grew at 2.9%, increasing from $180 in 1963 prices at the beginning of the period to $291 in 1967 ($459

39

TABLE 4.1. Peru: Growth of national product and components, 1950–1967

	Value (millions of 1963 dollars)[a]		Growth rate (percent per year)
	1950	1967	
Consumption	1029	2711	5.9
Government consumption	144	369	5.7
Gross investment	296	939	7.0
Exports	221	700	7.0
Imports	(238)	(1087)	9.4
Gross national product	1452	3634	5.5

Source: Banco Central, *Cuentas Nacionales* (1968), p. 22.

[a] At the 1961–1967 exchange rate of 26.82 soles per dollar.

in current prices). As the work force grew at a slower rate than the population, productivity increased at 3.2% annually. Inflation, measured by the implicit GNP deflator, proceeded at about 8% a year. It is widely agreed that exports played the key role in Peruvian growth, at least until 1964, a conclusion that will be examined in a later section. Exports, measured in 1963 prices, grew at 7.0% and accounted for 19% of GNP in 1967; the capacity to import (that is, exports corrected by the terms of trade) grew at 7.4% a year. Imports rose by 9.4% a year, while the irregularly growing deficit on current account was financed principally by long-term official capital inflows, which increased markedly after 1961. Gross private and public investment matched export growth at 7.0% a year, but government consumption did little more than keep pace with income, rising at 5.7% a year.[2] These 17-year rates mask some rather significant fluctuations in the principal aggregates over shorter periods, which will be treated later in this chapter.

Aggregate measures of economic growth are never adequate to describe the process, but in the case of Peru they may actually be deceptive. Peru is a textbook example of a dual economy. In 1961, the only year for which data are available, metropolitan Lima accounted for 40 percent of national income. Although Peru's income per capita was $192 in that year (at current prices), the Lima-Callao area had an income of $368 per person.[3] The more advanced sectors of the economy have been the export industries, principally fish products, minerals, cotton, and sugar, as well as the consumer goods, import-substituting industries of Lima. Except for minerals, these sectors are located along the coastal strip, while mining forms isolated enclaves both on the coast and in the mountains (sierra). In 1964, 60% of all exports originated at the coast and another 28% represented sierra mining.[4]

To give a better idea of the schism that marks the Peruvian economy, 1961 per capita income in the 10 coastal departments (which include some of the Andean region) was $259, while the other 13 departments, with 49% of the population, had per capita income of only $100.[5] These latter departments include the extremely rugged Andes, which dominate Peru's topography, and the extensive jungle (selva) of the Amazon basin. The sierra, rich in minerals, is a less-than-generous producer of agricultural products. Its 5.3 million people, 52% of the population in 1961,[6] include most of Peru's Indians, subsistence farmers who exist on the fringe of the economy and society, whose integration presents the country with its gravest problem. The selva is a potentially productive but remote, undeveloped, and scarcely inhabited region. Its development and settlement by sierra Indians has been a principal target of government policy.

Characteristic of underdeveloped countries, the income distribution by income classes is decidedly uneven. One economist has suggested that a Lorenz curve drawn for the country would be indistinguishable from the axes. The National Planning Institute of Peru has estimated a Lorenz curve, using 1961 income distribution by factor shares and sectors. Although the curve does not quite follow the axes, it does indicate that 2% of the population accounts for 40% of the income, while 11% of the population earns 60% of the income (see Table 4.2). By comparison, in Chile the wealthiest 10% earn about one-third of total income and in Venezuela, another classic case of a dual economy, they earn 46%.[7]

The pattern of Peru's national income by industrial origin is still very much that of a preindustrial country, although it has undergone significant change since 1950. In that year, agriculture and fishing together produced 23.0% of gross national product (1963 prices) and employed 58.9% of the labor force (Table 4.3). The indicated

TABLE 4.2. Peru: Income distribution by income classes, 1961

Income class (soles per year)	Percentage share of total		Cumulated percentages of	
	Income	Employees	Income	Employees
Below 3,000	1.4	9.2	1.4	9.2
3,000–5,000	8.0	32.7	9.4	41.9
5,000–10,000	9.9	22.9	19.3	64.8
10,000–20,000	21.2	24.5	40.5	89.3
20,000–30,000	2.9	1.8	43.4	91.1
30,000–50,000	12.8	6.0	56.2	97.1
50,000–100,000	3.6	1.0	59.8	98.1
Over 100,000	40.2	1.9	100.0	100.1

Source: Instituto Nacional de Planificación, *La Evolución de la Economía en el Período 1950–1964: Analisis y Comentarios* (Lima, May 1966), I, Chap. 3, p. 23.

TABLE 4.3. Peru: Origin of output and distribution of labor force, 1950–1967

Sector	Origin of national income in current prices (percent)		Origin of GNP in constant 1963 prices (percent)		Distribution of labor force (percent)	
	1950	1966	1950	1967	1950	1966
Agriculture	34.6	17.8	22.8	15.2	58.9	49.6
Fishing	0.6	2.1	0.2	2.1		
Mining	4.7	7.2	4.5	5.8	2.2	2.2
Manufacturing	14.2	15.0	13.6	19.5	13.0	13.7
Construction	3.3	4.8	5.1	4.5	2.7	3.8
Public utilities	0.4	1.1	0.6	1.0	0.2	0.3
Transport, storage and communications	4.0	4.4	35.6	37.5	2.7	3.2
Commerce	10.4	15.3			6.6	9.6
Banking, insurance and real estate	2.3	2.9			0.4	0.7
Services	9.3	12.7			9.4	10.4
Government	6.7	11.3	8.8	8.5	4.0	6.5
Owner-occupied dwellings	8.1	5.5	8.7	5.5	–	–

Source: Banco Central, *Cuentas Nacionales* (1968), pp. 16, 24, 30.

low productivity arises from the dominating importance of subsistence agriculture in a sector that also includes the highly efficient coastal farms and the fishing industry, both export-oriented. By 1967, agriculture and fishing produced only 18.3% of GNP; productivity had grown slightly less than the national average, so that 49.6% of the work force remained employed in that sector in 1966. The decline in agriculture's share of national product is even more marked, however, since the included fishing sector grew from 0.2% to 2.1% under the stimulus of demand from the fishmeal industry.

Meanwhile, manufacturing increased its share of GNP at constant prices from 13.6% in 1950 to 19.5% in 1967, while it employed 13.0% and 13.7% of the labor force in 1950 and 1966, respectively, and underwent a productivity increase of 5.1% per year. Productivity in the mining sector improved at the rate of 4.5% a year, allowing that export industry to increase its share of GNP from 4.5 to 5.8%, while it continued to employ only 2.2% of the labor force. Although employment in the sectors of transportation, communication, commerce, finance, and services rose from 19.1 to 24.2% of the labor force over 17 years, these sectors did not increase their share of national product very much in volume terms.[8]

To compare Peru's industrial structure with that of other economies, Thorbecke has used Chenery's regressions of sectoral value added per capita on population and per capita income, fitted for 51 countries. He finds that, as compared with the "standard" country with the same population and income per capita, Peru's agriculture was highly underdeveloped in 1960 (value added per capita 23% below the norm) and its mining highly overdeveloped (value added per capita more than five times the norm). The country was more industrialized than the "standard" country, with value added per capita for manufacturing running about 24% over the norm, while it devoted more resources than average to services, 26% above the norm.[9] The comparatively high concentration on mining merely reflects a resource endowment far more generous than that for most countries its size, but this is also a frequent cause for the type of economic dualism found in Peru. Furthermore, as Thorbecke notes, the comparatively advanced manufacturing sector, located largely near Lima and catering to the upper income groups, and the agricultural sector, whose comparative retardation reflects conditions in the sierra, testify to a sharply dualistic economy.

The Nature of Export Growth

Before presenting the case for export-led growth in Peru, the composition and behavior of the export sector will be described and possible reasons for this behavior analyzed. Aside from their expansion, exports are characterized by the complete dominance of raw materials and foodstuffs, a comparatively diversified composition, and the important changes that this composition has undergone in the 17-year period. In 1950 the current dollar value of exports was $193.6 million; by far the greatest foreign exchange earner, accounting for 35% of export earnings, was cotton (Table 4.4). If sugar (15%) and petroleum (13%) are added, the three largest export products earned 63% of the total value of exports. Lead, zinc, copper, and silver each accounted for 4 to 6%, while fish products added another 3%.

TABLE 4.4. Peru: Composition of exports, 1950 and 1967

	1950		1967	
Product	Value (million dollars)	Share of total (percent)	Value (million dollars)	Share of total (percent)
Fish and derivatives	5.7	2.9	204.0	27.0
Copper	10.2	5.3	198.3	26.2
Iron ore	–	–	62.1	8.2
Cotton	68.0	35.1	54.8	7.3
Sugar	29.7	15.3	53.1	7.0
Silver	8.0	4.1	42.3	5.6
Zinc	10.3	5.3	35.7	4.7
Lead	12.3	6.4	30.2	4.0
Coffee	1.0	0.5	29.1	3.9
Petroleum and derivatives	25.3	13.1	8.5	1.1
Wool	7.9	4.1	8.2	1.1
Others	15.2	7.9	30.9	4.1
Total	193.6		757.0	

Source: Banco Central, Cuentas Nacionales (1968), pp. 44–45.

By 1967, exports were valued at $757 million, an expansion of 3.9 times and a growth rate of 8.4% a year. The greatest growth had been in fish products, composed primarily of fishmeal feed, which then supplied 27% of all export earnings. The *compound* annual growth rate of volume exports of fish products was a spectacular 30%, while in value terms it was 24%. Copper production had also undergone a substantial expansion, largely the result of the opening of the Toquepala mine by the Southern Peru Company in 1960. In that year alone, copper exports more than tripled in volume, while over the 17-year period the growth rate in volume exported was 12.4% and in value, 19.1% a year. In 1967, copper accounted for 26.2% of total export earnings. Iron, in fourth place, had not been exported at all in 1950; in 1967, it supplied 8% of export value. Thus the first three foreign exchange earners accounted for 61% of the total. Cotton had fallen to fourth place, with only 8% of export value, probably because of an unusually poor year. Sugar, coffee (with negligible exports in 1950), silver, lead, and zinc each accounted for 4 to 7% of total export value. Petroleum had all but disappeared from the list, as limited resources and increased domestic needs made Peru a net importer of petroleum products. The concentration of earnings in the first three products decreased only slightly, but there were six products each earning between 4 and 7% of the total in 1965, against four in 1950, indicating a marginally more diversified export pattern.

What caused Peru's rapid export growth? The first step in answering this question is to choose between demand and supply conditions. To what extent was Peru merely the passive beneficiary of expanding markets and to what extent did it become a more efficient producer of its export products than its competition? One method, used by Lamfalussy in his study of export-led growth in Europe,[10] is to define the growth of demand for any commodity in any market as the percentage increase of imports of that commodity in each importing country. Then, the increment in a given country's export attributed to increased demand is calculated by applying these percentage increases to base-year exports by commodity and country of destination. The residuals between such hypothetical, demand-caused increments for each export good and the actual increments are attributed to "competitiveness," that is, supply factors. Of course, if the country is a major supplier of any commodity in world markets, as Peru is in fishmeal and copper, then this division between demand and supply runs afoul of the identification problem. Increased competitiveness will shift the world supply curve rightward, causing an increase in imports even if world demand does not grow, and some of the growth assigned to demand will in fact be due to increased supply. However, it is worthwhile to present a simplified version of the Lamfalussy calculation, in order to give an indication of the possible importance of increased competitiveness in Peru's export growth.

The 10 countries that are the most important markets for Peru's exports and the 12 most important export commodities were chosen for analysis.[11] Table 4.5 presents the results and lists the sources of the data. Over the 12 years for which data are easily obtainable, 1955–1967, total imports by those countries of 11 commodities (iron had to be excluded for lack of comparable data for both years) increased by 76.8% in current prices. This increase, applied to Peru's 1955 exports of the same commodities, can explain only 31.6% of the actual increase in Peru's exports to 1967. Furthermore, the growth of markets can explain over 40% of actual export growth in only three of the nine cases for which exports increased: sugar, zinc, and silver. Since increased consumption of both fishmeal and copper may have been due at least partly to Peru's shifted supply curve for these commodities, it seems safe to conclude that at least two-thirds of the country's export earnings are due to increased competitiveness, rather than to market conditions.

It is beyond the scope of a brief treatment of exports to make any quantitative evaluation of the sources of this increased supply, but at least two possible causes are obvious: resource discovery and increased productivity. The tripling of copper exports due to the opening of the Toquepala mine is clearly a case of increased exploitable natural resources, although the new mine may also have had a competitive advantage in utilizing the latest mining equipment. It is tempting to say that the fishmeal industry grew, in addition to external market stimuli, because of a newly discovered resource, but the existence of important quantities of fish off the Peruvian coast was known years before the rapid growth of the industry; in fact, fishmeal plants using whole anchovy were in production as early as 1950, six years before the boom began. Technological progress probably

Table 4.5. Peru: Export growth by commodities, 1955–1967

Commodity	(A) Export value 1955 (million dollars)	(B) Growth (decline) of nine country markets 1955–1967	(C) Calculated increase (decrease) in export value for 1967 using (B) (million dollars)	(D) Actual increase (decrease) in export value, 1955–1967 (million dollars)	(E) Fraction of increase in (D) explained by (C)
Sugar	37.0	0.292	10.8	16.1	0.68
Coffee	8.0	(.073)	(0.58)	21.1	<0
Cotton	68.1	(.169)	(11.50)	(13.3)	–
Wool	5.9	(.147)	(0.87)	2.3	<0
Fishmeal	1.4	7.08[a]	9.92	171.9	0.06
Fish oil	–	0.183[b]	0	14.9[c]	0
Iron	8.0	–[d]	–	54.1	–
Copper	29.3	1.109	32.5	169.0	0.19
Lead	26.2	0.004	0.10	4.0	0.03
Zinc	13.8	0.657	9.1	21.9	0.41
Silver	16.2	0.871	14.1	26.1	0.54
Petroleum products	22.1	2.06	45.5	(13.6)	–
All commodities except iron)	236.0	0.768[e]	181.2	574.5	0.316

Sources: Column B, except fishmeal: United Nations, *Commodity Trade Statistics*, Series D for January to December 1955 (New York, 1956); Vol. 1 for 1967 (New York, 1968). Columns A and D, except fishmeal and oil: Banco Central, *Cuentas Nacionales* (1968), pp. 44–45. Column B, fishmeal: Table 5.4. Columns A and D, fishmeal and oil: Table 5.5.

[a] Based on world export volumes.
[b] Includes animal oil.
[c] 1955–1966.
[d] Not available due to reclassification of relevant items.
[e] Includes constructed value for 1955 world exports of fishmeal, assuming 1967 unit value prevailed in 1955.

played the key role. In particular, in 1956 nylon nets began to replace the easily broken cotton ones, and the cost reduction was sufficient by itself to make the industry profitable in Peru. But the story of fishmeal exports must be reserved for the next chapter. It is clear from the discussion on sectoral growth (pp. 41–43) that labor productivity in all sectors, and particularly in mining and manufacturing (which includes fishmeal processing), increased substantially. However, it is total factor productivity that counts in world markets, and there is a presumption that mining at least is capital-intensive, reducing the importance of labor productivity.

Wilson Brown, in a doctoral dissertation completed at the Fletcher School, denigrates the roles played by increased markets, greater productivity, and natural resource discovery.[12] Instead, he traces export expansion to a major change in Peruvian government policy at the end of the forties, when the government backed away from an experiment in a controlled economy and moved toward free trade. From 1945 to 1948, the Peruvian government operated exchange controls and kept the sol overvalued in an attempt to transfer income from exporters, who were considered to be congruent with the wealthy class, to those who would benefit from cheaper imports. In 1949, the more conservative government of Odría, bolstered by a report from a mission of private consultants from the United States, reduced foreign exchange controls and freed the sol. It established a certificate system under which export earnings cleared against import and debt service payments in one market, while foreign investors and tourists had to obtain their foreign exchange in an open market that did not include export earnings. Illegal transactions and legal arbitrage kept the two rates together and the sol fluctuated freely until 1954, falling from 6.50 soles to the dollar in November 1949, to 16.10 at the end of the year and to 19.00 by 1954.[13]

Simultaneously, taxes on trade were reduced. Whereas import and export duties represented 17% of the value of trade in 1951, ten years later the fraction had fallen to 11%. Mining was particularly favored, as taxes on mineral exports fell from 12% of export value in 1949 to 3.5% in 1951 and remained at 2.1% in 1961. Thus the earners of foreign exchange in Peru were strongly favored by post-1948 government policy, and this was a strong contributory factor to the ensuing growth of exports.[14] Brown's underlying assumption, that increased and cheaper supplies of export products would increase export earnings, seems justified for Peru. It probably faces elastic demands for its exports, either because it was not a major factor in the markets for copper, iron, coffee, or cotton in the 1950's or because, as in the case of fishmeal, its exports had close, widely available substitutes.

The Role of Exports in Peruvian Growth

It seems pretty clear that the vigorously growing export sector provided a strong stimulus to the economy, but the precise nature of that stimulus is not easy to sort out. It will be recalled that the 17-year growth rate of exports (in constant 1963 prices) was 7.0%, compared with GNP growth of 5.5% a year. However, the growth of gross investment (public and private) matched that of exports, and in 12 of the 17 years investment was a larger fraction of GNP than exports. Thus, to the extent that investment was an exogenous variable, this, too, might have been a principal stimulant of growth. Government consumption, which increased at about the same pace as income, can be ruled out as a prime stimulus. Imports grew far more rapidly than any other variable (9.4% a year), so that import substitution does not seem to have been a major factor in income growth.

Perhaps the best way to determine the role of exports in Peruvian growth, and at the same time to decide if investment did act as an independent force, would be to capture the essential features of the Peruvian economy in an econometric model and then to simulate the economy's behavior with exports the only growing exogenous variable. A complete model would include the following sets of equations:

1. A production function and a factor supply schedule that determine output capacity; in addition to capital and skilled labor, essential imports could be considered a productive factor.
2. Aggregate demand equations that give the level of consumption, foreign and domestic investment, government expenditure, exports and imports.
3. Equations for monetary demand and supply and the determination of money wages, which yield the price level.[15]

In a perfectly competitive economy with flexible wages and prices, no liquidity traps, and demand schedules for investment or exports that are elastic with respect to interest rates or prices, national income will be determined by the first set of equations. The only role of exports under such a system is to stimulate or allow accretions in factor supplies. Rising exports may, for example, encourage investment if foreign investors are particularly sensitive to export sector behavior in making investment decisions, or exports may increase savings if they tend to raise the incomes of groups with higher marginal propensities to save. And, of course, exports play their permissive role of increasing the capacity to import essential, noncompeting imports and thus contribute to full-employment output. If, however, the economy is characterized by rigidities such as downward wage or price inflexibility, elastic liquidity preference schedules, or inelastic aggregate demand schedules for investment or exports, then the production function and factor supply equations will not in general determine equilibrium levels of national income. National income, and hence the degree of capacity utilization, will in that system depend on the aggregate demand and monetary equations. Then, in addition to their function as a determinant of incremental factor supplies, exports also help to determine the level of aggregate demand and thus national income.

Thorbecke and Condos, who spent considerable time in Peru advising the National Planning Institute and are thoroughly familiar with the data available, were unable to estimate a satisfactory production function relating capital stock or investment to output; they do not even mention attempts to include labor or imported inputs as factors of production. Recognizing this major limitation, they deal with three models of the pure Keynesian multiplier type. In such models, which implicitly assume that the economy operates below capacity, aggregate demand equations alone determine equilibrium levels of national income. Thorbecke and Condos conclude from their work that Peruvian growth over the period from 1950 to 1964 was export-led. To reach this conclusion, they make investment an endogenous variable and find that it is best explained by exports lagged one year and a variable related to the terms of trade, also lagged one year.[16] The problem with such an investment function is its lack of theoretical content.[17] It would have been far more satisfactory to use some variant of the accelerator principle, employing either first differences of exports directly if they are an important indicator to investors, or, more conventionally, first differences of national income. Profits in some form ought also to enter the equation. If one of these theoretically more satisfying specifications yields a good fit, then one could say with more confidence that exports, directly or indirectly, were an important causal factor in investment and therefore in income growth.

Using the newly available national income statistics of the Central Reserve Bank, I set out to replicate Thorbecke and Condos's results and to improve their investment function. It soon became apparent why they had used the theoretically unsatisfying variant. None of a score of variations on the accelerator theme, with exports, income, and profits in several configurations, yielded satisfactory coefficients of determination. Again, the Thorbecke and Condos version proved significant, explaining 85% of the variation in investment. We are left with a multiplier model, which is unsatisfactory to begin with, in which investment is correlated with lagged exports and the terms of trade. We must then decide whether such a theoretically ungrounded correlation implies causation or not.

A simple version of the Thorbecke-Condos model is presented in Table 4.6. To simulate export-led growth, the reduced form of the model was used with exports forced to grow at 7.0% a year and a 25% increase in the terms of trade. The simulation, carried on for 12 periods, yielded growth rates close to the 15-year rates discussed above for GNP (4.7% vs. 5.5%), consumption (5.7% vs. 5.9%), and imports (8.8% vs. 9.4%), but fell short of duplicating the rates for investment (5.0% vs. 7.0%) and government expenditure (3.8% vs. 6.7%). So, if the export-investment causality and the severe limitations of the model are accepted, exports can be said to explain most of Peruvian growth over the 15 years.

Still within the Keynesian framework, one can get a clear picture of the respective influences of exports and investment by looking at the growth rates of national income aggregates for short periods (Table 4.7). From 1950 to 1955, exports, measured in soles at 1963 prices, grew at 7.9%, with investment at 9.3% and GNP at 6.0%. During this period, export growth was attributable almost entirely to minerals. In 1956 there was a marked drop in export growth, so that the 1955–1958 rates were 4.8% for exports, 3.0% for GNP, and 3.9% for gross investment. So, up to 1958 it would appear that exports, investment, and income moved together. However, in 1958 a remarkable export boom began and was sustained, with the exception of one year, until 1964. During the six-year period, exports increased at the rate of 10.7% a year, due largely to the opening of the Toquepala copper mine in 1960 and the explosive growth in fishmeal production. During the same period, investment grew at

TABLE 4.6. Peru: Simple Keynesian income determination model, 1950–1967

Fitted equations: two stage least squares

$$C_t = -3170 + .372Y_t + .574C_{t-1} \qquad R^2 = .993 \quad (1)$$
$$ (1420) \quad (.126) \quad\; (.171)$$

$$I_t = -3780^{a} + .639X_{t-1} + 9610Z_{t-1} \qquad R^2 = .850 \quad (2)$$
$$ (3220) \quad\; (.075) \quad\;\; (2890)$$

$$G_t = 737^{a} + .673T_t + .715F_t \qquad R^2 = .940 \quad (3)$$
$$ (955) \quad\;\; (.107) \quad (.189)$$

$$T_t = 916^{a} + .140Y_t \qquad R^2 = .934 \quad (4)$$
$$ (647) \quad\; (.010)$$

$$M_t = -9320 + .258C + .937I_t^{b} \qquad R^2 = .993 \quad (5)$$
$$ (849) \quad\; (.042) \quad (.184)$$

Source: Banco Central, *Cuentas Nacionales* (1966 and 1968). Standard errors in parentheses.

Symbols (all variables in million soles at 1963 prices, except Z): Y = GNP, C = private consumption, I = private gross investment, G = government expenditures, X = exports, M = imports, F = net foreign aid, T = taxes, Z = terms of trade (1963 = 1.000).

[a] Not significant at the 0.05 level.
[b] Note that the equipment component of I_t is estimated from capital goods imports, so that the significance of this coefficient is a foregone conclusion.

an unimpressive 3.6% a year, leading to the conclusion that exports were primarily responsible for gross national product growth of 6.8% over those six years. Increased exports alone accounted for almost 30% of increased GNP; if both exports and GNP are adjusted to reflect the increased capacity to import resulting from improved terms of trade, then the increase in adjusted exports accounted for almost 40% of the increment to adjusted GNP.[18] However, from 1964 to 1967, public and private investment became the most important stimulative element, growing at 13.8% a year. Exports virtually stagnated and the capacity to import grew by only 3% a year.

The UNCTAD Secretariat has estimated an elaborate, 84-equation model for Peru, covering the period from 1950 to 1965, which has

TABLE 4.7.   Peru: Growth of national product and components by subperiod, 1950–1967

	Compound annual rates in percent per year				
	1950–1967	1950–1955	1955–1958	1958–1964	1964–1967
Gross national product	5.5	6.0	3.0	6.8	5.0
Gross investment (including government)	7.0	9.3	3.9	3.6	13.8
Exports	7.0	7.9	4.8	10.7	1.0
Capacity to import	7.4	5.4	0.1	15.5	3.0
Imports	9.4	12.4	2.7	9.0	12.2
Government consumption	5.7	5.5	2.9	7.8	3.8
Private consumption	5.9	6.3	2.1	7.2	4.7

Source: Calculated from Banco Central, Cuentas Nacionales (1966), p. 30; and (1968), p. 22.

two notable features.[19] First, unlike the simple multiplier models just discussed, this one includes a production function. Apparently unable to estimate a more conventional and more satisfactory relation, the model makes output dependent on net investment cumulated from 1950. It also recognizes the same kind of relation as found by Thorbecke and Condos between private investment, lagged exports, and lagged terms of trade. Thus, in this formulation, export growth induces private investment growth, which in turn adds to productive capacity.[20]

Second, the UNCTAD study found a strong negative relation between the income terms of trade (export value deflated by the import price index) and real wage income, and also found consumption out of real disposable wage income to be twice as high as consumption out of the real disposable income of nonwage earners. These two regressions together imply a strong positive relation between exports and savings; the study estimates that, for every 10% increase in export earnings, savings increase by 9%.[21] This illustrates the point made in Chapter 2 (p. 21) with respect to the two-gap (Chenery-Strout) model: if an export sector is both important to the economy and growing rapidly, it seems likely that export growth will always have an important impact, either by contributing foreign exchange to purchase needed imports, or by stimulating savings. In Peru, it appears that the savings gap is strongly affected by exports.

Export growth was important in another respect, which is more difficult to quantify. From 1949 until the middle of 1967, foreign exchange earnings were sufficient to enable Peru to maintain an open economy. The exchange rate was flexible until 1962 and, for the most part, not overvalued; import and export duties were low by the standards of less developed countries;[22] and controls over capital movements were relaxed. These policies not only helped stimulate exports, but also helped Peru avoid the distortions inherent in controlled foreign exchange regimes, with their overvalued rates and highly protective tariffs, all designed to promote import substitution. The open economy should certainly have led to greater static efficiency than otherwise, but its dynamic effect on development is not entirely clear. The following chapters, especially Chapters 7 and 8, will show that, for the fishmeal sector at least, outward-looking policies did promote development. But for the economy as a whole, export growth has left some of Peru's most critical problems very little closer to solution, as the next section will discuss.

Finally, although slightly beside the main points of this discussion, it is worthwhile to glance at the way in which Peru used its foreign exchange. The rapid rates of import growth show that foreign exchange earnings were used to increase considerably the fraction of national income spent on foreign goods. All classes of imports increased considerably from 1950 to 1967, but consumer goods imports decreased as a fraction of total imports (from 24% to 18%). The share of capital goods changed very little and the share of industrial raw materials and intermediate goods imports, the largest category, rose from 36% to 41%.[23] This behavior indicates some not very extensive substitution of domestic production for consumer goods imports, leading to increased demand for imported inputs into these substituting industries.

Export Growth and Economic Dualism

Having established that export growth was at least a very, if not always the only, important stimulus to Peruvian growth over the years from 1950 to 1967, the next step is to ask how this growth has affected the dualism that pervades the economy. In a country with an economic base as schizoid as the Peruvian, growth may not be enough. Equalization and integration are also legitimate goals, and economic growth may be asked to serve these ends. Hence the quality of development may be as important as its rate. Export industries, or any expanding sector, could contribute to the alleviation of dualism in the following ways:

1. By creating jobs, both directly through its own growth and indirectly through its stimulation of other industries, which can absorb surplus agricultural labor.
2. As a consequence of (1), by improving land-labor ratios in agricultural areas and thus increasing agricultural productivities.
3. By offering higher incomes than were paid in the sectors from which labor was drawn, thus contributing to a more equal distribution of income.
4. By opening-up productive opportunities in backward areas, helping to diffuse economic activity throughout the country.
5. By introducing people to the money economy, which may induce them to increase the productivity of the resources under their control.

The first means of alleviating dualism is obvious enough and can be expected to operate with any new or expanding industry, but it may not operate to a significant degree, as the discussion of Zambian mining in Chapter 2 made clear. The combination of items (2) and (3) implies the necessary condition that the expanding sector be one of higher marginal productivity of labor than the one losing labor. The fourth expresses the hope that, in the case of natural resource-based industries at least, nature does not lead to an intensification of whatever geographical concentration already exists. The last potential contribution centers about something like the demonstration effect.

It can be expected to work best in countries where export expansion has been based on the increased productivity of small farms. Once the notion begins to spread that increased productivity makes possible the acquisition of a whole new range of goods, economic incentives begin to work more strongly than they had previously and further increases in output can be expected from small-scale farms and rural industries.

It is fairly obvious from the discussion of export expansion in Peru that it could not have contributed very much to the last two goals. The two most dynamic sectors, fishmeal and mining, are carried out at the coast and in sierra enclaves, intensifying the existing geographic dualism. Although these industries may have introduced some new people into the market economy, the effect would have been limited to new employment and would not have had the kind of multiplier effect implied by item (5). That is, a new mine worker does not provide a demonstration to his farming neighbors to increase output in quite the same way as would another farmer newly producing for market. However, there might be some stimulus to additional local traders and small-scale producers from the increased consumption expenditures of workers in the sierra enclaves and fishmeal ports. Coffee, which does have a potential demonstration effect, has been a dynamic sector. However, in general, Peruvian export industries are not of the right kind to produce the widespread demonstration effect among small-scale producers that could substantially alleviate the condition of the sierra Indians and reduce dualism.[24]

One is left, then, with the possibility that the growing export industries may have created enough jobs at sufficiently high salaries to absorb surplus labor from the sierra (or from the Lima area, to which it migrates) and raise a substantial group of workers from subsistence to a higher place in the income scale, thus improving the income distribution. In a doctoral dissertation on the role of the foreign trade sector in Peruvian development, Vandendreis concludes that these goals were not well served by export industries over the period from 1950 to 1964.[25]

Table 4.8 summarizes the kind of indicative evidence Vandendreis is able to present on income distribution, updated to 1966. It shows that, while the share of agricultural independents in total income fell markedly, so did the fraction of the work force so employed.

TABLE 4.8.   Peru: Income distribution by functional shares, 1950–1966

	1950			1966		
	Share of total income (percent)	Share of labor force (percent)	Average annual income[a] (thousand dollars)	Share of total income (percent)	Share of labor force (percent)	Average annual income[a] (thousand dollars)
Agricultural inde-independents	21.5	40.3	191	11.1	32.7	388
Wage earners	21.3	35.0	217	23.4	33.2	797
Nonagricultural independents	14.2	14.3	354	16.4	14.8	1245
Salary earners	17.6	10.4	599	24.4	19.3	1428
Land and capital[b]	25.4	–	–	24.7	–	–
	100.0	100.0		100.0	100.0	

Source: Banco Central, *Cuentas Nacionales* (1968), pp. 14, 30.

[a] Converted at current exchange rates (15.43 soles in 1950 and 26.82 soles in 1963) from incomes in current soles.

[b] Residual.

The income and work force shares of wage earners and nonagricultural independents remained roughly the same, while salaried employees increased both their income and labor force shares markedly. Since the size of each group changed, it is not immediately obvious what happened to income distribution over the 16 years. An approximate evaluation can be made by constructing Lorenz curves from the data of Table 4.8, if it is assumed (probably incorrectly) that there is little overlap between the functional groups, which are listed in ascending order according to average annual income. (Because the number of individuals earning income from capital is not known, this group had to be excluded.) As Figure 1 shows, the curve for 1966 lies well below that for 1950 for low income groups, but slightly above it for high income groups. On balance, a somewhat less equal distribution seems indicated for 1966.

Considering the imprecision of the measure being used and the omission of capital shares, perhaps the strongest conclusion to be drawn with any confidence is that the income distribution did not improve markedly over a 16-year period during which exports were probably the most dynamic sector in the economy.

As for employment, Vandendreis presents data which show that in 1963 the export industries directly employed 392,000 workers, or 11.8% of the labor force, while producing 16.6% of gross domestic product. (The latter figure is lower than the 21.5% given by Central

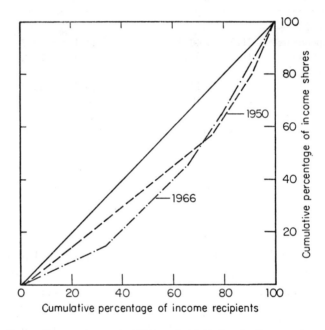

FIG. 1. Peru: Lorenz curves, 1950 and 1963 (excluding capital shares). Constructed from Table 4.8.

Bank data.) From 1950 to 1964, the labor force grew by just over 1 million workers. Vandendreis is able to account for increased employment in mining, fishing, and fishmeal processing of 48,000 over this time, or less than 5% of the national increase.[26] To this should be added an estimated 10,000 workers in industries supplying fishmeal (see Chapter 9), plus possible increases in employment in the agricultural export sector and in other supply industries. But the figure would remain well below 10% of the increment in jobs. This is not a large contribution from a sector responsible for one-quarter of the increase in GNP over the period. It is a strong indication of the capital- and resource-intensive nature of Peru's export industries.

It would not appear, then, that exports contributed very significantly to the alleviation of dualism in Peru's economy. The export-led growth of which this study speaks is, in the Peruvian context, the growth of only part of an economy. This is still a very significant phenomenon, because the growth was rapid and sustained and left the country with considerably more resources at its disposal. But the study of the fishmeal industry should be viewed against this background: its contribution to the urbanized economy may have been great, but its effects on the mass of rural society has been marginal.

5

The Fishmeal
Industry in Peru

In recent years the fishmeal industry has been the most dynamic of Peru's major export industries. Foreign exchange earnings from fishmeal increased a hundredfold from 1955 to 1964, and the product has been Peru's leading earner of foreign currency during the 1960s. The rest of this study will concentrate on this remarkable growth industry, describing its characteristics and tracing its influence on the Peruvian economy. This chapter discusses the world market for fishmeal, describes the processes of anchovy fishing and fish reduction, outlines the industry's organization, and concludes with a brief history of the industry in Peru. Subsequent chapters deal with the production function for fishmeal (Chapter 6), its linkages to the rest of the economy (Chapters 7 and 8), and its effects on factor markets (Chapter 9).

World Markets

Fishmeal is a protein-rich flour, the end result of cooking, drying, and milling either whole fish or parts of them. The meal is added to the prepared feeds of broiling chickens, laying hens, and pigs in Europe and North America. World imports of fishmeal, totalling 2.9 million metric tons,[1] were valued at $418 million in 1967 (see Table 5.1). This can be compared to world imports of such major agricultural commodities as wheat, valued at $4.5 billion in 1967; coffee, $2.5 billion; cotton, $2.5 billion; or bananas, $690 million.[2] This comparatively small world market has grown explosively in the last 10 to 15 years. World exports of fishmeal were only 693,000 metric

Table 5.1. World imports of meals and solubles of marine origin, 1948–1967.

	1948ᵃ	1958	1962	1963	1964	1965	1966	1967
	Volume (thousand metric tons)							
World	111	693	1637	1916	2353	2383	2439	2892
United States	38.7	105.4	234.6	347.9	402.9	250.2	410.1	594.3
Germany	3.3	136.6	345.4	311.2	414.0	436.9	400.0	502.5
United Kingdom	22.9	135.3	284.5	286.3	374.5	366.3	313.4	401.8
Netherlands	6.5	83.9	172.9	175.8	182.0	170.7	138.2	145.9
Spain	2.6	2.5	37.6	76.3	40.5	92.4	99.7	106.7
France	–	42.2	82.5	76.5	104.8	99.0	91.1	99.1
Italy	–	14.4	48.6	61.3	91.6	89.2	96.3	102.6
Japan	–	–	38.5	84.3	102.3	112.6	95.6	86.8
	Value (million dollars)							
World	15.3	103.4	213.2	247.4	312.5	370.1	425.0	417.7

Source: FAO, Yearbook of Fishery Statistics, 1963, 17 (Rome, 1964); 1967, 25 (Rome, 1968), Table H-2.

ᵃ Includes 94 countries; other years include 99.

tons in 1955, implying a compound growth rate of 17% a year to 1967. Moreover, in recent years up to 60% of world exports have originated in Peru.

The demand for fishmeal is rooted in the physiology of chickens and hogs, which, unlike cattle and sheep, have only one stomach and are unable to synthesize certain amino acids essential to their nutrition. Protein-rich fishmeal is able to supply these amino acids, in addition to vitamins and minerals and an unidentified factor that promotes growth in young fowl and pigs. The growth factor is important in raising broilers, since it reduces the time and therefore the costs involved in fattening them for market; and in hogs, since consumers prefer lean pork, which in turn requires early slaughter and thus rapid growth.[3] The amount of fishmeal used in each case depends on its price relative to other protein sources, principally soy bean and meat meals, although at very high or low prices the response to price changes may become quite inelastic.

The point is illustrated in Figure 2, which depicts an informed individual's demand for fishmeal to be used in broiler rations. (Prices

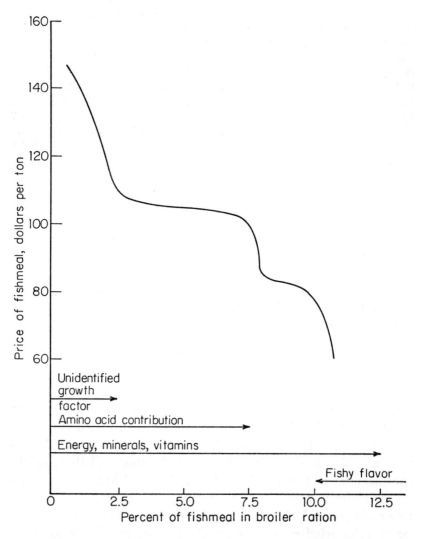

FIG. 2. Demand curve of informed individual buyer of fishmeal for broiler feeds, Chicago market, November 1960. From G. R. Allen, "The World Outlook for Fishmeal," in FAO, *Future Developments in the Production and Utilization of Fishmeal* (Rome, 1961), II, p. 7.

reflect the Chicago market during November, 1960.) At prices above $110 per ton, fishmeal cannot compete with soy or meat meal as a protein source. But it still has value as a source of the unidentified growth factor as long as no more than 2.5% of the ration is composed of fishmeal. Since no other additive is as effective in supplying this factor, the demand for fishmeal is rather inelastic in the range from 0 to 2.5% of the total ration. At prices below $110 per ton, fishmeal becomes an economic source of protein, up to a limit of 7.5% of the ration. Thus, over the range from 2.5 to 7.5% of the feed, for which the amino acid contribution of fishmeal is effective and paramount, there are good substitutes and the curve is highly elastic. The amino acid contribution of amounts in excess of 7.5% is no longer important and fishmeal must compete merely as a supplier of vitamins, minerals, and energy, so the curve drops off rapidly to another elastic region at roughly $82 per ton. Finally, when more than 10% of the ration contains fishmeal, the end product may begin to taste more like fish than chicken, so the demand curve goes into a steep decline.[4]

The world demand curve for fishmeal is, of course, the horizontal summation of all such individual demand curves. But it is not a simple step from knowledge of the demand curve for one rational buyer, using fishmeal for a specific purpose in a given market, to the aggregate curve. The vertical position of the curve will vary from place to place, depending on the prices of competing meals, and the shape of the curve will be different for different uses. For example, the unidentified growth factor is not important in feeding laying hens, so for this use the first inelastic portion will be missing. Moreover, not all buyers fit the model of perfect rationality or are fully informed of the nutritional contributions of the various additives, so their demand curves may look very different.[5] And over the longer run, all of these curves can be expected to display more elasticity than in the short run. If the period is long enough, price movements alone cannot explain changes in the amount demanded; the hog and chicken population, as well as technological change, become major considerations.

Apparently, very little quantitative work has been done on world or country demands for fishmeal. Allen makes some general comments on the elasticities involved, which he calls "informed guesses": at prices around $125 per ton cif in Europe, the short-term price elasticity is probably between 1 and 1.5, while the long-run elasticity may be as high as 3.[6] However, Allen's informed guesses are not borne out by elemenatary econometric analysis, using annual data for 1958–1967 on world fishmeal exports and unit values, United States soy meal prices, growth indices for the major fishmeal-consuming industries, and a time trend. Regressions using these variables in several combinations showed price elasticities of demand (using fishmeal prices relative to those for soy meal) in the range of −0.48 to −0.59. The results were excellent, explaining 97% of the variation in exports, and price coefficients were significant at the 0.1 level.[7]

If these elasticities are reasonable, then price declines of up to one-fifth from the mid-1950s to the mid-1960s could have explained only about a 10% increase in fishmeal imports. Even if the long-run price elasticity were as high as three, declining prices could account for

TABLE 5.2. Growth of fishmeal markets, 1948–1966

| | Production in selected western countries[a] | | |
	Pork (thousand metric tons)	Poultry meat (thousand metric tons)	Eggs (billions)
1948–1952 Average	7,220	2,544	–
1955	8,454	3,159	113.4
1958	8,602	4,372	121.8
1960	9,373	4,732	121.6
1961	9,552	5,579	129.1
1962	9,978	5,533	132.4
1963	10,257	5,752	134.3
1964	10,554	6,095	141.0
1965	10,211	6,550	137.0
1966	10,225	7,189	139.5
Growth rates (percent per year), 1955–1964	1.8	7.8	1.9

Sources: Pork and poultry meat production: FAO, *Production Yearbook* (Rome, 1958–1968). Egg production: Commodity Research Bureau, *Commodity Yearbook* (New York, 1960–1968).

[a] Belgium, Denmark, Germany, Italy, Netherlands, United Kingdom, Canada, and United States, plus France and Japan for egg production only.

only a 60% increase in imports. In fact, fishmeal imports grew by a factor of 4.3 from 1958 to 1967. Some of this growth can be attributed to the growth of the major fishmeal-using industries: pork, poultry, and egg production. However, only poultry production has grown at all rapidly since 1955, achieving an 8% growth rate from 1955 to 1966 (see Table 5.2). Therefore, much of the 18%-a-year increase in fishmeal consumption from 1958 to 1967 must be due to technological change, primarily in the form of increased and more widely applied knowledge of the nutritional needs of livestock. The regressions reported in n. 7 support this. Although production indexes and price explain 97% of the variance in fishmeal exports, the elasticity of exports with respect to the production index would have to be about five in order to explain the growth of fishmeal exports. Moreover, a simple time trend does just as well in explaining fishmeal growth. Unfortunately, but not surprisingly, using the production index and time trend together does not help sort out the relative effects, because the collinearity of the two time series renders the coefficients insignificant.

Peruvian Production: Fishing

In Peru, fishmeal is manufactured almost entirely from anchovies, which abound along the 1400-mile coast. The abundance of this and other marine life is due to the Humboldt Current, a stream of cool water, 120 to 180 miles in width, which originates in the southeast Pacific, encounters the west coast of South America in northern Chile, and flows along the coast almost to Ecuador, where it turns west just south of the Equator. It was along this current that Thor Heyerdahl navigated the Kon-Tiki from Peru to Polynesia. In addition to its counterclockwise movement around the Pacific, the Humboldt Current is characterized by an upwelling of cool water, from a depth of as much as 1000 feet. This upward flow is responsible for the relatively low temperature of the water (at least 18°F below normal for the latitude). Plankton, the animal and vegetable organisms that form the basis for all marine life, flourish in these cool waters. Because the plankton exist in such quantity, anchovy also thrive in the current. And the anchovy in turn provide food for many other species found near the Peruvian coast: bonito, tuna, corvina, and others that have been exploited by Peru's fishing industry for human consumption. Probably the most famous exploitation of the schools of anchovy until recent times was by the guano industry; the fertilizer dug from islands off the coast of Peru is dropped there by enormous flocks of wild sea birds whose principal food was the anchovy.[8]

As will become clear in Chapter 6, the cost of producing fishmeal is strongly influenced by the cost of catching the fish. Thus Peru's industry has depended very importantly on both the abundance of anchovy and their location close to shore. Timing is important. Unpreserved fish will substantially decompose within 24 to 48 hours of being caught, the period being shorter the smaller the fish and the higher the water temperature. That places an upper limit on the allowable elapsed time between catching and processing the fish, but there is also a continual loss of oil and protein content, which makes it important to get the fish into port in the shortest time possible. The proximity of anchovy, which are located in a range of from a few miles to perhaps 200 miles off the coast, enables a boat to leave port early in the morning, fish, and return before nightfall, depositing the catch at the plant in time for processing to begin without requiring preservation of the fish. Thus, small, relatively simple boats can be used.

The largest boats employed in numbers to catch anchovy in Peruvian waters are about 95 feet in length, with a hold capacity of between 180 and 350 metric tons of fish. The most commonly used boats are 65 feet or slightly more in length, with a capacity for roughly 120 tons of fish. However, there has been a steady trend in favor of larger vessels, as indicated by Table 5.3. Whatever the size, these boats are purse seiners (*bolicheras* in Spanish), so called because their nets, extended in the water to form a shallow cylinder, are closed at the bottom in a manner resembling the pulling of the drawstring on an old-fashioned purse. The boats have been constructed of either wood or steel plate; the first reinforced fiberglass boat went into service in 1969. In 1963 wooden boats accounted for over 80% of the registered fleet, but three-quarters of the 409 *bolicheras* constructed from 1964 to 1967 were metal, and the principal builder of wood boats began producing fiberglass *bolicheras* in 1969.[9]

As the boats have grown in size and durability, they have been

TABLE 5.3. Peru: Composition of the fishing fleet, 1960–1968

Length (feet)	Boats catching fish during							
	January 1960		December 1963		May 1966		December 1968	
	Number	Percent	Number	Percent	Number	Percent	Number	Percent
35–39	28	8	–	–	–	–	–	–
40–44	42	13	3	–	–	–	–	–
45–49	54	16	13	1	–	–	–	–
50–54	68	20	53	6	12	1	1	–
55–59	59	18	69	8	22	2	3	–
60–64	71	21	244	27	217	18	110	10
65–69	7	2	419	47	667	56	530	48
70–74	1	–	38	4	114	9	100	9
75–79	4	1	38	4	73	6	85	8
80–84	2	1	3	–	86	7	203	19
85–89	–	–	–	–	–	–	3	–
90–94	–	–	8	1	11	1	45	4
95–99	–	–	–	–	–	–	2	–
Total	336	100	888	98[a]	1202	100	1082[b]	98[a]

Sources: 1960–1966: Sociedad Nacional de Pesquería, unpublished data. 1968: Pesca, 18 (April 1969), 13.

[a] Less than 100% due to rounding.
[b] Excludes 90 boats with unknown length.

outfitted with more sophisticated equipment. In addition to a marine engine and nylon net, *bolicheras* are now equipped with a radio, an echo-sounder for finding fish, a power block for retracting the net, and a pump for transferring the fish from the net to the hold; none of these was standard equipment a few years ago. A fully equipped, 200-ton capacity, metal purse seiner, built in Peru as almost all of the boats are, cost close to $200,000 in 1967. These boats are taken to sea by a crew of between 10 and 14 men, including the captain. There has been little change in crew size over the years, so that as the size and sophistication of the boats have increased, labor productivity has also risen. Each crew, with the exception of the motor technician, is paid entirely under a piece rate system.

The boats put to sea shortly after midnight and usually arrive at the suspected fishing grounds around daybreak. The search for anchovy is based partly on the experience of the past few days, partly on the use of the echo-sounder, which reflects sound waves off air bubbles inside the fish to give readings on the depth of the fish, and very largely on the intuition of experienced captains. When the fish have been located, the nylon net is ejected into the water and spread, often with the help of a skiff carried by the *bolichera,* into a cylinder with a circumference of about 1000 feet and a depth of about 200 feet. Lead weights drag the lower edge of the net downward, while rubber floats keep its top edge on the surface. Once the fish have been surrounded, the bottom of the net is closed and part of the full net is hauled onto the deck by the hydraulically operated power block. As the fish are concentrated near the surface, they are pumped into the hold of the boat by means of a pump developed for the purpose in Peru; the transfer was previously accomplished with small nets. Two or three good net-loads of fish will fill the hold of a boat and, since it takes two hours or more to deploy, recover, and empty a net, it is obviously advantageous to fill the hold with as few net-loads as possible.[10] When the hold is full, or, in any case, shortly after dark, the *bolichera* returns to port. On arrival it puts in at a dock or anchored barge, either of which is equipped with a pump to transfer the fish from the boat to a pipeline. The pipeline may carry the fish directly to the plant if the latter is located close to the shore, or it may send the fish to waiting trucks, which then transport it to the plant. Costs are, of course, higher if poor plant location requires that trucks be used.

In spite of the seemingly great abundance of anchovy off the coast of Peru, there have been persistent fears about the possibility of over-exploiting the resource. In 1960, the United Nations Special Fund helped establish an organization, now called the Marine Institute of Peru (*Instituto del Mar del Perú*) to carry out scientific investigations of the country's marine resources. These investigations have raised the specter of overfishing in the Humboldt Current and have led to an enforced limit of about 9.5 million metric tons of anchovy to be landed each year. To maintain the limit, the Peruvian government has restricted the fishing of anchovy, both by prohibiting fishing altogether during the poor months of June, July, and August, and by suspending it periodically, or restricting it to weekdays, during the good fishing season in February and March.[11]

The evidence supporting these prohibitions (*vedas*) comes primarily from biological research, which has led to an estimate of the anchovy population of about 12 to 13 million tons. Allowing for reproduction and for consumption by other marine species and by the guano birds, whose preservation has been part of government policy since the beginning of the fishmeal boom, 9 to 10 million tons per year are left for the fishmeal industry. In addition to biological considerations, statistics showing (1) an increasing percentage of voyages made each year on which no fish were caught, and (2) a decreasing average catch per ton of registered fleet capacity, have been interpreted to indicate that any increased effort in the form of more voyages per year may very well lead to a decrease in the total weight of fish landed.[12]

The evidence of decreasing average catch was not corroborated by an elementary econometric analysis, using data supplied by the National Fishing Society. In any case, decreasing average catch with increasing fishing effort (capital services) is sufficient to demonstrate decreasing marginal product, but not decreasing total product. However, if the total catch were really constant or decreasing with increased fishing effort, this would imply a zero or negative marginal product. With any marginal cost above zero, marginal cost would exceed marginal revenue and the point of uneconomic fishing would already have been passed. This state of affairs is possible, even likely, because fishermen are not charged for access to a scarce resource, the anchovy stock, and the cost of depleting this asset is not part of their profit-maximizing calculation. In short, the pure statistical case for overfishing is not convincing, but there is a presumption, based on economics, that overfishing has probably been occurring.[13]

Peruvian Production: Processing

The reduction of anchovy to fishmeal consists basically of cooking, pressing, drying, and milling the fish until a dry meal is achieved. The liquid extracted in the process is separated into solids which are recycled and become part of the meal; fish oil, an important by-product; and water containing solid material which can be recovered to improve the yield of meal from fish. A schematic diagram of the process, including the optional but economically desirable subprocesses for improving yields, is presented in Figure 3.

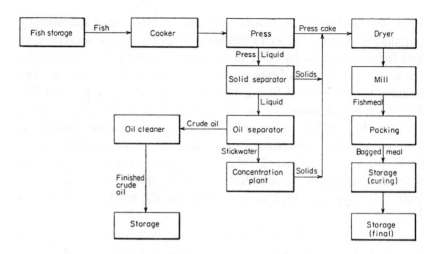

FIG. 3. Schematic diagram of the fish reduction process. Diagram after Sharples del Pacífico, S. A., *Elaboración de Harina de Pescado para Alimento de Animales* (Lima, June 1964), p. 3.

The raw material (fresh anchovy), delivered to the plant either by pipe or by truck, is weighed and then stored in large, open concrete tanks until the processing equipment can accommodate it. The whole fish is conveyed from the tank to one or more cookers, where it is submitted either directly or indirectly to steam at 80 to 100°C. A helicoidal transporter carries the material through each cooker to a press, where a tapered screw squeezes the liquid from the cooked fish. The press emits a moist, cohesive, solid substance, descriptively called the "press cake," which passes to a long, rotating horizontal cylinder, where the cake is dried by means of forced hot air. Like the cookers, the dryer may be of a direct- or indirect-heat type. The rotation of the outer shell of the dryer about a helical axis forces the cake through the dryer to a mill, where it is ground into a dry meal. The meal is sent to a packing station, put into hundred-pound jute or treated-paper sacks, and sent to a yard for storage. The sacks must be spaced to permit an ample flow of air around them, allowing oxidation to take place with a minimum rise in temperature, and must be stored for at least 21 days. Were this not done, the tightly packed meal, either in storage or in the hold of a ship, would be liable to burn spontaneously.

The process just described is the minimum required to produce fishmeal. However, the liquid squeezed from the cooked fish by the press contains both fish oil and fish solids, which can be recovered. The oil is sold and the solids recycled to improve yields. The liquid is sent from the press to a centrifuge, which separates out the insoluble solids and sends them back to the dryer, where they are treated along with the press cake. The remaining liquid is sent to another centrifuge, which separates the oil from what is called stickwater, a liquid containing soluble solids with high protein content. The oil is sent to a cleaner, actually a third centrifuge, through which hot water is passed to remove the remaining solids. The resulting crude oil is stored and sold, either to a refining plant or directly for export. Most of the fishmeal plants in Peru have the optional equipment described so far, which recovers the insoluble solids and produces fish oil as a by-product. However, perhaps only a fifth of the factories operate with stickwater, or concentration, plants, which evaporate much of the stickwater to recover the soluble solids. The concentrated solids, like the insoluble solids from the first centrifuge, are sent back to be mixed in with the press cake before it enters the dryer.[14]

To illustrate the importance of the recovery equipment, a Peruvian manufacturer of centrifuges has estimated that, without any of this optional equipment, a reduction plant can theoretically produce 1.5 tons of meal from 10 tons of anchovy. With the centrifugal equipment installed, the same plant should be able to produce 1.9 tons of meal from the same amount of fish, in addition to which it will recover 0.24 tons of salable fish oil. If a concentration plant is added, the yield from 10 tons of fish will rise to 2.3 tons of meal.[15] In addition to this production equipment, plants located near population centers such as Callao or Chimbote may be required to install deodorizers to treat the gasses discharged from the dryer. The treatment reduces but does not eliminate the fish-like odor which does nothing to improve the quality of urban life along the Peruvian coast.

A single line of basic equipment, consisting of a cooker, press, dryer, and mill, can process up to 40 metric tons of fish per hour. The throughput usually depends on the capacity of the press, although other bottlenecks are possible. A reduction plant may consist of only one such line, but more often they have two or more. The dryer, which may process 50 to 60 tons per hour, will sometimes be fed by two presses. In the middle 1950s a plant with a 10-ton capacity was considered fairly large, but today that would be a very small plant. Capacities of 30 to 60 tons are usual and the largest plants can process over 100 tons per hour; 40 tons is about the average. An average plant with, say, two lines would cost about $1 million in 1967 prices, and the addition of a stickwater plant would add about $250,000.

To operate this equipment, about 15 workers are required, a number that apparently does not vary much as a plant grows from one to as many as three lines. Automatic control equipment is now being installed in many plants to regulate such variables as the temperature in the cooker or dryer. However, as one owner explained, most of the control is still done by experienced operators who know the correct texture of a press cake and adjust the equipment accordingly. These workers need not be highly skilled, but they require at least informal training on the job to become efficient operators. In addition to the operators, unskilled labor is required to sack and handle the fishmeal and skilled maintenance crews must be employed; both groups tend to increase with output. A typical 40-ton plant, operating with two shifts, may employ 75–85 people, including a small administrative staff, which is usually located in Lima.

Location and Organization

The Humboldt Current runs along the entire coast of Peru and fishmeal plants can be found just about wherever the current is. The first important concentration of plants was in Callao, the port that serves Lima, where 31 plants were in operation as early as 1960. However, by 1966 the remarkable growth of Chimbote, a port some 260 miles north of Lima, had put it in first place with 34 active processing factories. The zone between these two centers contains another 59 plants, so that 85% of the 147 plants producing fishmeal in 1966 were concentrated within the 260 miles between Callao and Chimbote. However, there are a couple of plants working close to the Ecuadorian border in the north, and there has been considerable development of fishing in the southern zone, right to the Chilean border.[16] In fact, Chile has also entered the fishmeal business and has become one of the four or five leading exporters.

Fishing is not uniformly good along the coast and the fortunes of any one zone vary from season to season or even from month to month. The fish had been abundant and close to shore in the southern zone for several years, until the 1966–1967 season when they became rather scarce. The Chilean industry particularly was hurt. The central region plants, which before 1967 had been incurring the higher costs of operations with a scarcity of fish, benefited from the shift of anchovy away from the south. Chimbote, meanwhile, has had more uniformly good fishing than the other ports. The reasons for these shifts are not well understood, so fishmeal production is plagued by an important stochastic element.

One consequence of the high-risk element inherent in the availability of fish has been the general tendency of anchovy processors to achieve greater control over the raw material market by operating their own fleets of *bolicheras*. Although fishing used to be dominated by independent boat owners who sold their catch to the factories, the great majority of fishmeal producers now directly own at least part of the fishing fleet they need to operate their plants close to capacity. Data do not exist for earlier years, but a sample of 51 plants, processing about 60% of the catch, revealed that 70% of the fish caught in 1966 were landed by boats belonging to fishmeal plants.[17] The consensus among plant owners is that they would prefer not to worry about the additional organization and higher fixed costs involved in operating individual fleets. However, the independent fishermen have proved unreliable, not always keeping their contracts and quickly deserting areas of poor fishing. Thus a plant maintains a fleet to guard against low capacity utilization or shut-down in case the fishing in its area worsens.

In a smoothly functioning, competitive market this behavior would be inexplicable. Decreases in the supply of anchovy should be reflected in higher prices paid by the plants in the zones affected. It would be immaterial to the processors whether fish were supplied by independents at higher market prices or by owned fleets at higher costs.[18] However, constant references by processors to the unreliability of independent fishermen point to a possible explanation for plant-owned fleets. Fishermen may behave in cobweb-theory fashion, overreacting to changes in the supply of fish. If, for example, the supply curve for fish shifts upward due to poor fishing (that is, it costs more to land a given quantity), fishermen may nevertheless assume that the previous equilibrium price will still prevail in their zone. At this low price, many independent boats will desert the zone, driving the quantity supplied below the new equilibrium amount. Continued cobweb behavior may converge to the new equilibrium, but another supply shift will start the process over again. Although the long-run average price and quantity of fish may reflect equilibrium conditions, they would mask sharp short-run fluctuations in supply. Thus it would appear that plants run their own fleets essentially to smooth these fluctuations and to eliminate the higher cost of processing that they probably entail.

However, the only long-run protection against poor fishing is to spread the risk by operating plants in two or more different zones. There is at least that reason for the multiplant firms that accounted for over 60% of production in 1968. (Cost considerations in general will be discussed in the next chapter.) The largest producer is Luis Banchero Rossi, a Peruvian who entered the industry in its early stages; he operates eight plants and in 1968 produced 254,000 metric tons of meal, or 13.2% of total Peruvian production. The next two producers were International Proteins Corporation of the United States, with five plants and 6.1% of 1968 production; and the Peruvian partners, Madueño and Elguera, with four plants and 5.8% of production. The top 20 firms, operating 54 of the 120 active plants, produced 67% of the fishmeal in 1968. There is some evidence of increasing concentration, but only since 1966, when the first 20 companies operated 44 of the 147 active plants and produced 55% of the fishmeal. From 1960 to 1966, there seems to have been a reduction in concentration. In 1960, the five largest firms produced a third of the output, compared to 28% in 1966 and 35% in 1968, while in eight months of 1963 the ten largest accounted for 45%, compared to 40% in 1966 and 48% in 1968.[19] The largest plant in Peru, owned by Banchero, produced 61,000 metric tons of meal, or 3.2% of total output in 1968.[18]

The concentration percentages taken alone may be misleading. Superimposed on the market structure described above are a strong trade association, the National Fishing Society (*Sociedad Nacional de Pesquería* or SNP), a large cooperative marketing group, the Fishing Consortium of Peru (*Consorcio Pesquero del Perú*), and the world quota arrangements of the international Fishmeal Exporters Organization (FEO), of which Peru is a member. The Fishing Society was founded in June 1960, in the middle of a serious slump in the world market for fishmeal. In October, delegates were sent to the first meeting of the major fishmeal exporting countries, held in Paris. That meeting produced the FEO (the acronym happens to mean "ugly" or "improper" in Spanish), whose purpose was to promote sales of fishmeal, to act as a clearing house for information on fishmeal production and markets, and to establish a system of export quotas for participating nations. Peru, Chile, South Africa, Angola, Norway, and Iceland are members.

Quotas are determined by the members, after each has submitted estimates of how much it can sell in world markets in the coming period. Decisions must be unanimous and members are free to change their estimates quarterly.[20] Thus the term "quota" implies a stricter regulation of markets than in fact exists. Peru's exports have grown rapidly while under the FEO system, and the producers do not feel that the industry is particularly constrained by these arrangements. Since Peru's quota is 60% of world exports, there is not much room to grow by increased market share without affecting world prices; so the discipline of FEO quotas does not add substantially to the constraints inherent in Peru's world market position.

The Peruvian government ratified the Fishing Society's participation in the FEO and also agreed to allow the society to act as its agent in assigning export licenses in Peru to conform to the world market quotas. These have been set by granting each producer a share of the quota for the coming quarter equal to the fraction of total production represented by his production for the previous period, allowances being made for new plants or those with additional capacity. Therefore, each producer is encouraged to process as much as he profitably can: individually he cannot affect world market prices, while his additional output either yields a higher quota in the following period or helps to maintain his quota in the face of generally rising production. Thus, in spite of the quota system, the elements of a competitive market seem to have been preserved within Peru.

However, acting both as the accepted instrument of government in market control and the accepted voice of the fishmeal producers, the Society collectively wields considerable market power, and its internal organization is of some interest in assessing the concentration of power in the fishmeal industry. Voting procedures have been arranged to give some additional weight to the interests of the large producers. Ten of the twenty directors representing the fishmeal industry are elected on the basis of one vote for each member, but in voting for the other ten, members cast one vote for each ton of production during the past 15 months. Five directorships are reserved for other fishing interests, for a total of 25 elected directors. On other matters put to the general membership, producers have one to three votes, according to whether they produced less than 0.6%, from 0.6% to 1.50%, or greater than 1.50% of total production in the previous 15 months.[21]

Such a bare statement of by-laws does not begin to suggest to what extent the extra voting power of the bigger firms actually does control the decision-making process of the association. As one indication of the influence of large producers, it might be noted that 12 of the 20 directors in 1966–1967 represented the 14 firms with more than 1.5% of 1966 output, while 16 directors came from the largest 20 firms at that time.[22] This is some indication that the interests of the bigger companies are better served in the Society, but it is not conclusive evidence. A more complete assessment would require detailed analysis of the control of key committees, the precise issues on which the interests of the large and small producers diverge, and a history of actual votes taken on these matters. Such an exercise is well beyond the scope of this study.

A third institution, the Fishing Consortium, was also a child of the market crisis of 1960. This cooperative was formed after the meeting in Paris in order to organize the marketing of Peruvian meal. There had been an active trade in fishmeal contracts, and it was widely believed that the price fall in 1960 was caused by speculation in this paper. The cooperative's aim was to reduce the scope for speculators by keeping Peruvian meal out of their hands and, in particular, to prevent traders with extensive short positions from covering at favorable prices. Its system of payments to producers conforms to the quota system described above. Each member sells his output to the Consortium, which places its supplies on world markets. Producers are paid a fraction of all proceeds for a given period, based on the fraction of total fishmeal at the disposal of the Consortium that they had provided during the period. Thus each member receives an average price for his output. No fishmeal is handled physically by the cooperative; storage and shipping is handled by the member plant. When it was formed, the Consortium included virtually all the producing firms. In early 1967, only 62 plants were members and these represented 59% of production.[23] Since December 1966, however, those outside the Consortium have been formed into three alternative marketing channels, the object apparently being to compromise between competition and orderly marketing. The other three channels are groupings of producers who agree to market all their fishmeal with a single trading company.

History of the Industry in Peru

The dynamic development of the fishmeal industry was sketched briefly at the beginning of this chapter. Tables 5.4 and 5.8 bring together a set of data which summarizes the growth record of the industry since 1955; sources are indicated on the tables. In 1955, Peru exported only 18,700 metric tons of fishmeal, compared with a world total of 415,000 metric tons. Yet nine years later, when Peruvian production hit a temporary peak, 1.55 million tons were produced and 1.43 million tons exported, and Peru had captured 60% of the world market (Table 5.4). With 1956 as a base year, over the eight spectacular years of growth to 1964, production grew by a factor of 50.5 and export volume by a factor of 51.3, which represent compound growth rates of over 50% per year (Table 5.6). Exports of the by-product, fish oil, grew even more spectacularly, as increasing numbers of plants installed the equipment necessary to extract oil (Table 5.5).

Table 5.5 also indicates that the fishing industry had roots in Peru predating the rise of fishmeal production: in 1950, Peru exported 21,600 metric tons of fish products, mostly canned and frozen fish for human consumption, which were worth $5.7 million. But from 1958, when Peru exported 30,400 tons of fish products other than fish meal or oil, to 1966, there was very little change in the volume of these products exported. The rapid growth of anchovy meal production may very well have drawn resources from a potential expansion of other kinds of marine production. Perforce the statistics on

TABLE 5.4. World production and exports of fishmeal, 1955–1967

Thousand metric tons (unless otherwise noted)

	1955	1958	1960	1962	1964	1965	1966	1967
Production								
World	1259	1396	2144	2885	3654	3601	4067	4596
Peru	20.1	126.9	588.3	1117.4	1553.4	1282.0	1470.5	1816.0
(Percent of total)	(1.6)	(9.1)	(26.0)	(38.8)	(42.6)	(35.6)	(36.2)	(39.5)
United States	332.1	332.7	343.3	383.4	287.3	304.8	267.4	249.8
Japan	141.6	170.7	312.7	317.7	353.1	344.5	361.3	412.8
Norway	197.8	126.5	158.2	107.6	188.1	319.6	421.8	491.7
South Africa	43.7	97.5	96.2	212.3	260.6	274.4	267.8	354.6
USSR	36.0	40.0	85.1	91.5	144.7	202.6	238.5	294.9
Exports								
World	415	596	953	1652	2367	2384	2375	2941
Peru	18.7	105.8	507.0	1055.9	1426.4	1412.7	1302.0	1594.7
(Percent of total)	(4.5)	(17.8)	(53.2)	(63.9)	(60.2)	(59.2)	(54.9)	(54.3)
Norway	148.7	106.9	101.2	59.9	182.8	259.7	257.5	495.0
South Africa	57.3	89.4	126.7	207.4	244.9	232.8	173.4	288.8
Iceland	26.6	55.2	54.4	71.5	126.0	147.8	172.7	132.8
Chile	8.7	10.2	24.2	72.2	146.4	66.9	183.4	113.7
Value of world exports, fob (million dollars)	—	81.0	85.9	170.7	259.0	298.4	347.1	350.0
Unit value of world exports (dollars per metric ton)	—	135.9	90.1	103.3	109.4	125.2	146.1	119.0

Sources: 1958–1967: FAO, *Fishery Statistics*, 1959–1967. 1955: FAO, *Future Developments in Fishmeal*, II, pp. 7–8 (for 1955 exports only).

TABLE 5.5. Peru: Exports of fishmeal, fish oil, and all fish products, 1950–1967

Year	Fishmeal exports			Fish oil exports			Exports of all fish products		
	Quantity (thousand metric tons)	Value (million dollars)	Price (dollars per metric ton)	Quantity (thousand metric tons)	Value (million dollars)	Price (dollars per metric ton)	Quantity (thousand metric tons)	Value (million dollars)	Price (dollars per metric ton)
1950	3.7	0.3	7.5	0.0	0.0	—	21.6	5.7	265.9
1955	18.7	1.4	75.2	0.0	0.0	—	47.3	11.8	248.7
1956	27.8	2.5	89.7	1.7	0.2	94.2	61.0	14.9	244.9
1957	61.6	5.0	81.7	4.3	0.4	97.7	97.7	18.4	188.4
1958	105.8	10.1	95.5	1.6	0.2	101.0	137.2	17.9	130.4
1959	277.6	31.1	112.1	17.2	1.7	97.2	338.5	42.5	125.7
1960	507.0	38.7	76.3	35.0	3.7	105.6	575.4	50.0	86.9
1961	708.3	49.6	69.9	102.3	10.8	106.0	849.9	69.7	82.1
1962	1055.8	99.9	94.6	128.0	11.6	90.5	1219.5	119.8	98.2
1963	1038.3	104.5	100.6	125.5	8.1	64.6	1199.7	120.2	100.2
1964	1426.1	143.4	100.5	110.6	14.1	127.3	1565.5	165.7	105.8
1965	1413.0	155.5	110.0	137.5	22.8	137.5	1581.4	185.7	117.4
1966	1302.0	181.6	139.4	87.4	14.9	170.7	1421.7	205.7	144.7
1967	1594.7	173.3	92.0	—	—	—	1812.4	204.0	112.5

Sources: Fishmeal and oil exports, 1955–1966: Superintendencia General de Aduanas, Estadística del Comercio Exterior, (Lima, 1956–1967). Fishmeal exports, 1950: Sociedad Nacional, unpublished data. Fishmeal exports, 1967: FAO, Fishery Statistics, 25 (1968), h-38. Fish product exports: Banco Central, Cuentas Nacionales (1968), p. 44.

80 / Fishing for Growth

TABLE 5.6. Peru: Fishmeal production, 1955–1968

| | | Thousand metric tons | | |
| | | Fishmeal | | |
Year	Anchovy: Capture	Production	Exports	Stock[a] at year-end
1951	–	7.2	6.0	–
1955	58.8	20.0	18.7	–
1956	118.9	30.6	27.8	–
1957	325.9	64.5	61.6	–
1958	739.1	126.9	105.8	–
1959	1946.8	332.4	277.6	45.9
1960	3313.1	558.3	507.0	77.0
1961	5010.9	835.1	708.3	156.7
1962	6691.5	1112.6	1055.8	192.9
1963	6634.8	1129.4	1038.3	156.4
1964	8863.4	1547.9	1426.1	260.5
1965	7242.4	1282.0	1413.0	237.4
1966	8529.8	1466.4	1301.8	375.2
1967	9824.6	1804.7	1594.7	–
1968	10,262.7	1915.4	–	–

Sources: Capture; production, 1961–1967: FAO, *Fishery Statistics* (various). Exports, 1955–1967: Table 15. Production, 1951–1960; exports, 1951; and stock: Sociedad Nacional, unpublished data. 1968, *Pesca* 18 (March 1969), 18.

[a] Additions to stock will differ from the surplus of production over exports by the amount of local sales and losses, not shown.

fishmeal plants and the fishing fleet (Tables 5.7 and 5.8) also show explosive growth. The 27 plants existing in 1956 had grown to 175 by 1965, and their capacity had multiplied by a factor of 52. Likewise, over the ten years for which data are available, 1954 to 1963, the number of registered *bolicheras* increased by a factor of 12 and their capacity by a factor of 45.

Statistics, of course, cannot write history. Unfortunately, no complete history of the fishmeal industry in Peru has been written and the few articles existing on the subject are quite sketchy. What follows is not authoritative and is far from being a comprehensive account of the industry. Rather, it is a compilation of events, culled from published articles and the author's notes of personal interviews with a few of the participants. It may help to put a little flesh on the skeleton of economic analysis, which will be the concern of the ensuing chapters.

The modern fishing industry in Peru began during the early part of World War II. The abundance of several varieties of fish off the Peruvian coast was becoming apparent just as the war brought a heightened demand for fish liver as a rich source of vitamins A and D. Peru began to supply this market using bonito, but producers found that the fillet, which was a waste product in producing fish liver and oil, could be profitably canned and sold in the United States

TABLE 5.7 Peru: Fishmeal plants, 1956–1968

| Year | Number of plants | | Capacity of existing plants (metric tons of fish/hour) |
	Licensed	Operating during year	
1956	27	–	139
1957	39	–	242
1958	53	–	568
1959	68	–	880
1960	89	77	1560
1961	101	101	2282
1962	118	117	4119
1963	154	147	6553
1964	171	157	7134
1965	175[a]	150	7281
1966	176	154	7321
1967	155	131	7590
1968	169	120	–

Sources: Number and capacity of licensed plants, 1956–1961: I. Tilic, Capacidad de Producción de la Industria de Harina de Pescado en el Perú (Lima, 1962), pp. 3, 6. Plants operating, 1960–1965: Pesca, Anuario 1965–66 (Lima, 1966), p. 118. Licensed plants and capacity, 1963–1966: Sociedad Nacional, unpublished data. Capacity, 1962: Instituto Nacional de Promoción Industrial and Banco Industrial del Perú, Situación de la Industria Peruana en 1964 (Lima, 1965), p. 113. Plants licensed, 1965: Oficina Sectorial, unpublished data. 1967–1968: Pesca 16 (May 1968), 25–26, and 18 (March 1969), 17–18.

[a] Inferred from two sources of possibly inconsistent data.

TABLE 5.8. Peru: Fishing fleet, 1954–1968

	Registered bolicheras		Bolicheras *catching fish during month of December*[a]	
Year	Number	Total hold capacity (metric tons)	Number	Estimated total capacity (metric tons)
1954	126	3,100	–	–
1955	175	4,700	–	–
1956	220	6,800	–	–
1957	272	9,800	–	–
1958	321	14,100	–	–
1959	426	21,600	–	–
1960	731	48,700	467	42,100
1961	846	60,100	521	47,400
1962	1070	86,100	735	75,200
1963	1523	140,000	888	98,000
1964	1642	–	762	88,100
1965	1788	–	921	110,300
1966	1932	–	1249[b]	151,500[b]
1968	–	–	1172	162,000[c]

Sources: Registered *bolicheras*, 1954–1963: Lora, *Crecimiento de la Flota*, p. 17. Registered *bolicheras*, 1963–1966 (by adding construction data to 1963 registrations): "Bolicheras de Gran Capacidad," p. 16. Active *bolicheras:* Sociedad Nacional, unpublished data. *Bolicheras* fishing, 1968: *Pesca* 18 (April 1969), 13.

[a] Covers 85–90% of the total catch.
[b] March.
[c] Probably a low estimate.

as tuna. The war's end brought a small boom in exports of bonito to the North American market, but by 1949 tuna supplies in the United States had increased enough to reduce the market for bonito significantly. Moreover, a United States Food and Drug Administration ruling, that Peruvian bonito could no longer be labeled as "tuna," further reduced its market.[24] Some producers began to use bonito scraps to produce a low-protein fishmeal, which was the entry of that product to Peru. As the reduction plants might have excess capacity, other species, especially herring and anchovy, were fished to produce meal. In 1950, the first plant devoted entirely to the reduction of whole anchovy was built in Chimbote, utilizing used equipment imported from California. Called *Pesquera Chimu,* it was a joint venture of the Wilbur-Ellis Company of San Francisco, which had been interested in Peruvian fishing before the war, and Manuel Elguera, who had been assistant superintendent for one of the first commercial fishing ventures in Peru (and is now the third largest producer of fishmeal, in partnership with Arturo Madueño, another pioneer).

The biggest problem in the early 1950s was the cotton net then in general use. Water-absorbent, weak, and subject to rot, cotton nets were heavy and awkward to handle when wet, and lasted only about two to three weeks. The heavy costs of these nets made anchovy fishing a doubtful proposition and retarded its development in Peru. About 1956, nylon nets for anchovy fishing were introduced to the market. Resistant to rot and mildew, with a tensile strength about six times that of cotton, and not water-absorbent, nylon nets have about half the dry weight of equivalent cotton nets and last from two to five years, allowing for the replacement of sections of netting over time. Yet a nylon net could be purchased for only about twice the price of a cotton one. Not only was there a dramatic saving on fishing costs, but stronger and lighter nets permitted the use of larger boats and possibly afforded some scale economies in fishing. It is perhaps more than coincidence, then, that the major expansion of the industry dates from 1956. It is symbolic that, just after the introduction of the nylon net, Luis Banchero entered the fishmeal industry, establishing *Pesquera Humboldt* in Chimbote in partnership with the Wilbur-Ellis Company. Banchero's story is the story of fishmeal in Peru. He entered the industry at the very beginning of the boom and rode it to the top. In 1966 he was the largest producer, *Pesquera Humboldt* was the largest plant, and Chimbote the most important center of fishmeal production.

By 1959, Peru's exports of canned and frozen fish reached an all-time high, but by then fishmeal and anchovy oil exports accounted for almost seven times the value of exports of other fish products. The first great fishmeal boom covered the years from 1957 to 1959. In the most lackluster of those three years, 1958, export volume grew by 70% and in no year did export value fail to double; in 1959 it tripled. Unit values for fishmeal rose from $90 in 1956 to $112 in 1959. Although no cost data exist for the period, it is widely agreed that profit margins were wide, perhaps ranging up to 50% or more.[25]

About this time the commercial banks began to take an interest in the industry; producers were easily able to service loans at high interest and found it profitable to expand capacity even though expensive credit was required. These years also saw the beginnings of the capital equipment industry, which came into existence to supply the reduction plants and fishing fleets. The need to move whole anchovy into and out of boats in quantities unachieved previously in any country led to the development of a specialized fish pump by the Peruvian company, *Hidrostal,* which utilized a helical impeller to avoid cutting the fish in transit. The patented invention has since been exported to fishmeal-producing countries all over the world. And at least four engineering companies that had previously supplied other industries had begun to produce fishmeal processing equipment by 1959.

Output expanded by a further 83% in 1960, but prices fell markedly, from $140 in late 1959 to as low as $58 in mid-1960, while the average unit value for Peruvian fishmeal exports dropped to $76 for the year.[26] Several factors were responsible for the fall, most obviously the marked increase in world output of fishmeal (Table 5.4), in the face of a slowdown in egg, poultry, and hog production in Western Europe and the United States. Competition from soybean and meat meal also intensified. But the precipitous price decline was partly due to speculation in fishmeal contracts.[27] In particular, one European trader, who took an especially bearish view of increasing Peruvian output, systematically sold large amounts of fishmeal short, obtaining enough meal at low prices from the unorganized Peruvian producers to keep going profitably for about a year.

Faced by what appeared to be a capricious world market, producers formed the National Fishing Society late in June 1960, and sent a delegation to attend the meeting of major fishmeal-exporting countries in Paris early in October.[28] At least one influential member of that delegation was publicly on record as opposing any market control scheme,[29] and in fact the interest of a fast-growing national export industry would normally be opposed to controls. Nevertheless, the Society's delegation adhered to the Paris agreement, which applied the flexible quota system described earlier (p. 75) and established the Fishmeal Exporters Organization to implement them.

Peruvian producers were probably willing to follow the Paris agreement chiefly because quotas were so informal and because 60% of the world market was reserved for Peruvian meal. More positively, however, it appears that the Peruvians were persuaded by South African arguments that the market was capable of absorbing additional production, but that better market organization was needed to stabilize prices at profitable levels and to avoid the kind of speculation for which the 1960 market was blamed.[30] The loose quota system of the FEO at least provided a formal channel for the exchange of information on production and markets among the major exporters. This first step in market organization was followed by the formation of the Fishing Consortium of Peru, in December 1960, to handle the marketing of most of Peruvian production. The Consortium was able to end the speculative attack on fishmeal by preventing the largest trader from covering his short position. It has not, of course, been able to eliminate all speculators, as some producers, who assume speculation is usually destabilizing, had evidently wished and thought possible. On the contrary, trading in fishmeal contracts is now well established in futures markets created in New York and London in 1966 and 1967, respectively.

The recovery after 1960 pushed prices to about $100 a ton fob by April 1961, although unit values of fishmeal exports fell even further, to $70, probably due in part to delivery of meal that had been sold forward at unfavorable prices during 1960. Still, the industry did continue to expand at a substantial rate during 1961: export volume grew by 40% and plant capacity was increased by 77%.

This was also the period of explosive and entirely unforeseen growth in Chimbote. An unofficial estimate by a city engineer put the population at 17,000 in 1954 and at perhaps 28,000 in 1959. The 1961 official census lists 68,000 for the district of Chimbote, but city officials estimate that by 1962 it may have reached 85,000.[31] At the end of 1958 there were about 14 fishmeal plants around Chimbote Bay, but by the end of 1962 the number had grown to 31.[32] Chimbote became an unplanned city of dirt streets and *barriadas,* the shanty towns that are a common feature of urban life in Latin America. It was not until 1966 that the main streets of Chimbote were paved and sufficient electrical generating capacity became available to meet industrial, but not domestic, needs.

During 1962, the unit value of fishmeal exports rose to $95, the highest level in three years. Growth continued, as production rose by 30% and export volume by almost 50%. The favorable results of 1962 stimulated another investment boom the following year. In many ways, 1963 was the most remarkable of the eight years of rapid growth. Thirty-six new plants were constructed that year, and the registered fishing fleet swelled by 40% with the addition of 453 *bolicheras*. Virtually all the boats and an increasing fraction of the processing equipment were being supplied by Peruvian manufacturers, so that the expansion of capacity stimulated a growing capital goods industry. No complete figures exist, but by 1963 there were at least six Peruvian producers of processing equipment, some of whom undertook complete plant construction as well.

The real boom, however, was in boat building. Peru's progress in boat construction came sharply into focus in 1961, when one manufacturer built a *bolichera* at the biannual International Trade Fair, held just outside Lima. It had become clear by then that a man with limited capital could share in the profits being made in fishmeal if only he could buy a *bolichera* and hire a crew to man it. Apparently it was not difficult to raise the capital required, if widely told stories of the period are to be believed. According to one story, a potential boat owner could purchase an engine from an importer for 25% down, for which he not only got the balance on credit, but might also get credit to cover the cost of the hull! Whether the story is true or not, there was a mad dash for boats. One hundred and fifteen were added to the registered fleet in 1961 and 224 in 1962. By the end of that year the backlog in one of the biggest shipyards covered 18 months of production. Banchero, unwilling to wait that long to put profitable boats into the water, started his own shipyard, which turned out to be a successful one.

In early 1963, *Pesca* did a survey of the shipyards then operating and presented photographs of 42 different yards with a total annual capacity of over 1200 *bolicheras,* more than enough to double the number of registered boats in one year. At that time, they found 382 purse seiners under construction. Most of these yards were small and produced wooden boats.[33] In the dry Lima climate, construction could take place outdoors on an empty lot or even in the street. Wood could be purchased from local suppliers on credit, so that in-

vestment in plant and inventory was negligible. But the capital structure of the shipyards was too fragile for survival. Eight months later,
Pesca made another survey and found only six shipyards producing
bolicheras. In 1967, they found eight yards operating, four of which
were producing over 20 boats a year; only one of these four built
wooden boats.[34]

The widespread failure of the small shipyards is partially explained
by the paradox of that frenetic year, 1963. Investment in all aspects
of the fishmeal industry reached a peak, but it was also the first
year in the history of the industry in which export volume actually
dropped, and production increased very little in spite of the great
increase in capacity. The reason apparently lay in poor fishing, particularly in the second half of the year. The banks seem to have
become nervous even before the decreased landings of fish. *Pesca*,
noting that the fishmeal firms owed an estimated $150 million to
banks and suppliers, reported a cutback in bank credit, particularly
in the form of unrenewed short-term loans, as early as June, 1963.[35]
In the beginning of 1964, the Consortium was having difficulty meeting its forward commitments from depleted Peruvian stocks and was
forced to purchase fishmeal on the world market at high prices,
causing losses to its members. The adverse effect on cash flows became
a serious problem in the heavily leveraged industry. But the crisis
was short-lived. Fishing improved substantially and 1964 turned out
to be the most productive year to date for the industry: 1.55 million
metric tons was produced and 1.43 million tons exported. Landings
of over nine million tons of fish of all species made Peru the leading
fishing nation in the world.[36]

However, the years of sustained rapid growth ended with 1964.
Export volume actually fell slightly in each of the two succeeding
years, although rising prices kept export values increasing. The end
of the long boom was signaled at first by growing fears of overfishing.
In 1965, the Marine Institute called attention to the possibility that
the limits of anchovy exploitation had been reached,[37] and in August
of that year the government prohibited fishing for one month, the
first such *veda* in the history of the industry. In 1966 the prohibition
lasted three months, but these were the invariably poor fishing months
of June, July, and August. The government's imposition of a six-week
veda during the height of the fishing season in February and March

in 1967 and subsequent years has established an official limit of about 9.5 million tons of anchovy landings each year.

Thus, unless mollifying biological considerations arise or the policy of preserving guano birds is changed, the fishmeal industry will have to depend for most of its future growth on increased yields from a given raw material input, and this of course requires technological change. Moreover, the imposition of a fishing limit caught the industry just at the end of its great expansion. Its capacity to process 7000 metric tons of fish per hour means that, working two ten-hour shifts for 250 days per year, it could theoretically handle 3.8 times the allowable catch.[38] Allowing for seasonal fishing, which may make it difficult to utilize more than 50% of capacity in the long run, the existing plants could still handle almost twice the allowable limit. Excess capacity has clearly become a problem.

But biological limits were not the only problem of fishmeal in 1966. It was a year in which producers, having seen world prices rise to new heights during 1965 and being mindful of the Consortium's costly, overextended forward position during early 1964, avoided forward sales, only to watch prices fall during late 1966 while stocks climbed to record levels. It seems certain that at some point falling prices passed rising unit costs. Excess capacity, increased taxes, higher duties on imported inputs, a wage settlement in favor of fishermen, and Peru's general inflation all contributed to the rising costs. Prices, hovering at just over $100 per ton fob in the first half of 1967, showed no tendency to rise enough to allow most firms to operate profitably at current average costs, estimated by the National Fishing Society to be $130 per ton.[39] Given the industry's debt-heavy capital structure, widespread bankruptcy again became a distinct possibility.

One implication of the 1967 fishmeal crisis is unmistakable. The basic problem of the industry has changed. Before 1963 the approach was to rush as much fishing and processing capacity as possible toward completion to take advantage of the highly profitable conditions then prevailing. High margins put a premium on speed and the opportunity cost of caution was high. Now, however, the halcyon days are over and the main task is to promote technological change that will increase yields and reduce costs in the face of narrow (or negative) margins. This is a different phase of development and may require different talents. It also requires further investment, but it is doubtful that many of the fishmeal operators still have access to debt financing on the scale necessary. Those exigencies probably help to explain the increasing concentration of ownership and the reduction in active plants that have occurred since 1966.

Causes of Growth: A Summary

Scattered throughout this chapter have been references to the factors that stimulated the fishmeal industry in Peru. We pause at this point to place them in the context of staple theory. In their study of Canada, Caves and Holton gave three categories of stimuli to the export sector: increased foreign demand, resource discovery, and technological change.[40] The second and third are two different causes of a shifted supply curve, while the first refers to shifts in the demand curve.

In the case of Peruvian fishmeal, there was unquestionably an increase in external demand during the period of growth from the mid-1950s and into the early 1960s. It was caused in part by rising incomes in the industrialized countries, which led to an increased demand for pork and poultry products and thus to a greater derived demand for protein-rich additives to the feedstuffs of these animals. More important, however, the demand for fishmeal and related products shifted upward because of new and more widespread knowledge of the value of these nutrients in the raising of chickens and hogs. As incomes continue to rise, especially in the developing countries, and as commercial farming practices spread to other countries, the demand for protein-rich feeds should continue to increase.

Resource discovery in the conventional sense was not an element in fishmeal industry growth. Caves and Holton had in mind the mineral discoveries in Canada or, perhaps, the sharply improved access to large quantities of fertile land in western Canada. However, knowledge of the Humboldt Current and its rich resources certainly dates back to the guano trade of the middle-nineteenth century if not earlier, and access was never a problem in the tranquil seas near the coast where fish abound. The only element of discovery was in finding the most advantageous way to exploit the resource. Large-scale fishing and reduction of anchovies grew naturally out of earlier efforts in freezing and canning, spurred on by favorable markets and, after

1956, low costs. Thus it requires a fairly contorted interpretation to give much credit to resource discovery.

Technological change occurred most dramatically in fishing, especially with the introduction of nylon nets to replace costly cotton ones in 1956. Unfortunately, no reliable data are available to measure the cost saving involved, but it is generally agreed to have been crucial and the rapid growth of the industry does in fact date from the introduction of nylon. In addition to netting, there have been other important improvements in fishing: echo-sounders to facilitate the location of fish, pumps to replace small nets in transferring the fish from the net to the hold, and power blocks to recover the net, allowing the use of larger nets. The latter two developments also led to the use of larger boats and possibly to economies of scale in fishing, although there are no data to test that presumption. Technological change in processing has not been so marked, although there has probably been an improvement in the quality of the equipment; there has definitely been a trend toward greater recovery of the oil and soluble materials, both of which improve yields and profitability. Now that a fishing limit has been established, the future growth of the industry will depend entirely on technological change in processing to improve yields of fishmeal from anchovy.

6
The Production
Function for Fishmeal

The staple theorist's analysis of economic growth centers upon the production function of the major export industry. It is used to explain the growth path taken by an economy or the reasons why development failed, even though primary exports grew vigorously. In order to delineate the effects of fishmeal export growth on Peruvian development, it is necessary to take a multifaceted approach to the production function for fishmeal. Many of the more important aspects of fishmeal production cannot be captured mathematically; these have been covered in Chapter 5. This chapter will add two more types of description, both mathematically based. First, to get an idea of the types and quantities of inputs required, a Leontief production function will be presented. Then, after an unsuccessful attempt to estimate a Cobb-Douglas production function, an estimated cost function will be employed to provide information on economies of scale. The results of this chapter will be employed in the next three, which cover the industrial linkages between fishmeal and the rest of the economy and the effects of fishmeal production on factor markets.

Leontief Production Function

The fixed coefficient (Leontief) production function has the virtue of giving a good picture of the expenditures on current inputs to the industry, and will be used in Chapter 7 to help explain the development of Peruvian industries that supply fishmeal producers. For the purposes of this section, the fishmeal industry is taken to include both fishing and processing.

Ideally, a Leontief function would be estimated econometrically, taking as large a sample of firms as possible and regressing each input on output to find its coefficient. In practice, point estimates are generally used instead, the coefficient being the ratio of the sum of inputs for all firms in the sample to the sum of their outputs. In this study, it was necessary to use a less elegant method, since no single body of reliable data exists that will give the point estimates required. There were available three censuses of fishmeal producers, a cost breakdown published by the fishing trade association, a study on fishing costs by the Marine Institute, and information on the fishing costs of one producer.[1] Taken together, these sources are flawed by inconsistent reporting, use of possibly unrepresentative samples, aggregation of dissimilar items, and coverage of several years. Not too surprisingly, they yield several conflicting results.

Situations like this call for art rather than science. The author's approach was to select from the sources indicated, trying to find consensus where possible on each item, using what appeared to be the most reliable source when there was disagreement, or using compromise figures when there was little to choose between conflicting ones. The process was so tortuous that no attempt has been made to outline it here. The outcome of this deliberative process is a synthetic Leontief production function, which is probably most representative of conditions during 1964, although 1962 data were relied upon heavily for the fishing data. The result is presented in Table 6.1.

A few words of warning follow. First, the greatest disagreement among the sources was on the fraction of fishmeal value represented by purchases of fish, the range being from 0.40 to 0.52. The figure chosen was constructed from the 1964 census of fishmeal producers and a likely prevailing price for fish in that year. However, this figure is not so critical as its size implies, since it is only used as a weight in consolidating fishing items with processing; changes in the weight of plus or minus 10% do not make a great difference in consolidated coefficients. Second, the residual for fishing apparently includes interest, since no allowance was made for it elsewhere. Interest payments were probably very large in fishing throughout the period from 1960 to 1964, since the fleet was growing rapidly and debt finance accounted for a large fraction of the investment. In consolidating fishing with processing, half the fishing residual was arbitrarily as-

TABLE 6.1. Peruvian fishmeal: Leontief production function, approximately 1964

| | Input coefficients | | |
	Fishing	Processing	Consolidated
Fishing			
Fuel and oil	.047		
Maintenance and repair			
Boats	.153		
Nets	.055		
Insurance	.025		
Crew wages and benefits	.380		
Depreciation	.135		
Taxes (stamp)	.004		
Other expenses	.032		
Residual (including interest)[a]	.169		
Total revenue	1.000		
Processing			
Raw material (fish)		.460	–
Fuel and lubricants		.040	.062
Power (purchased only)		.005	.005
Sacks			
Jute		.038	.038
Paper		.014	.014
Maintenance and repair			
except nets		.061	.131
nets		–	.025
Transportation		.043	.043
Insurance		.004	.016
Taxes (except on income)		.075	.077
Interest[a]		.054	.093
Depreciation		.034	.096
Wages and benefits		.125	.299
Other expenditures		–	.015
Residual[a]		.046	.085
Total revenue		1.000	1.000

Sources: Dirección Nacional de Estadistica y Censos, *Primer Censo Nacional Económico 1963: Censo de Manufacturas* (Lima, 1966); Oficina Sectorial, unpublished census data for 1964 and 1966; Sociedad Nacional, *Crisis de Pesquería;* I. Tilic, *Costos y Beneficios en la Industria de la Pesca Anchoveta* (Lima, 1963).

[a] In consolidating fishing with processing, an arbitrary assignment of half the fishing residual was made to interest. Considering capital-output ratios, debt equity ratios and interest rates prevailing, this assignment is plausible, but could be 30% higher or lower with equal plausibility.

signed to interest, rather than to residual, on the ground that a plausible if crude estimate was better than none at all. The amount is within reason, given the capital-output ratios reported by Tilic, the heavy debts of the industry and the prevailing interest rates.[2] Third, and most obvious from what has just been said, very little faith should be put in the residual as a measure of profit. It is merely a residual, nothing more, and there are no reliable estimates of profit margins on sales to confirm the figure given.

With reference to the consolidated figures, one-third of output value (including meal and oil revenues) is spent on material inputs, which provide a potential market for Peruvian industry. As might be expected in what is basically an extractive industry, gross value added[3] is high; it constitutes 65% of output value, while net value added is 55%. However, of the value-added items, only wages is likely to have strong consumption linkage effects. This component is about 30%, or 23% if social benefits are excluded. The net share of capital is unconfidently given as 18%, or 27% if depreciation is included.

One of the problems with the Leontief approach is that it does not handle investment naturally or conveniently. No allowance for it is made above, except in the limited sense that depreciation reflects past investment. Yet the most obvious stimulus given the Peruvian economy by the fishmeal industry has been its purchase of investment goods manufactured in Peru, and it is necessary to extend the treatment here to include capital goods. In order to get average capital coefficients for the industry, data for 1964 from Tables 5.5 through 5.8 have been used. They show that, for each ton of fishmeal produced, the industry employed:

1. 0.0042 metric tons per hour of active plant capacity.
2. 0.00101 boats, assuming 1000 boats were active at some time during the year.

To put this in more natural terms, the average plant had a capacity of 41.7 metric tons per hour and produced 9900 tons of meal from 56,500 tons of fish, which were caught in nine boats with an average capacity of 106 tons (if the firm owned its own *bolicheras*). This plant had a theoretical capacity to process 200,000 tons of fish if it worked 20 hours a day for 250 days a year. With seasonal fishing, it would have had a difficult time processing as much as 100,000 tons. Nevertheless, the average plant had about twice the capacity it needed, so that the coefficients used above are not truly Leontief coefficients, which give marginal inputs demanded per unit of additional output.

To put these estimates into the same units as those in Table 6.1, the following estimated 1964 prices were employed: $19,700 per metric ton of installed plant capacity; $116,000 for a boat including a net valued at $20,000; and $110.20 for a ton of fishmeal plus 0.1 ton of fish oil.[4] The coefficients, then, turn out to be 0.75 dollars invested in plant and 1.06 dollars in boats for each dollar of output, which give an average capital-output coefficient based on gross output value of 1.81. Using value added, the average capital-output ratio is 2.78.

In order to approximate marginal capital-output ratios, the 1964 census was used to select, on the basis of average cost, the 36 most efficient firms in each of several annual output categories.[5] A series of linear regressions was run using output, in metric tons of fishmeal, as the dependent variable; and raw materials, labor and capital, in turn, as explanatory variables; the fitted equations are presented in Table 6.2. The author used three different proxies for capital stock (Eq. 4 to 6): gross book value of fixed assets, gross book value deflated by an investment goods price index, and plant capacity. After the results are adjusted to place output in value terms, the resulting estimates of the marginal capital-output ratio for processing run from 0.39 to 0.59. No estimates of ratios for fishing are possible with this data. Obviously, the 36 low-cost producers are far more efficient users of capital than the average. However, these marginal coefficients are suspect. In the fixed coefficient model, regressions of output on capital stock are certain to yield a true marginal capital-output ratio only if the capital constraint is binding, that is, if no excess capital is employed in production. It is clear from data already presented that this condition does not hold in the fishmeal industry, and the poor fits of the regressions on capital stock, compared with the fit of output vs. raw material (fish) inputs in Eq. 1, further confirm that observation. However, the estimates based on 36 low-cost firms will have to be accepted as the closest possible approximation of the true value.

The estimates of labor coefficients run into the same problems.

TABLE 6.2. Peruvian fishmeal: Leontief production function for processing, 1964[a]

Fitted equations: ordinary least squares		
$Q = -301^{b} + .179M$ (434)　(.004)	$R^2 = .983$	(1)
$Q = 741^{b} + .571L_m$ (1758)　(.051)	$R^2 = .745$	(2)
$Q = -1320^{b} + 72.9L_h$ (3500)　(16.6)	$R^2 = .533$	(3)
$Q = 1370^{b} + .729K_b$ (2680)　(.123)	$R^2 = .509$	(4)
$Q = 1970^{b} + .577K_d$ (2220)　(.081)	$R^2 = .601$	(5)
$Q = -4810^{b} + 460K_c$ (2740)　(58)	$R^2 = .650$	(6)

Symbols: Q = output, metric tons of fishmeal per year; M = raw material, tons of fish per year; L_m = labor, man-days per year; L_h = labor, hours per year; K_b = capital, gross book value of fixed assets, thousand soles; K_d = capital, gross book value deflated, thousand soles, deflated by Banco Central investment goods price index for the year in which each plant was constructed; K_c = capital, plant capacity, tons per hour.

[a] Thirty-six observations, except 19 for Eq. 3; standard errors in parentheses.

[b] Not significant at the 0.05 level.

Production is seasonal, but labor regulations prevent hiring on a seasonal basis. Thus the labor required to operate the plant at peak loads must be retained as an overhead throughout the year. Moreover, long-term adjustment is also restricted by legislation. The estimated marginal ratio of raw material to output is more certainly correct, since Eq. 1 in Table 6.2 represents the binding constraint of the Leontief production function. The coefficient of M, 0.179, indicates that 5.6 tons of fish are processed by these efficient firms for every ton of meal produced. This is a slight improvement over the industry average of 5.8.

The analysis of the following two chapters would be aided by a comparison of the factor intensity of fishmeal with those for other industries in Peru. Data comparable to that developed in this section are not available for other industries, so it is necessary to resort to the 1963 census of manufactures for a set of consistent data on manufacturing industries. Table 6.3 presents two indicators of capital or labor intensity, and one of labor skills intensity for nine industries and for the average of all industries in the census. To facilitate comparison, a set of rankings, with the most intensive industry ranked first, is given alongside each indicator. The conclusion is that fishmeal processing is highly capital-intensive compared with other manufacturing in Peru, with a capital-labor ratio of $9700 per employee,

TABLE 6.3. Peru: Factor intensity of manufacturing industries, 1963

Industry	Capital-labor ratio[a] (thousand dollars per employee)	Rank	Average wage[b] (dollars per year)	Rank	Wage share of gross value added[b]	Rank
All manufacturing	4.6	5	950	7	0.26	5
Food (except fishmeal)	4.4	7	830	10	.19	7
Textiles	3.6	8	1020	5	.39	1
Paper	6.3	4	1100	4	.19	7
Chemicals	4.6	5	1170	3	.29	4
Petroleum products	42.0	1	2190	1	.13	9
Basic metals	14.0	2	1570	2	.16	10
Machinery (non-electrical)	1.6	10	970	6	.38	2
Transportation equipment	1.8	9	930	8	.34	3
Fishmeal processing	9.7	3	850	9	.23	6
Fishmeal (including fishing)[c]	8.4	3	1100	4	between .30 and .38	2 or 3

Source: Dirección Nacional, Censo de Manufacturas, 1963.
[a] Fixed assets at original cost, divided by number of employees.
[b] Includes nonwage benefits.
[c] Using the capital-output ratio from text, p. 95 and assuming 13,000 fishermen each earn $1340 per year, per discussion in Chap. 9, p. 147.

over twice the average. However, this judgment must be qualified, since fishmeal plant is probably uniformly newer than the fixed assets of other industries and its higher coefficient most likely reflects inflation as well as capital intensity. Fishmeal's below-average wage is probably explained by the heavier dependence on unskilled workers than other industries in the group. The low ranking in wage share, sixth, is consistent with its capital intensity and below-average wage. When fishing is consolidated with processing, the fishmeal industry maintains its capital-intensity ranking based on capital-labor ratios. However, the high average wage received by fishermen[6] gives the consolidated industry a high labor-intensity ranking, when the wage share is used as a measure.

Neoclassical Production Function

It would be advantageous to estimate a neoclassical production function, which allows for variable factor proportions, for two reasons. First, if the fit for such a function is significantly better than that for a production function with fixed factor proportions like the Leontief, then it could be argued that Peruvian entrepreneurs in fishmeal have had sufficient innovative capacity to respond to changing relative factor prices by adjusting factor proportions. If the linear function were to fit better, however, it could mean either that innovative capacity is lacking, relative factor prices have not changed substantially, or factor substitution is technically infeasible. Second, a neoclassical function is also capable of indicating the strength of increasing or decreasing returns to scale for the plant or industry.

Unfortunately, excess capacity in the fishmeal industry precludes any estimate of a long-term production function. Regressions employing a Cobb-Douglas function showed that virtually all the variation in output can be explained by raw material inputs; coefficients for labor and capital were statistically insignificant.[7] Moreover, production functions inevitably omit a fourth potentially important variable, management, because of the difficulty of measuring managerial inputs. In an industry like Peruvian fishmeal, in which a wide range of management performance is observed, differences in the quality of management might explain much of the variation in output. Because it was not possible to avoid the overcapacity problem or to get at the management variable, the Cobb-Douglas production function yielded no new insights into the characteristics of the fishmeal industry. The estimation of cost functions proved a more useful tool.

Cost Structure

Economies or diseconomies of scale are central to understanding the stimulus of fishmeal growth on other sectors of the economy. Sharp diseconomies would explain the large number of fishmeal plants and firms that has been characteristic of the industry. Economic plant size is a major determinant of the demand for entrepreneurs and helps explain the nature of the demand for capital goods.

Cost curves, although a much cruder theoretical device, are also capable of overcoming some of the estimating problems involved in fitting production functions. A relation giving costs as some function of output subsumes a whole set of equations, including the production function and market equations for the factors of production. Thus factors excluded from the production function, particularly management, are automatically accounted for by using the cost function. However, the kind of fundamental disequilibrium that dominated the production function regressions cannot be completely purged from estimates of the cost curve. Disequilibrium will probably be manifest by generally higher costs, which may not be critical for an investigation intent primarily on economies of scale, and by greater indeterminacy in estimates of the cost curve, as discussed below.

The definitions and concepts of cost theory are almost impossible to apply rigorously in any real situation. Four discrepancies arise between the theory of the firm and any observations the economist is able to make on the long-run cost curves of real enterprises. First, not all real firms are efficient in the economist's sense of minimizing costs for any desired output. Thus the costs observed at any output are likely to lie above the theoretically correct minimum cost for that output, imparting a consistent upward bias to the estimates. The size of this bias can be reduced, but not eliminated, by using a select group of efficient firms; those in this study were chosen, on the basis of low average cost, from the 119 for which there are data. The selection process will be described below.

Second, the economist's concept of cost includes a minimum return to keep managerial or entrepreneurial factors in the industry. The accountant's definition of cost includes no profit element and so understates the concept used by economists. However, in the case of the comparatively small, often family-run, enterprises that mark the Peruvian fishmeal industry, the problem may disappear. High salaries to owners, the use of family members in high positions or as paid directors, and the purchase on company account of goods meant for family consumption are all ways in which the owner can extract his minimum necessary profit. These expenditures are, of course, included as costs in company accounts. The extent to which such practices are common in Peru is not known, but they are widely alleged to occur there and certainly are common practice in small businesses in other countries.

The third discrepancy is more fundamental. For the purpose of explaining Peruvian responses to the stimulus of fishmeal production for export, the relevant concept is the long-run cost curve. The point of interest is the decision whether to enter the industry or not and, if so, with what size unit. Such entry decisions are made with no capital committed and no costs fixed, conditions that define the long-run cost curve and differentiate it from short-run curves. On the other hand, no existing firm actually makes rational decisions based on its long-run cost curve, since existence implies capital stock and fixed costs, which make a short-run curve relevant. Thus any observations of actual cost-output relations will be along short-run curves. These will not be coincident with the desired long-run cost curves, unless the firm happens to be in short-run equilibrium at an output for which the curves are tangent.

The implications of this are seen readily from Figure 4. The curve AC_L refers to the long-run average cost for the industry, while MC_L is long-run marginal cost and P_0 gives the level of minimum AC_L. Three plants of different size are in existence, with short-run average and marginal cost curves given by AC_S and MC_S. At a price greater than P_0, say P_1, all firms are in equilibrium with positive profits. Firm 3 happens to be optimum, equating $MC_S = P_1$ at Q_3^1, where $MC_S = MC_L$ and AC_S is tangent to AC_L. Hence the observed average cost is the desired one. But this is fortuitous for a firm already in operation; firms 1 and 2 are in short- but not long-run equilibrium, and for them observed AC_S is noticeably greater than the desired AC_L. At prices less than P_0, like P_2, when firms lose money, but presumably still cover variable costs, the same phenomenon holds: the observed AC_S is above

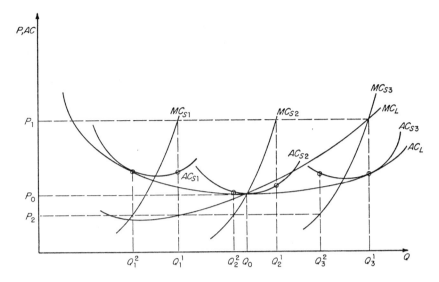

FIG. 4. Long-run and short-run average cost curves.

the desired AC_L, although for firm 1 the difference is not large. Thus the observed short-run costs are systematically above long-run costs. However, there is no way of knowing just how much this upward bias is going to be. As long as it does not operate differentially along the long-run curve (giving, for example, a greater bias for greater plant size), it should not mask economies or diseconomies of scale, particularly if these are sharp.

The final problem in observing cost curves is resolved in favor of the observer, rather than the theorist. In perfect competition, which is considered the relevant model for the fishmeal industry, the economist would not expect to see any plants constructed with minimum short-run cost less than that of firm 2 in Figure 4. For any price greater than P_0, the entering firm ought to construct a plant to produce output greater than Q_0, with $P = MC_S = MC_L$, since the option of building an optimal plant is open. At prices below P_0, no new firms should enter at all, since profits would be negative and there are no fixed costs to consider. Thus a plant like firm 1, with $MC_S = MC_L$ at outputs less than Q_0, should never be built under perfect competition. If such plants were never constructed, then it would not be possible to observe anything of the downward-sloping portion of the average cost curve. In fact, however, there is every expectation that such plants do exist, for two obvious reasons. First, an entrepreneur may not be aware of all the possible plant sizes and may not realize that by building a larger plant he can make greater profits. Second, and more probable, the entrepreneur may lack one or both of two critical factors, capital or management. Capital markets are poorly developed and indigenous management probably is scarce in Peru. An entrepreneur may not be able to finance or manage a plant of optimum size, but, with prices above P_0, he still finds it profitable to build a smaller one. Considering the boom nature of fishmeal industry growth in Peru, with high profits and many small-scale entrants, it is very likely that entrants into the industry built suboptimum plants to earn profits right away, rather than wait until funds or management could be found to build larger plants. Because more distant profits were less certain, it may not have been irrational behavior at all. Moreover, it might be seen as profit maximization if capital market and management constraints were considered.

As previously noted, the available data consisted of the 1964 census returns of 119 fishmeal plants, which included cost and some balance sheet information. The data on costs were altered, where necessary, to ensure consistency, especially in the treatment of fishing costs and depreciation. The costs derived are those for producing both fishmeal and fish oil, although the output of oil is not considered in any of the cost models; the cost of any fish sold unprocessed was, however, subtracted from total cost. Accounting years differed among reporting plants and, considering the nonnegligible rates of inflation in Peru, it was thought best to use only the 87 plants with common accounting years ending in December. These were screened to yield a sample of the 25 most efficient plants.[8]

In order to determine if economies or diseconomies of scale are important in the industry, two types of mathematically equivalent cost equations were fitted:

$$C = a + bQ + dQ^n + u \tag{1}$$

and

$$AC = \frac{C}{Q} = \frac{a}{Q} + b + dQ^{n-1} + v \tag{2}$$

where C is the total cost in 1000 soles, Q is the fishmeal output in metric tons per year, AC is the average cost in 1000 soles, and u and v are disturbance terms. The exponent, n, was tried at both 2 and 3. If coefficient d turns out to be positive and significant, then, after some output, the higher power of Q begins to dominate and average cost rises. Decreasing costs may be evidenced by a significant, positive, and large coefficient, a, in the face of no significance to d, or even by a negative and significant d. In addition, a variable representing capacity utilization was tried to see what, if any, effects this factor may have had on costs. A selected set of results is given in Table 6.4.

Unfortunately, the regressions do not provide unambiguous answers to the questions being asked. It is possible to find either increasing or decreasing costs at high values of output, depending upon which regressions one trusts and how hard one is willing to search. Looking first at the basic equations (set I of Table 6.4), we find that the results are very different, depending on whether the regressions in total or average cost are considered. Those using total cost do not give significant values for the constant term, a, while regressions in average cost consistently yield significant a coefficients, indicating a marked downward-sloping section to the average cost curve at low output. This difference may arise because the intercept term in total cost equations is very small compared with values of C at high outputs and will not weigh very heavily in the process of minimizing squared deviations. When the total cost is normalized to give average cost equations, however, the small values of C close to the origin are divided by comparatively small values of Q; the resulting ratios, C/Q, receive greater weight in regressions of AC on functions of Q. Note also that, in shifting from total to average cost equations, no significance is lost in the b term, which becomes the constant in the average cost equations.

It is on the more critical question of rising *vs.* falling average costs for high outputs that ambiguity sets in. The equations in AC fail to provide any significant values for the coefficient, d, of the terms in Q and Q^2, although d is always positive. On the other hand, the total cost equations have consistently negative, though mostly insignificant, ds. In the one case in which the negative value of d is significant at the .05 level (Eq. IC1), the average costs falls by 15%

TABLE 6.4. Peruvian fishmeal: Cost function for processing, 1964[a]

I. Basic equations

A. $C = 2569^b + 2.326Q$ $R^2 = .972$ (1)
     (1367) (.082)

     $AC = 2967Q^{-1} + 2.247$ $R^2 = .597$ (2)
     (509)   (.111)

B. $C = -167^b + 2.789Q - .101^b(10^{-4})Q^2$ $R^2 = .975$ (1)
     (2053) (.279)   (.058)

     $AC = 3278Q^{-1} + 2.120 + .0630^b(10^{-4})Q$ $R^2 = .608$ (2)
     (642)   (.193)   (.0785)

C. $C = -30^b + 2.676Q - .174(10^{-9})Q^3$ $R^2 = .977$ (1)
     (1666)   (.169)   (.075)

     $AC = 3083Q^{-1} + 2.209 + .0683^b(10^{-9})Q^2$ $R^2 = .600$ (2)
     (575)   (.139)   (.1472)

II. Capacity utilization

B. $C = -61^b + 2.602Q - .190^b(10^{-4})Q^2 + .00610^bQ \cdot U$ $R^2 = .976$ (1)
     (2072)   (.364)   (.125)   (.00756)

     $AC = 2882Q^{-1} + 2.417 + .167^b(10^{-4})Q - .00804^bU$ $R^2 = .644$ (2)
     (682)   (.276)   (.104)   (.00548)

C. $C = 1452^b + 2.038Q - .384(10^{-4})Q^3 + .0109^bQ \cdot U$ $R^2 = .980$ (1)
     (1811)   (.413)   (.146)   (.0065)

     $AC = 2636Q^{-1} + 2.516 + .215^b(10^{-9})Q^2 - .00616^bU$ $R^2 = .622$ (2)
     (702)   (.310)   (.198)   (.00560)

Symbols: C = total cost, 1000 soles; Q = fishmeal output, metric tons per year, $AC = C/Q$ = average cost, 1000 soles, tons per year; S = plant size (capacity); tons per hour; U = capacity utilization, percent.

[a] Twenty-five observations; standard errors in parentheses.
[b] Not significant at the .005 level.

as the output rises from 10,000 to 50,000 metric tons a year. However, in no case does the addition of terms in Q^n or Q^{n-1} improve the fit by more than one percentage point, and in most cases the improvement is considerably less. Hence linear cost equations of the form, $C = a + bQ$ or $AC = a/Q + b$, explain almost as much variation in cost as do the higher order equations. In the absence of strong and consistent statistical evidence to the contrary, the most tenable conclusion is that total cost is close to linear, so that marginal cost is roughly constant and average cost falls rapidly toward an approximately constant value. Looking at Eqs. IA1 and IA2, which are fairly consistent, we note that, at $Q = 10,000$ metric tons, the average cost has fallen to within 12% of its minimum value of about 2300 soles ($86) per ton, while at 40,000 tons, average cost is only 3% above the minimum. Cost differences are not major at high outputs; in going from 20,000 to 30,000 tons, for example, average cost falls by only 2%. Note that there are only three observations for outputs over 30,000 metric tons per year, so that the shape of the fitted cost curve is much more certain for lower outputs. A plot of actual values and the fitted curve of Eq. IA2 is presented in Figure 5.

The addition of a term, U, representing the percentage of capacity utilization during the year, does not alter the results. The utilization term indicates at what point along the short-run average cost curve a firm is producing. Presumably, average costs will fall as U rises over some range, but rise again as capacity is approached. Thus it is not clear a priori what sign U ought to have in the regressions, except that the fishmeal industry is known to be considerably over-capitalized and most firms are probably producing in the range where greater utilization drives the average costs down. In two of the four

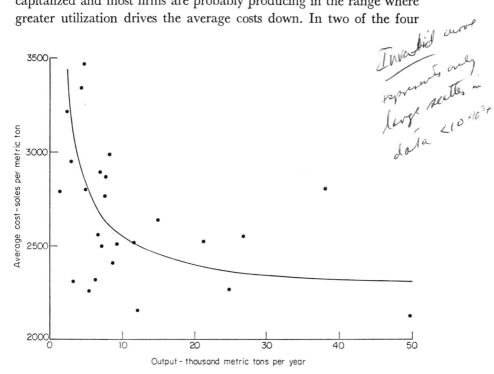

FIG. 5. Fish-processing cost function: Actual versus fitted values.

equations of set II, the coefficient of U was negative, contradicting that expectation, but it was never statistically significant. The utilization term failed to change the conflicting pattern of d coefficients noted above; the d coefficient of Eq. IIC1 is significantly negative.

Nothing has been said so far about economies of scale at the firm level. All the data used in the regressions refer to plants and only two of them are part of multiplant firms. (For some reason, efficient multiplant firms tend to use accounting years ending in June, so they were more numerous in the samples that had to be discarded for lack of sufficient observations.) Because multiplant firms were not sufficiently represented in the sample of lowest-cost firms, the entire population of 119 plants that reported to the 1964 census was utilized to determine if horizontally integrated firms had a cost advantage over independent plants. All of the 28 plants belonging to firms with two or more plants[9] were selected for the test. Two attributes were controlled: accounting year and output for that period. Then 28 independent plants were selected from the remaining 91 in the survey, so that both controlled attributes were as much alike as possible in the two sets of plants. That is, the set of independent plants contained as many companies using a July to June accounting year as did the set of integrated plants and also contained as many plants producing within each of three output categories (0 to 10,000 metric tons a year; 10,000 to 25,000; and over 25,000). To the extent possible, plants were chosen randomly for the group of independents, but it was impossible to match attributes without some nonrandom selection.

Observations from each of the two groups were paired according to their ranking within each group by annual production, and for each pair the difference in average costs was calculated. Using that sample of differences in average costs, the t statistic, the mean divided by the square root of the ratio of sample variance to sample size, was computed to test the hypothesis: the mean of the differences was not significantly different from zero, that is, the two groups do not have different average costs.[10] The mean of the differences was positive, indicating that the multiplant firms had higher average costs than the independents, but the t statistic was only 1.06, so that it was impossible to reject the hypothesis. In other words, the average costs of the two groups are statistically indistinguishable. This shows rather conclusively that there are not, under Peruvian conditions at least, any economies to be gained by horizontal combinations of fishmeal firms.[11]

The conclusion of this investigation into the cost structure of Peruvian fishmeal firms is that large-scale operation, at least beyond 20,000 tons per year, does not lower costs markedly. Furthermore, large multiplant firms seem to have no cost advantage over single-plant operators. Thus the proliferation of small firms cannot be seen as an irrational response to the stimulus of profitable fishmeal markets. Given high profits, apparently unlimited fish before 1964, and small-scale economies, it made sense to enter the industry with companies producing, say, between 10,000 and 20,000 tons of fishmeal per year. The point should not be pushed too far. Many plants (46 in the 1964 census sample of 119) produce less than 7000 tons a year and probably face rapidly falling costs, although many of these were intended to produce more. At the other end of the scale, there is no strong reason in the estimated cost structure not to build large plants, since no sharp diseconomies are evident. Thus the cost structure as depicted here is fairly neutral and permissive. It does not compel a narrow range of rational economic decision-making, so that Peruvian capital and entrepreneurial markets were free to respond in their accustomed way.

7
Backward Linkages

The stimulative effects of a rapidly growing staple industry on the domestic economy can be artificially but conveniently divided into two classifications: those that act through commodity markets and those that act through factor markets. This chapter traces the backward linkages of Peruvian fishmeal to determine the nature of its direct stimulus to supply industries. Chapter 8 deals with three other types of commodity market stimulus: forward linkages, factor payments that lead to a demand for domestically produced consumer goods, and the construction of social overhead capital resulting from fishmeal industry growth. To give a balanced picture of the marginal social product arising from fishmeal development, Chapter 8 will also touch on some external diseconomies of the industry. Chapter 9 delineates the impact of fishmeal production on the factor markets for labor, capital, entrepreneurship, and foreign exchange.

The boundary of this division of impacts is sometimes fuzzy. For one thing, social overhead capital could as easily be classified as a factor of production. Also, the question of foreign exchange markets is inextricably involved with the input-output study of this chapter. Any injustice done to the ananysis of export-led growth by this classification will be rectified in the final chapter, which relates Peruvian fishmeal to other staple industries.

An Input-Output Table

Fishmeal production has been largely, if not entirely, responsible for the establishment of four new industries in Peru: construction of boats, production of fish nets, fabrication of processing equipment, and manufacture of jute sacks. In addition, it has been an important market for several larger industries, such as paper, petroleum products, transportation, and insurance. In order to document these backward linkages, Table 6.5 presents the fragment of an input-output table for Peru relating to the fishmeal industry.[1] The first column, giving the inputs to the integrated industry of fishing and fish processing, is taken directly from the Leontief function of Table 6.1. The second column gives the import content of production for those domestic industries supplying the fishmeal sector directly. Although not properly a part of the input-output schema, this information will help evaluate the leakages from the economy on the second round of expenditure. Normally, such leakages would be included automatically in calculations using the inverted matrix of a full input-output table for Peru.[2] Skipping over to column 7, the imports listed are first-round imports: those purchased directly by fish-processing firms. Thus a Japanese boat would be included in column 7, but a foreign radio installed in a Peruvian boat is counted in column 2.

The figures given in the sixth column for gross fixed investment are intended to indicate a possible long-run equilibrium level, but should not be viewed with great confidence.[3] Investment in boats is based on an average of the three low-key years following the hectic performance of 1963 and includes a large element of replacement. That for netting is merely a residual between a fairly firm estimate of the total market and the purchase for net repair given by column 1. Investment in processing equipment is based on the yearly replacement and renewal of 10% of the capacity needs found in the Leontief production function regressions of Table 6.2; that is, it is assumed that existing capacity will be renewed at capital-output ratios established by the most efficient firms in the industry.

The fishmeal and oil row is based on actual 1964 outputs for two reasons. First, coefficients of column 1 come from the concocted Leontief function of Table 6.2, which is closer to 1964 results than any other. These estimates are probably pretty close to those of 1965 and early 1966 as well. Second, 1964 output and prices were as close to long-run expectations as those for any year for which detailed data were available. The entries in the table for fixed investment and imports, however, are based on more recent conditions, in order to give some indication of the continuing impact to be expected from fishmeal. Thus the table represents a conservative estimate of the impact of a static industry on the economy. Any important changes, such as improved markets, technological improvements, or an easing of the limit on fishing, will lead to stronger linkages than those shown in the table and elaborated below. For example, the recent introduction of fiber glass boats may accelerate replacement and stimulate the boat-building industry beyond the levels foreseen in Table 7.1.

The statistical information of this chapter has a rather tenuous base. Much of the data has been extracted from interviews, many of which yielded conflicting or widely divergent information. Often the precise coverage of a value is unclear. Or, in cases where the information was considered trustworthy, it frequently gave different results than did official census information. Thus the columns of Table 7.1 are products of averaging, compromising, and other inelegant methods that force themselves on the investigator in situations of necessarily small samples and scattered estimates. All that can be said in defense of the final result is that the figures presented are plausible ones and that macroeconomic evaluation is not very sensitive to large changes in individual components of the input-output table.

The Supply Industries

Fishmeal's supply industries fall into two classes. The first four, shown in Table 7.2, excluding those listed as "maintenance and repair," are substantially smaller than the next four, as a glance at the second column of the table will show. Boats, netting, processing equipment, and jute bags are industries that grew and prospered simply because fishmeal did. Table 7.2 shows that all sales of the net manufacturing industry and almost all those of the boat construction industry were to anchovy fishermen. (The public sector's naval shipyard is excluded from these considerations.) Half the output of three jute-processing firms and almost 40% of nine equipment manufacturers' production went to fishmeal processors; in the latter case the dependence was unquestionably much greater in the 1960 to 1963 period when fishmeal investment was heavy.

The same cannot be said about the other industries supplying the fishmeal producers. Fishmeal's demand for paper products, petroleum products, transportation and storage, power, or insurance is certainly a healthy share of the estimated output of these sectors. But the shares are of the order of a few percent, not 40% or more, and the demand is fairly homogeneous with that of all other sectors in the economy for these goods and services. The more important stimulus to petroleum, paper, and insurance arises from the growth of national income due to fishmeal exports. The same holds for power, except in isolated areas where fishmeal is the dominant industry, a problem discussed in the next chapter. Finally, the demand for transportation and storage, as well as for maintenance services, involves a different set of considerations. In these industries, the stimulus has been to a diverse set of small operators. These include contractors who handle the bagged fishmeal from the time it leaves the factory for storage until it arrives at the dock for export; small contractors who perform repair services; and larger producers in the boat and processing equipment industries. Thus no well-defined, new industries have been created. As a practical matter, gathering data from such a diverse collection of small contributors is a hopeless task. For these reasons, little more will be said about industries other than the four clearly defined ones that depend primarily on fishmeal.

Shipyards

Typical of all capital goods industries, boat construction has faced an unstable demand. Table 7.3 presents estimates of the gross investment in *bolicheras* from 1957, based on increments in the number of registered boats as given in Table 5.8. (See the note to Table 7.3 for complete references.) Purchases of boats for anchovy fishing rose by a factor of almost six from 1957 to the boom year of 1960, when 305 were added to the fleet. The investment in boats fell precipitously in 1961, quite possibly in reaction to the decline in fishmeal prices during 1960, but in each of the succeeding years it doubled, reaching a peak of 453 new boats in 1963. The fishing crisis in late 1963, as well as shrinking investment opportunities, limited purchases of new purse seiners to less than 150 a year in each of the next three years. Although boats have an economic life of only four to nine years, the increasing capacity and sophistication of the boats

TABLE 7.1. Peruvian fishmeal: Input-output table, 1964–1966 (millions of dollars, except in parentheses)

	Intermediate goods			Final goods			Source of output	
	(1) Fishmeal and oil[a]	*(2)* Import content of supply industry production[b]	*(3)* Livestock	*(4)* Exports	*(5)* Investment (inventory)	*(6)* Investment (fixed)	*(7)* Direct imports[c]	*(8)* Gross domestic output[d]
Fishmeal and oil[e]	—	—	2.4 (22MT)	157.5 (1426MT)	11.4 (104MT)	—	—	171.3 (1552MT)
Fishing boats—construction[f]	12.0 (.070)	9.8 (.50)	—	—	—	19.7 (133/yr)	—	19.7
Fishing boats—maintenance and repair[g]	4.2 (.025)	6.0 (.50)	—	—	—	—	—	12.0
Netting[h]	—	1.4 (.40)	—	—	—	3.3 (6.6T/yr)	4.1 (770T/yr)	3.4
Processing equipment—construction[i]	—	[0.6 (.6) / 1.1 (.30)]	—	—	—	7.4	[5.6 / 3.7]	[1.8 / 3.7]
Processing equipment—maintenance and repair[j]	10.4 (.061)	3.1 (.30)	—	—	—	—	—	10.4
Bags (jute)[k]	6.7 (.039)	0.1 (.02)	—	—	—	—	5.0 (17mn/yr)	1.7
Bags (paper)[m]	2.4 (.014)	0.6 (.25)	—	—	—	—	—	2.4
Petroleum products[m]	10.6 (.062)	1.0 (.09)	—	—	—	—	—	10.6
Power[n]	0.9 (.005)	—	—	—	—	—	—	0.9
Transport and storage[p]	7.4 (.043)	0.4 (.06)	—	—	—	—	—	7.4
Insurance	2.7 (.016)	—	—	—	—	—	—	2.7
Taxes	13.2 (.077)	—	—	—	—	—	[3.4 / 2.9]	—

Labor	51.3 (.299)	—	—	—	—	—	—	—
Capital (gross)	47.0 (.274)	—	—	—	—	—	—	—
Total[a]	168.8 (.985)	$\begin{bmatrix}23.0\\23.5\end{bmatrix}$	—	—	30.4	—	$\begin{bmatrix}14.7\\12.8\end{bmatrix}$	$\begin{bmatrix}73.0\\74.9\end{bmatrix}$

a Coefficients in parentheses from Table 6.1, the Leontief production function.

b Imported intermediate goods, which are *also included* in the output figures of columns 1 and 6. Excludes duties to the extent possible; taken from information developed later in this chapter unless otherwise noted. Figures in parentheses give fractional import content.

c Refers only to goods imported directly by fishing and fish-processing sector. These estimates *include* import duties, which are *also* shown separately below the line in the tax row (90% on netting imports, 35% on equipment, and nothing on jute bags). The column total is the sum of the entries above the first solid line.

d Equals the sum of columns 1 + 3 + 4 + 5 + 6, less column 7. The column total refers only to intermediate inputs to the fishmeal industry.

e Using 1964 outputs and price, the latter taken at $110 per metric ton, to include fish oil; 1964 is considered a more normal year than either 1965 or 1966, which saw a sharp but temporary rise in world prices for fishmeal.

f Investment taken as 133 boats per year, the three-year average for 1964–1966; uses 1966 average price of $148,000 per boat.

g Import content of second column assumed same as for fishing boats; this is probably an overestimate in what is a more labor-intensive operation, but no better estimate was available.

h Table 6.1 coefficient for netting used in repair was maintained and the residual between the weight of netting implied by that coefficient and a known total market of 1500 long tons was attributed to investment in nets; used weighted average 1966 price of $2.49 per pound, allowing for imports and domestic production, in going from values to volume, except that imports alone were priced at $2.66 per pound, which includes duties (see note c).

i Investment estimated using Table 6.2, regression 6 (Leontief function in plant capacity) to find marginal capital-output ratio, and assuming that replacement will take place at a rate of 10% a year on a capital base found using this ratio. Adjusted to 1966 prices using Central Bank investment price index. Direct imports of column 7 carried at two extreme values per discussion below, pp. 119–120.

j Import content assumed same as for processing equipment, again probably an overestimate.

k Table 6.1 coefficient used, which is consistent with the National Fishing Society estimate of 22.8 sacks per ton of meal; one-third of market allocated to paper sacks at 5.45 soles each and the balance to jute at an average price of 7.6 soles each. Imports equal four-fifths of total jute bag consumption at 7 soles per bag, on which no duty is charged.

m Import content per *Censo de Manufacturas 1963*.

n Purchased only; much power is generated by the processing plants themselves.

p Import content estimated as 25% of maintenance costs as determined by a survey done for Venezuela by R. M. Soberman, *Transport Technology for Developing Regions* (Cambridge, Mass., 1966), pp. 66–68.

q The sum of all entries below the dashed line (that is, excluding fishmeal and oil industry outputs), except for column 7 (see note c). Note that factor payments have not been carried over to column 8, so that column 8 gives a total of all intermediate inputs to fishmeal production.

TABLE 7.2. Peru: Dependence of domestic supply industries on fishmeal, estimates for 1963–1966

Industry	Sales to fishmeal[a] (million dollars)	Industry sales (million dollars)	Ratio, fishmeal/industry
Fishing boats[b]	19.7	20.2[e]	.98
Netting	3.4	3.4	1.00
Processing equipment[b]	3.7[d]	9.5[e]	.39[e]
Jute products	1.7	3.4[f]	.50
Paper products	2.4	49.5[g]	.05
Petroleum products	10.6	116.8[g]	.09
Utilities	0.9	45.0[h]	.02
Transportation	7.4	184.0[h]	.04
Insurance	2.7	n.a.	−

[a] From Table 7.1.

[b] Excludes maintenance and repair.

[e] Figure allows $500,000 for exports per Table 7.6; there may also have been some boats built for other fishing in recent years; the naval shipyard is excluded. The "fishing boat industry" is a fiction, since two of the largest firms also do general metal fabrication and this part of their sales is excluded (though largely included under processing equipment).

[d] Maximum value from Table 7.1.

[e] Based on actual ratio of fishmeal to total sales for 1966 for nine firms interviewed; actual total sales of the nine were $12.5 million.

[f] Estimated by one mill operator; conforms closely to known jute mill capacity.

[g] Estimated from 1963 census figure, increased by 1.70, the ratio of money GNP for 1966 to that for 1963.

[h] Value added for the sector, 1966; note the noncomparability between these estimates and the previous ones, all based on gross output.

being constructed in Peru probably mean that even the reduced gross investment since 1963 represents some increase in the available capacity for catching fish.

Table 7.3 also converts the estimated figures on investments by boats into annual investment values. The prices used are intended to reflect the considerable improvements in boat quality over the years, while eliminating increases due to general inflation. To give a rough idea of the relative magnitude of this single investment goods market, during the admittedly extraordinary peak year of 1963, estimated gross investment in fishing boats represented 5.6% of gross investment for the entire Peruvian economy.

Virtually all of this substantial market has been supplied by Per-

TABLE 7.3. Peruvian fishmeal: Gross investment in boats,[a] 1957–1966

Year	Increase in number of boats[b]	Price indicating quality changes related to 1963[c] (million soles)	Gross investment at 1963 prices	
			(million soles)	(million dollars)[d]
1957	52	0.95	50	2.6
1958	49	1.01	50	2.0
1959	105	1.04	109	3.9
1960	305	1.18	360	13.9
1961	115	1.38	158	5.9
1962	224	1.50	336	12.5
1963	453	2.02	916	34.2
1964	111	2.54	282	10.5
1965	144	3.06	441	16.4
1966	143	3.58	511	19.1

Sources: Prices, 1957–1962: estimated using Tillic, *Costos y Beneficios,* p. 21, and Lora, *Crecimiento de la Flota,* pp. 17, 22. Price, 1966: estimated using data from personal interviews and *Pesca,* "Bolicheras de Gran Capacidad," p. 16. Price deflators: Banco Central, *Cuentas Nacionales* (1968), p. 26.

[a] Excluding nets but otherwise complete.

[b] Equal to the annual differences of registered boats as given in Table 5.8. It is not known to what extent, if any, this series reflects boat mortality or retirement, but the discrepancy between active and registered boats (Table 5.8) would indicate that many sunk or retired boats remain on the register.

[c] This price series was constructed to reflect quality changes only and not movements in the general price level for investment goods. Interviews and the sources listed above yielded estimates for 1951, 1961, 1962, and 1966; values for the other years came from interpolation. Prices for 1951–1961 are highly conjectural.

[d] Converted at current exchange rates.

uvian shipyards. Lora reports that in 1963 only about 1% of the registered boats were imported[4] and there is no reason to think that the figure has risen since. Peru, with the largest annual catch of any country in the world, provides a relatively large market for small and comparatively simple fishing boats that were within the capabilities of a comparatively inexperienced national industry. The surviving, successful firms have limited the number of models produced and have been able to achieve scale economies by maximizing the number of repetitive tasks performed. The extent to which Peruvian shipbuilding is competitive in world markets will be discussed below.

Although practically all fishing is done in Peruvian boats, these *bolicheras* have been built with imported steel or wood, propelled by imported marine engines, and outfitted very largely with imported equipment. Just what fraction of total value is represented by imported inputs is very hard to say, since the estimates available vary from 25% to 70%.[5] In Table 7.1, a 50% import content is assumed, since it was the estimate best supported with cost information and is close to the midrange of all estimates. It would appear, by the way, that the figure has been rising over the years. Most of the technological change in boats has been introduced by way of imported equipment, while some, but not very much, import substitution seems to have taken place. There is scope for considerable substitution in the form of domestically produced steel plate, one of the major inputs into metal boats.

As discussed in Chapter 5 (see pp. 86–87), the boat construction industry experienced a rapid build-up, involving many small firms, until early 1963. Then there was a sharp contraction, which only the larger and more efficient firms survived. Two of the four or five well-established producers manufactured over 30 boats each in 1966. In almost all cases, as expected, boat manufacturers owed their existence entirely to the fishing industry. However, two of the largest firms were basically metal fabricators that produced, among other things, fishmeal processing equipment before entering boat manufacturing. One of these firms failed in 1967, but the survivor retains the potential to supply industries other than fishmeal, as indeed it is doing to some extent. The defunct producer had also been a major factor in reduction plant engineering.

Netting

Figures supplied by Peruvian manufacturers indicate that the fishing industry consumes from 1300 to 1700 short tons of nylon netting each year, which, at the 1967 weighted average price of $2.49 per pound for netting imported and manufactured in Peru,[6] amounts to a median value of $7.5 million per year. The industry sells netting, rather than nets (which are assembled by fleet operators), and its product could be considered either intermediate or capital goods. A net has a life of perhaps three years, but during that period about three-quarters of the net is replaced. The Leontief coefficient for net repair expenditure of Table 6.1 indicates that 56% of sales may be due to replacement—this is the fraction used in Table 7.1. However, this figure could easily vary from year to year, since the investment in new nets is strongly influenced by the investment in boats and because there is probably considerable scope for deferring purchases of new nets in favor of further repair of old ones.

The large Peruvian netting market was supplied entirely by foreign, especially Japanese, manufacturers until 1963, when the first of four local manufacturers was established. Estimates differ, but in 1966 about 45% of Peruvian consumption was supplied by the local firms and this fraction was expected to rise considerably.[7] Although the industry owes its existence in Peru completely to fishmeal production, one of the companies supplying netting is not specialized in that field, which is a comparatively small part of its synthetic fiber business. The industry is heavily dependent on import duties, as discussed below.

Plant and Equipment

The total value of output from nine Peruvian firms that construct plants and fabricate processing equipment for the fishmeal industry was half of that for the shipyards in 1966. However, the industry is far less homogeneous than shipbuilding, and it is extremely difficult to give a reliable picture of its size. Table 7.4 presents estimates of the annual gross investment in plant and equipment since 1957. These probably undervalue investment for 1965 and 1966, primarily because replacement and quality changes are not accounted for. (See note *a* to the table.) Investment in plant and equipment generally exceeded that in boats (Table 7.3) until 1965.[8] However, a large fraction of processing equipment is imported.

Before estimating the size of that fraction, a description of the industry is necessary. Two rather different sorts of firms are involved. One type is the engineering company with the capability both to fabricate processing equipment and to erect reduction plants. There were six active companies in this category in 1967, with sales of $3.7 million in 1964 and $2.8 million in 1966.[9] The two largest firms were responsible for over 70% of this output, although a different firm was in second place in 1964 than in 1966. The dominant firm

TABLE 7.4. Peruvian fishmeal: Gross investment in plants, 1957–1966

| Year | Increase in capacity (metric tons per hour) | Estimated investment in 1963 prices[a] | |
		(million soles)	(million dollars)[b]
1957	103	54	2.8
1958	326	173	6.9
1959	312	164	6.1
1960	680	358	13.4
1961	722	380	14.2
1962	1837	967	36.2
1963	2434	1281	47.9
1964	581	306	11.4
1965	147	77	2.9
1966	40	21	.8

Sources: Price to convert capacity increases to investment values: Oficina Sectorial, unpublished data; and Banco Central, Cuentas Nacionales (1966), p. 34, and (1968), p. 26. Increase in capacity calculated from Table 5.7.

[a] Annual differences in installed capacity priced at $19,700 (529,000 soles) per metric ton. This price was derived from data in the 1964 census of the Oficina Sectorial, giving the fixed assets and installed capacity of nine plants completed during 1964; the estimated 1964 price was deflated by the investment goods price index of the Central Bank. No allowance could be made for (1) decreasing unit construction costs as average plant size increased over the period, (2) increased quality of processing equipment, or (3) investment in replacement equipment and in stickwater plants (which increase recovery yields), especially in the later years. These errors are likely to be offsetting for the early years of the period, but probably cause considerable underestimation of investment of 1965 and 1966, due largely to the third factor.

[b] Converted at current exchange rates.

in this field was founded in 1960, primarily to supply processing equipment, and then branched out into metal boats two years later. With demand from the fishing sector falling off during 1967, it was unable to utilize its comparatively large capacity sufficiently to continue operations, and closed.[10] The other five firms have longer histories, which predate the fishmeal boom. They produced mining equipment,[11] manufactured small metal parts, and constructed metal structures. Thus fishmeal was not responsible for creating these companies. However, in two cases, their efforts were redirected towards the manufacture of production equipment, and the fishmeal market certainly helped all six firms to grow or avoid failure when other business was slack. In a very real sense, then, fishmeal has been responsible for the expansion or maintenance of a Peruvian capability to produce processing equipment with a wide range of applications.

The second category of firm in the processing equipment industry includes three producers, each specialized in a narrower range of products: fish pumps, centrifugal separators, and electric motors. Sales of these firms to the fishmeal industry were running around $2.2 million after 1963, while their total sales were about double that figure. Separators and pumps, but not electric motors, were manufactured primarily to supply fishmeal processors. In addition to markets outside Peru (see below), the pump and centrifuge firms find ready markets for their equipment in Peruvian industries other than fishmeal, so that only a little more than half of combined sales has been to fishmeal producers.

The problems of estimating the share of the plant and equipment market taken by imports have been implicit in the foregoing. First, the size of the market is not accurately known, especially for 1965 and 1966, because of the limitations inherent in the gross investment estimates of Table 7.4. (See note a to the table.) Second, the only figures available for sales of domestic equipment firms are an unsatisfactory mixture of 1963 and 1964 sales and a more accurate estimate for 1966 (see n. 9). Third, the firms producing pumps, centrifuges, and motors may supply either the processors directly or the plant and boat builders. If they sell to fish processors, then their output should be added to that of the metal fabricators to get total local production; but if they sell to plant and boat builders, these sales should not be considered, since they would be included in sales of the fabricators.

The path chosen out of this thicket was as follows: the bogus 1964 sales data for local producers were used, since the gross investment estimate for that year is unquestionably better than for 1966, and all sales of the second-category equipment companies were used, giving an upper limit estimate.[12] Thus local suppliers sold $5.9 million worth of fishmeal plant and equipment during 1964, which is 52% of gross investment in reduction plant and equipment, as estimated in Table 7.4. The 1964 survey data[13] gives a very different picture of direct imports and provides a lower limit for the market share of domestic producers. The 119 responding firms gave total investment in plant and equipment of $9.7 million, a figure reasonably close to that shown in Table 7.4. Of this, however, only 25% is attributed to domestic sources. It is not possible to interpret this figure precisely. Some of the reported imports were probably bought directly from foreign suppliers by the processors, but others were probably purchased through domestic companies as part of contracts for construction of plants. To the extent that reported imports refer only to direct purchases from overseas, the 25% figure gives a lower limit to sales by domestic equipment suppliers. Both the upper (52%) and lower (25%) limits are carried in Table 7.1; in the macroeconomic calculations below, the difference turns out to be small.

Second-round effects present no such estimating problems. The consensus among equipment manufacturers is that imported inputs represent 30% of the value of their sales, a figure with which the 1963 census of manufactures agrees. Thus, allowing for second-round effects, the domestic component of total investment would be 36% using the upper limit estimate for first-round domestic sales, and 18% using the lower limit.

Paper and Jute Sacks

The fourth industry showing the impact of fishmeal demand has been the production of paper and jute sacks, in which the meal is bagged for storage and shipping. The total demand from fishmeal producers in 1966 was about 33.5 million bags.[14] Close to one-third of the sacks consumed by the fishmeal industry are of paper; these are produced by one large Peruvian manufacturer who supplies over 75% of the total domestic paper market. Although fishmeal stimulated this particular product line, it in no way played a role in establishing the industry, which was initiated 12 years before the first fishmeal plant was constructed and sells only a small fraction of its output to fish processors. Treated paper sacks have won a share of the fishmeal container market because they are cheaper and limit the rise in temperature of newly produced meal. On the other hand, when handled roughly, they split more easily than jute bags.

The fishmeal industry consumes about 22.5 million bags of jute a year. Because Peru is capable of growing jute in its undeveloped and otherwise largely unproductive jungle region, it was government policy to encourage the establishment of a national jute fiber industry. In 1967, ten-ounce imported jute sacks, of the type used for fishmeal, could be delivered to users, duty-free, for 7.10 soles each; duties brought the price to about 11.50 soles. Nationally produced bags sold for 9.60 soles, but domestic producers had insufficient capacity to supply the market created by this substantial differential. In view of the situation, regulations permitted users to import four sacks duty-free for each domestic one bought, a ratio that permitted Peruvian producers to operate close to capacity.[15]

Fishmeal producers bought 4.5 million nationally produced jute bags in 1966, at a value of $1.61 million. However, fishmeal is only part of the market for jute sacks in Peru. Guano, rice, salt, sugar, coffee, and other commodities produced in the country can also be stored and transported in jute bags. Thus, in 1963, fishmeal was responsible for 45% of the national consumption of jute sacks,[16] and in 1966 it probably purchased about half of national production. Although national production in 1966 could have been absorbed by Peruvian industries other than fishmeal, its added demand stimulated at least one entrant into the jute bag industry and has opened the way for further expansion of the industry. In 1967 the jute sack industry consisted of three firms, one of which produced over half the national output.

The most attractive feature of the jute industry as a development vehicle is that it reaches into the jungle, creating a cash crop for farmers without other viable alternatives and bridging the dual economy. The 3345 metric tons of fiber produced in 1963 is calculated to have been capable of occupying 2856 fully employed farmers, although a greater number of underemployed persons probably took part in production. Calculations based on that same year demonstrate that, if all imports of jute bags were replaced by national production, a total of 16,800 persons would be fully employed producing jute fiber, all in the *selva*. This possibility fits perfectly with the aim of developing the jungle region as a cure for land pressure in the sierra. Vertical integration is expected to permit some economies, possibly reducing such prices by about a fifth.[17] This would bring the price of domestic jute bags to within 10% of duty-free imports. Because of the low import content of domestic production and the high welfare payments to workers, shadow pricing, especially of foreign exchange and labor, might show expanded jute production to be economic.

Nature of the Stimulus

The production function for fishmeal encouraged these industries. Fishmeal is relatively capital-intensive in Peru and its capital stock is composed of many small units of equipment: boats, cookers, presses, dryers, and so forth. In the case of boats, fish abounding in calm waters close to shore allowed the use, at least in the beginning, of small and relatively simple *bolicheras,* the kind of product that gave a fledgling industry a chance to develop. The size of the resource meant that enough boats were demanded to support an industry of at least three and possibly more firms that, with standardized designs, could take advantage of the economies of a production line operation.

The production of processing equipment was stimulated because the production function of fishmeal called for, or at least allowed, the existence of low-capacity processing lines. If each of roughly 150 plants have two lines, then over nine or so years there was a demand for about 300 processing lines, each with at least four pieces of substantial equipment, ignoring oil separators, concentration plants, and other auxiliary equipment that adds to demand. Peruvian companies supplied from one-quarter to one-half of this equipment. Although no cost data are available by which to judge scale economies, it may be supposed that, in the job-shop operations which characterize equipment manufacturing, economies of scale have severe limits, since several different types and sizes of equipment are offered. However, there is probably a critical market size, below which it is not profitable to learn or hire the skills necessary to produce specialized equipment. The Peruvian market has been extensive enough for at least three or four firms to achieve that size.

To some extent, the absence of important, or at least realized, scale economies in fishing and processing may also have been a factor in the stimulation of Peruvian boat and equipment manufacturers. Scale economies at the plant, but especially at the firm level, would probably have led to large firms composed of many small fishing and processing units, so that the number of separate pieces of equipment demanded might have been roughly the same. However, it is also probable that such an industry of large firms would have been dominated by foreign capital, entrepreneurship, and management, since in Peru these factors seem available primarily for comparatively small-scale ventures. In that case, foreign firms might very well have directed their purchases of capital equipment overseas, for several reasons. First, had their investment been compressed into a shorter time period than the eight years it took for entrepreneurs to respond on a small scale, Peruvian industry might not have had the capacity to meet the demand, nor the time to learn the necessary skills. Second, foreign companies might have been prone to utilize established supply channels in their home countries, particularly if quantity discounts were involved. This tendency would have been reinforced by the inchoate nature of the Peruvian metal fabricating industry. Finally, large foreign firms making substantial investments in the country might have been able to obtain concessions from the government on the importation of capital equipment, with some exoneration from duties. This has been the pattern in Peruvian mining. Although this is not an airtight case, it is plausible that small units investing in small amounts created more favorable conditions for Peruvian suppliers than large, especially large foreign, units would have done.

In the manufacture of fish pumps, the production function for fishmeal stimulated not only investment, but innovation. No existing pump met the need to move large amounts of small, whole fish into and out of boats fast enough to begin reduction before decay advanced very far. When a Peruvian firm, under contract with a fishmeal producer, developed a new pump to do the job without cutting the fish, a substantial business developed around this patented invention.

Competitiveness of Suppliers

It is germane to inquire into the competitiveness of these supply industries. To the extent that they depend more on tariff protection than low costs, they are creatures of the state as much as of the fishing sector. The degree of tariff protection is shown in Table 7.5. It is invariably greater than 30%, which is the usual ad valorem rate applied to constructed cif value (fob plus 20%); specific duties are often added. The duties on boats, nylon netting, and jute sacks are

TABLE 7.5.   Peru: Duties on imports competing with domestically
manufactured fishmeal inputs, 1964–1966

Item	Duties		Total[b] (percent) based on	
	Ad valorem[a] (percent)	Specific (soles per kilo)	Constructed[c] cif	Actual cif
Fishing boats, 30–400T	60	–	60	–
Fish netting	30	45.00	–	90
Fish pumps (with motors)	30	2.00	34	–
Centrifuges	30	1.00	30	–
Processing equipment	30	2.00	34	–
Bags (jute)	30	8.00	–	60

Sources: Ministerio de Hacienda y Comercio, Arancel de Aduanas: Importación (Lima, 1964), and personal interviews.

[a] Applied to a constructed cif value = 1.20 × (fob value).

[b] Approximate, since within any class the value-weight ratio and thus the impact of the specific duty may vary.

[c] Actual cif value not known; the constructed cif value is explained in n. (a).

all over 60%, reaching 90% for netting. The duty on jute sacks is somewhat misleading; it need not be paid by a firm that buys one domestic jute bag for each four it imports, a ratio calculated to keep domestic firms close to full capacity.

There is no doubt of the need for duties in the jute bag and nylon netting industries. These are part of Peru's textile industry, which has the reputation of suffering from high costs due to unproductive labor. Japanese netting can be landed in Callao for $1.40 a pound, against the local price of $2.31, while imported jute sacks sell for 26% less than domestic ones. High Peruvian labor costs are probably part of the explanation. In 1964, Peruvian textile workers were paid wages 39% above those of more experienced labor in Japan, and about three times the wages of Pakistani and Indian textile workers.[18] However, as mentioned above, there may be substantial economies from vertical integration of the jute industry.

There is some question, though, whether the more efficient producers of boats and processing equipment require high duties. Managers of the larger firms producing boats and reduction equipment of all kinds protest that they are, in fact, competitive on the west coast of Latin America. A small but continual flow of boat, centrifuge, and fish pump exports, mainly to Chile but also to other fishing countries, attests to their claim (see Table 7.6). Peruvian producers may be pricing their exports below their domestic sales, following the model of a discriminating monopolist facing an overseas market with more elastic demand than his domestic one, but then the same can probably be said about foreign competitors. And even in that model, rational exporters do not sell at prices below marginal cost, which ought to be the basis for judging their competitiveness in any case. Thus it can be said that efficient producers of boats and fishmeal equipment in Peru probably have marginal costs that are within unit transportation costs of their Japanese, European, and North American competitors' prices.

If so, then high duties on those products may have any of four explanations. First, efficient producers may be able to obtain them in order to raise demand and reduce elasticity within their home market, permitting greater profits. Or, if these are decreasing-cost industries in Peru, with marginal cost below average cost, competition in world markets may lead to sales at prices below average cost, especially if demand is very elastic, so that marginal revenue is close

TABLE 7.6.   Peru: Exports of fishing and processing equipment, 1959–1965

| Year | Boats | | Reduction equipment | Pumps[a] and centrifuges | Total (thousand dollars) |
	Number	Value (thousand dollars)	(thousand dollars)		
1959	2	26	–	–	26
1960	3	51	–	–	51
1961	2	102	–	–	102
1962	7	358	–	–	358
1963	9	555	–	294	849
1964	8	501	–	433	934
1965	2	n. a.	141	285	426
Totals	33	1593	141	1012	2746

Source: Superintendencia General, Comercio Exterior, 1959–1965.

[a] It is suspected that these items were omitted from, or obscured in, customs statistics for the years before 1963, since the author has knowledge of exports beginning in 1959.

to price. Then tariff protection may be required to make up for these losses on exports by charging higher prices in the home market. Alternatively, the duties may be designed to protect less efficient producers, meaning that it is only inframarginal producers who compete on world markets. The argument has also been advanced that imperfections in international capital markets necessitated tariff protection against foreign suppliers, whose access to cheaper credit facilities tied to exports enables them to offer a package of goods and credit which Peruvian suppliers cannot match. At likely prevailing loan terms, this makes sense only if boat purchasers have very short planning horizons.[19] Finally, the duties on netting and equipment, which are still imported in quantity, could also be for revenue purposes.

Macroeconomic Assessment

The focus of this study is the impact of fishmeal development on the Peruvian economy. In order to assess that influence, the magnitude of the backward linkages being discussed ought to be compared with relevant magnitudes for the whole economy. The first step is to calculate the share of gross output that, after several rounds in the input-output chain, can be attributed to value added in Peru. The lack of a complete Leontief table for Peru prevents this analysis from going beyond second-order effects, but Table 7.1 can be used to get that far. Exports of fishmeal and oil in 1964 earned $157.5 million in foreign exchange, while total fishmeal and oil production was valued at $171.3 million at world prices. Adding gross fixed investment induced by fishmeal on the hypotheses of Table 7.1, and subtracting fishmeal purchased by the livestock industry, we find that the total final output due to fishmeal is $199.3 million. This represents 4.0% of estimated 1966 GNP of $5.04 billion and 5.6% of that for 1964 in current prices.[20] The seventh column of Table 7.1 shows that, of these final goods related to fishmeal, a maximum value of $11.3 million, net of duties, was directly imported as first-round expenditures by fishmeal operators. Of the goods supplied by Peruvian industry on the first round, column 2 shows that another $23.0 million (the estimate consistent with the maximum one just used for direct imports) leaks out in the form of intermediate goods imported by Peruvian suppliers on the second round of expenditures. Thus, after subtracting all direct imports by fishmeal operators and intermediate goods imported by suppliers (all first- and second-round imports), $165.0 million has been spent on domestic goods and factors. This is 83% of the gross value of final goods related to fishmeal, including fishmeal output for export and inventory plus investment in reduction and fishing equipment; it is equivalent to 3.3% of GNP for 1966 in current prices or to 4.7% of GNP for 1964.

If some crude assumptions are allowed, one can gain a rough idea of the foreign exchange cost of imported intermediate goods and raw materials on subsequent rounds of expenditure. Let S be the value of goods supplied to the fishmeal industry by Peruvian manufacturers, $73.0 million from the last column of Table 7.1. The fraction, m, of this value that represents imports of intermediate goods to the suppliers (net of duties) is 0.315, which was calculated using the ratio of the total of column 2, Table 7.1, to S. Assume, as a pure guess, that another 0.3 of S is spent on intermediate goods inputs from domestic suppliers, and let this fraction be called d. If the fractions, m and d, apply to all other sectors of the economy, then the sum of all third and later-round imports would be $9.9 million.[21] Adding this to the figures for first- and second-round imports, fishmeal demand leads ultimately to goods imports of $44.2 million. Thus total imports, net of duties, account for only 22% of the value of final goods related to fishmeal.[22]

It is also worthwhile to compare the investment demand of the fishmeal industry with that for the entire economy. One possible comparison utilizes the sixth column of Table 7.1, which shows total gross fixed investment of $30.4 million; this is 4.5% of private gross fixed investment for the economy for 1966.[23] A better idea of the dynamic effect of fishmeal development on national investment can be obtained from Table 7.7, which summarizes the data from Tables 7.3 and 7.4. Investment in nets, concentration plants, and plant renewal is neglected, because the data are lacking. As expected from the history related in Chapter 5, the table shows investment, in 1963 prices, rising, with only one hesitation, to a peak of $82 million in 1963, from where it plummets to a sustained level close to $20 million in the next three years. During the peak year, fishmeal investment accounted for over 15% of total gross fixed investment for Peru, a rather spectacular performance for an industry whose gross output

TABLE 7.7. Peruvian fishmeal: Gross investment[a] in fleets and plants, 1957–1966

Year	Investment in fishmeal fleets and plants (million soles)	Investment in fishmeal fleets and plants (million dollars)	Private gross fixed investment, Peru (billion soles)	Ratio, fishmeal to Peru (percent)
1957	104	5.5	13.1	0.1
1958	223	8.9	11.3	2.0
1959	273	9.9	9.1	3.0
1960	718	26.9	9.9	7.3
1961	538	20.1	12.1	4.5
1962	1303	48.6	14.0	9.3
1963	2197	82.0	14.1	15.6
1964	588	21.9	13.0	4.5
1965	518	19.3	14.9	3.5
1966	532	19.8	16.2	3.2

Sources: Private gross fixed investment for Peru: calculated from Banco Central, *Cuentas Nacionales* (1968). Fishmeal investment from Tables 7.3 and 7.4.

[a] 1963 prices.

value was under 4% of gross national product in 1963. Aside from the growth years of 1960 and 1962, when investment in fishmeal was 7.3 and 9.3% of national investment, respectively, the contribution was respectable but not outstanding.[24]

8
Other Linkages

Forward Linkages

A forward linkage is established when the output from one industry, A, encourages production in another industry, B, primarily because of reduced prices of principal inputs. This mechanism may not work effectively by itself, but is potentially powerful when coupled with a backward linkage, or demand pressure, acting on industry B.[1] In the case of fishmeal in Peru, it is difficult to find any such coupled effect at work. Technically, of course, the forward linkage from fishing to fish processing has all the textbook ingredients. Anchovy inputs dominate the cost structure of the reduction industry, accounting for from 40 to 50% of the value of the final product. World demand for protein additives to livestock feeds, which rose markedly during the 1950s, did not stimulate production in Peru until the introduction of the nylon net substantially lowered the cost of this dominant input. A more perfect illustration of Hirschman's thesis would be hard to imagine. Yet this is a highly artificial and contorted interpretation of the fishmeal industry, which includes not only processing factories, but fleets of *bolicheras* as well. It is equally plausible to view fishing development as a linkage backward from processing, the search for better nets and other improvements having been stimulated by the demand from existing fishmeal producers or those on the verge of entry. In fact, the pioneers who searched for cheaper fishing methods were processors as well.

The obvious place to look for a more meaningful forward linkage would be the livestock industry in Peru. From 1960 to 1965, output

129

from slaughtering and meat preparation in Peru increased by 30%,[2] while, according to an unofficial but reliable source, the annual production of pork grew by a total of 22% and of chicken by one-third. These are fairly modest increases, although there are signs, obvious to the visitor in Lima, that the market for chickens is a healthy and expanding one: restaurants specializing in chicken seem to flourish and large chicken farms can be seen from the roads leading out of the capital. Even assuming that fishmeal faces a growing if still small market in Peru, it does not follow that the availability of a cheap protein source was a major stimulant to chicken production. Under plausible assumptions, the reduction in the cost of chicken production due to the availability of cheaper Peruvian fishmeal would be no more than 1.3%.[3] At capital-output ratios which might range from 1.5 to 3.0,[4] the increased yield on investment would range from 0.9% down to 0.4%. It seems unlikely that, in a capital market supporting interest rates upward of 10%, a difference in yield of less than 1% could be responsible for substantial new investment and growth. Hence it is possible to discount the importance of this forward linkage from fishmeal to chicken raising.

A less direct, but possibly important, form of forward linkage runs from suppliers, set up to serve the fishmeal industry, to other potential industrial consumers of their products. Several firms in the processing equipment industry either began as fishmeal suppliers or were able to continue profitable operations as a result of the fishmeal investment boom, while the jute sack industry owes its existence primarily to fishmeal demand. Yet in neither supply industry does sales to fishmeal firms comprise more than half of total sales.[5] Processing equipment manufacturers supply boilers, pumps, evaporators, condensors, storage tanks, and other equipment for the cotton, sugar, food oil, mining, and petroleum industries, and also build transportation equipment and steel structures. Jute bags are sold to package coffee, tea, fertilizer, and rice; jute is also used as a fabric for rugs and curtains, among other things. A forward linkage could be established if locally produced processing equipment or jute products, available at a low cost, made it possible for one of the above-mentioned consuming industries to produce profitably. Such a determination would require detailed information beyond the scope of this study.

Most of the using industries listed above predate the fishmeal industry, and so do not qualify as forward linkages. We cannot say to what extent these might have been expanded, or the others established, as a consequence of locally available processing equipment or jute sacks, priced cheaply to take advantage of excess capacity or to penetrate new markets and diversify production. This may have happened in the case of processing equipment, but is rather unlikely in the case of jute, since sacks probably are not an important cost in the consuming industries. One exception to the latter would be the jute fabric industry, which is actually part of the jute sack industry and seems to have been started precisely to reduce dependence on fishmeal demand.

Consumption Linkages

Consumption out of factor payments is not, strictly speaking, part of backward linkages. However, when a consumption function, detailed enough to show purchases by sector, is inserted into a Leontief table, the results are indistinguishable from backward linkages, except that these work on the second round of expenditure rather than the first. Baldwin stresses the pattern of factor payments and the consequent consumers' behavior as a key aspect of staple theory. He contrasts the skewed income distribution of plantation agriculture and the small wage bill of capital-intensive mining, both of which lead to a narrow market for mass-produced consumer goods, with the more equal distribution and larger labor share of family farms, which stimulate domestic consumer goods industries (see Chapter 2, p. 7). Two questions are involved, then: the consumption pattern of staple industry workers and the size of the wage bill.

For fishmeal in Peru, the latter is more easily answered than the former. Referring again to Table 7.1, we find that labor's share of fishmeal output is given as 29.9%; if we eliminate social benefits, which probably do not influence consumption patterns substantially, the fraction is reduced to 22.6%.[6] Thus, in a year like 1964 the wage bill would be $38.7 million, which is 1.5% of Peruvian consumption for that year. If we put social benefits back into the equation to make a consistent comparison, the total payments to labor of $51.3 million would be 3.5% of wage and salary payments in Peru for 1964 and 2.6% of 1966 payments.[7] In the absence of any data on the matter, we can make only a rough estimate of the contribution to consumer demand due to wage payments by fishmeal's supply industries. Assuming that 20% of the value of intermediate and investment goods purchased by the fishmeal industry represents labor's share,[8] then we can add another $14.6 million, to give total wage payments and social benefits in fishmeal-related activities of $65.9 million, equal to 4.6% of 1964 wage and salary payments and 3.3% of 1966 payments.

Note that these comparisons ignore the potential earnings of labor in alternative employment. Skilled and semiskilled workers could probably have found employment at slightly lower wages in other industries had fishmeal not existed. However, about 65% of the labor used in fishing and reduction is unskilled, largely migrant labor with low opportunity costs. Moreover, many of the semiskilled laborers in processing and the skilled laborers in the supply industries were trained on the job. So the wage comparisons overstate the case for fishmeal's contribution to consumer demand, but probably not by much. In any case, unless the fishmeal workers' consumption is concentrated on a few goods or in new, undeveloped, and isolated areas, the wage payments of the industry are not large enough relative to the rest of the economy to be identified as a primary stimulus for investment in consumer goods industries. The impact of fishmeal, like that on the insurance and petroleum industries, is diffuse.

It is not possible to be precise about expenditure patterns. No one has made a study of the consumption behavior of fishermen or fishmeal workers. Budget studies done to establish consumer price index weights for the Lima area are of little use, except perhaps in application to salaried personnel, who receive about a fifth of the total outlay for wages and salaries. To apply these budget studies to fishmeal industry employees would assume that they behave as the urban average, in which case special linkage effects can be ruled out and the percentages calculated above reveal most of the story. However, many fishmeal workers and fishermen, especially those employed outside Callao, are recruits from rural areas. Their annual incomes, which do fit within the range covered by the Lima studies, are unlikely to be spent in the same way as those of workers in Lima with a longer history of wage employment. The only clues to the differences come primarily from the casual observations of fishmeal operators.

The one formal study which touched on the topic showed that just over half of 600 fishermen interviewed in Chimbote owned their own homes,[9] indicating at least the start of the habit of investment in consumer durables, even though these homes may be very humble indeed.

Beyond that, the expected stereotypes of the new industrial worker, as seen by his employer, color the picture. One plausible observation was that banking services are not used much, especially by fishermen. Despite the large payrolls that are met each Saturday in Chimbote, banks do not notice any significant increase in deposits early the following week. Part of the blame may be laid to the banks themselves, which maintain the traditional banker's hours even though the fishermen are at sea during those times. A bank open on Saturday might begin to attract a whole new group of clients. On the other hand, workers in at least one location have started cooperatives under union auspices, and one company has been making loans for houses, with good repayment experience.

Still, there is a consensus, which may not mean much, that consumption patterns in towns like Chimbote and Tambo de Mora run toward wine and women. The one industry that inevitably seems to thrive in good fishing season is one that never enters the input-output tables of the world, unless it might be buried deeply under "services." Although North's phrase, "residentiary industry," seems singularly appropriate to this service, it is certainly not the sort of consumption linkage he or any of the staple theorists had in mind (or at least in print). Moreover, the brothels may be the source of an unsuspected leakage from the economy. It is alleged, and on this the author has no personal knowledge, that most of the prostitutes have been imported from neighboring Latin American countries and even further afield. If so, then to the extent they are savers they will probably remit some of their incomes home, to the detriment of Peru's balance on current account.

Fishing development in Chimbote, Tambo de Mora, and other centers away from Lima has probably led to the establishment of small-scale industry in food and some services. But it is unlikely that anything more substantial has resulted from the fishing boom. The industrial census for 1963 lists only seven establishments in Chimbote in the food industry, other than fishing, and none has over 25 employees. There are also five furniture makers, two printers, and nine automobile repair shops, none with more than 20 employees. Otherwise no consumer goods industries are listed.[10] In the highly centralized Peruvian economy, whatever demand exists for nonperishable consumer goods is probably supplied from Lima.

It would appear, then, that the consumption linkage from fishmeal in Peru does not play the role attributed to it by Baldwin and North for Africa and North America. The income distribution generated by fishmeal does not show the very sharp skewness that these authors observe in plantation agriculture. Nor does fishmeal display the extremely high wages and low labor content characteristic of copper mining and other enclave industries. Instead, the wage pattern in fishmeal is not sharply different from that for other Peruvian industries, and not capable of markedly altering existing consumption behavior.

Overhead Capital

One of the most important external economies of the American and Canadian wheat industries was the construction of railroads, as discussed in Chapter 2. Unlike the development of the wheat economy in the open lands of North America, fishmeal production has grown along a coast that already supported two substantial primary product export industries (cotton and sugar) and was supplied with a reasonably good coastal highway. Most of the road was paved before fishmeal began its rapid growth, and it is generally agreed by government officials that the fish industry played a very minor role in the decisions leading to the improvement of this road south of Lima in recent years.

However, Peru's lines of communication to the exterior have always been at least as important as those to the interior, and fishmeal growth has had a measurable impact on port development since 1960. Table 8.1 provides a comparison between port traffic and the share of fishmeal cargo for 1958 and 1965. During that interval, the flow of cargo through Peru's ocean ports, measured by the weight of imports plus exports, increased by a factor of 2.3. In five ports, Chimbote, Supe, Huacho, Chancay, and Pisco, the dependence on fishmeal grew to between 40 and 100%, and in each case traffic more than tripled. To accommodate the increased burden on port facilities, the govern-

Table 8.1. Peru: Port development, 1960–1970

Port	Cargo flow, imports plus exports (thousand metric tons per year)		Fishmeal exports as a percentage of cargo for		Port works executed and planned[a]	
					Value (million dollars)	Years start-finish
	1958	1965	1958	1965[b]		
Paita	81[c]	120	1.9	2.3	5.2	1965–
Pacasmayo	37[c]	43	0	0	0.8	–
Salaverry	185[c]	185	0	0	15.4	1959–1967
Chimbote	203	622	26.2	61.2	11.0	–1969
Supe	28	187	14.3	68.9		
Huacho	40	180	12.5	41.0	8.4	–1973
Chancay	10[c]	86	69.0	100.0		
Callao	1673[c]	3009	n. a.	7.8	30.1	–1970
Pisco	82	310	2.3	61.8	10.8	–1968
Matarani	107[c]	210	0	0	1.8	1966–
Ilo	10	326	7.0	18.0	3.4	–1969
Totals	2340	5278	12.3[d]	22.1	87.9	–

Sources: Cargoes, 1957 and 1965: Superintendencia General, Comercio Exterior, 1957, p. 54 and 1958, p. 38. Cargoes and fishmeal exports, 1958: Panorama Portuaria (1960), 23, 26–27. Fishmeal production, 1965: Pesca Anuario 1965–1966. Port works: Mundo Pesquero, "Callao se Moderniza," 3 (October 1966), 27–30; Mundo Pesquero, "Los Puertos del Perú," 3 (June 1966), and Instituto Nacional de Planificación, Plan Desarollo Económico y Social, 1967–1970: Inventorio General de Proyectos (Lima, 1966), IV, pp. 577–608.

[a] As of 1967.
[b] Fishmeal production; understates exports, since stocks fell by 2% of production in 1965.
[c] 1957.
[d] Excludes Callao.

ment has spent or planned to spend, mostly before 1970, the sum of $87.9 million, of which $30.2 million has been allocated to the five ports mentioned. In addition, a fishmeal dock was completed at Callao in 1962.

The plans for Supe, Huacho, and Chancay, which are located between Lima and Chimbote, are particularly interesting. Officials envisaged a new port, in an improved location, which will augment all three existing ones. It is expected that this port complex will begin to handle an increasing share of the import traffic which now congests Callao. In this instance, the demand for overhead capital, almost entirely from fishmeal, may have very tangible linkages if this decision leads to a new congeries of import-centered activities along a previously export-dominated stretch of coastline. The works for the five predominantly fishmeal ports would, if completed over a ten-year period, involve an average annual expenditure of $3.0 million a year, which represents 3% of public sector investment for 1965. This is a significant fraction, but over half of the contemplated improvements and extensions were only in the planning stage, and it is hard to say how much will actually be completed.

There is a general feeling in Peru that the growth of the fishmeal industry took everyone, and in particular the government, completely by surprise. The history of social overheads in Chimbote, boom town par excellence, confirms the belief. City officials estimate that the population had grown to 85,000 by 1962. Yet, until 1966, only the main road through town was paved; in that year only a six-by-six grid of roads in the center of Chimbote received tarmac. Although the Rio Santo hydroelectric scheme provided sufficient power for the steel mill, which predated fishmeal as Chimbote's major industry, many of the fishmeal plants were forced to generate their own power until 1966, when the second stage of the hydroelectric project was completed. The new workers have been less well served: only an estimated 25% of the population had potable water in 1967, and 80% were without sewage facilities. The city is noted for the *barriadas* that crowd the area between the coastal highway and the bay. It is clear from the record in Chimbote and from the development schedule for harbors that fishmeal led and investment in infrastructure followed, a sequence that Hirschman calls "development via shortage" of social overhead capital.[11] The importance of this linkage for the development of other industry can only be guessed at this stage, when the construction of overhead capital is really just getting started.

External Diseconomies

The linkages backward from fishmeal have not all been creative ones. Fishmeal has been responsible for several external diseconomies which, although not easily measurable, ought to be mentioned. The most obvious diseconomy has affected the guano industry, with which fishmeal shares a common resource. The public corporation in charge of guano exploitation has been concerned for the guano bird population ever since the first fishmeal plant was opened. Their alarm was not without cause. Although the bird population is subject to sharp fluctuations that cannot be explained by anchovy fishing, it is equally clear that the years since the fishmeal boom have been substantially less productive ones for the guano industry. From 1958 to 1966, the peak bird population was an estimated 25 million, which was 16% below the *minimum* level for the previous ten years and 60% below the maximum. Production figures show a similar decrease: the 1958–1966 high of 206,000 metric tons is below the 1950–1957 low of 218,000 metric tons and 39% below the peak.[12]

Fishing interests do not fully accept that the decline is permanent or that the fishing of anchovy is the principal cause. However, even granting these points, they argue that the process by which birds produce guano, which is deposited on off-shore islands, wastes so much of the fish consumed that one anchovy consumed for guano has a marginal revenue product only 12% of that for the anchovy caught for fishmeal.[13] The obvious policy conclusion which the Society would like to draw is that the guano birds ought not to be protected, but instead the limit on anchovy fishing ought to be raised to allocate all of the sustainable annual catch to the fishmeal industry.

Other external diseconomies are obvious, even to the casual visitor to any of the fishmeal-producing ports. Chimbote is archetypical. The visitor who drives up from Lima can begin to smell the exhaust from the reduction plants several miles before the outskirts of town. When he reaches the city, a new and worse smell begins to dominate the air: the scenically beautiful bay is contaminated by rotting fish and waste from the processing plants. Analysis has allegedly shown some of these fumes to be toxic, leading to fatigue, numbness, bronchial infection, and allergic skin eruptions. The haphazard placement of plants all around the bay makes it difficult to control the fumes, even with mandatory decontamination equipment that cleans the exhaust from the driers. The contamination of air and water has, of course, ruined Chimbote as a tourist center. Its scenic bay and location on one of Peru's main tourist routes were assets that the fishing industry has devalued considerably. These costs are common in any history of industrialization, but the particular problem with the fishmeal industry is that its production has led to operations all along the coast, with pervasive effects for both good and ill.

9
Factor Markets

Two aspects of factor markets are important for staple theory. First, the demand for factors of production may lead to external economies, as when an industry, intensive in a scarce factor, creates additional supplies of that factor; it may, for example, be forced to train skilled workers. Second, it is necessary to consider the societal responses of the country to the stimulus of increased demand from the export sector. Levin concentrated on factor supply when he studied Peru's mid-nineteenth-century export economy:

The supply of factors which would be needed for the guano trade . . . was insufficient in 1840 Peru. Entrepreneurship was a scarce and socially repressed quality. Manual labor was highly immobile, and though existent among the mountain Indians and some urban guilds, was not responsive to money incentives, and therefore unattainable. Capital was especially scarce . . . Even high returns could not bring out enough labor, capital and entrepreneurship to launch and operate the guano-export trade. Scarcity and immobility made the domestic supply of these factors inadequate.[1]

Although the natural resource is the same, the result has been very different in Peru during the middle of the twentieth century. The purpose of this chapter is to offer some evaluation of the impact of fishmeal and its satellite industries on the markets for labor, capital, entrepreneurship, and foreign exchange, and to indicate the effectiveness of Peruvian responses to these stimuli. The industry demand and factor supply aspects are considered together in the discussion of each factor market to avoid an artificial division of the material.

Labor

The first step in discussing any of these factor markets is to obtain an indication of its magnitude. Table 9.1 presents two sets of estimates of employment due to the fishmeal industry; sources are noted in the table. Employment in fishmeal processing was probably between 13,400 and 16,000 in the 1963–1966 period, while 12,800 to 13,300 were probably employed as fishermen. Thus a reasonably certain estimate of the average employed in fishmeal in the mid-1960s is 28,000, plus or minus 2000.

Confidence wanes considerably when workers in supply industries dependent on fishmeal are brought into the picture. The statistics of Table 9.1 result from a mixture of different estimating techniques applied to data for different years from 1963 to 1966. The figure of 1611 workers producing boats and processing equipment for the fishmeal industry, combined because one large firm covers the two categories, is probably a good approximation. The estimate of 550 to 810 for the two textile industries, netting and jute bags, is less certain, and the rest of the estimates are very crude, being based largely on aggregate data for various years, as indicated in the notes to the table. Moreover, the figures for satellite industries are dominated by two categories, transportation and maintenance, about which very little is known, at least in their specific relation to fishmeal. So the estimate for all supply industries of 10,000, plus or minus 2000, is an order of magnitude only. This gives a rough estimate for persons employed in the fishmeal and related industries of 38,000, with a subjective 80% confidence interval of plus or minus 4000. However, there is an element of conservatism in these calculations, since they ignore all second- and subsequent-round effects in the Leontief multiplier chain; only industries in the input column of the fishmeal sector are included.

For Peru, 38,000 employees is a moderate, but not overwhelmingly impressive, number. The national accounts set the country's labor force at 3.6 million in 1965, of whom 1.8 million are employed outside of agriculture and 492,000 are in manufacturing.[2] Fishmeal's contribution to nonagricultural employment is 2%. Its share of employment in manufacturing is 4%, excluding fishermen and transportation and utility workers, who are considered part of different sectors; if fisher-

TABLE 9.1. Peru: Employment due to the fishmeal industry, 1963–1966

	Low estimate		High estimate	
Fishmeal industry (1964)				
Fishing[a]	12,800		13,300	
Processing[b]	13,420		16,039	
Total		26,220		29,339
Supply industries				
Boat and processing equipment				
manufacturing[c]	1,611		1,611	
Textiles (netting and jute sacks[d])	546		812	
Paper[e]	135		135	
Petroleum[e]	72		72	
Power[f]	306		306	
Transport and storage[f]	4,300		4,300	
Maintenance—boats and plants[g]	1,480		5,000	
Total		8,450		12,236
Total due to fishmeal		34,670		41,575

[a] Low estimate is based on crews of 12 (including motorman and captain) in boats catching fish during 1964, taking unpublished Sociedad Nacional data for four months (March, June, September, and December) and allowing for (a) the probability that some different boats were among the successful ones each month and (b) the coverage of the data (about 90% of total catch); high figure is from Elijalde, *Industria Pesquera*, p. 57 and relates to 1963.

[b] Low estimate from 1964 census of fishmeal plants; high estimate is by Oficina Sectorial, "Estadistica Pesquera 1964 y 1965," mimeo (Lima 1966), p. 31. A third estimate, 14,830, can be derived from the *Censo de Manufacturas 1963*, by allowing for more active plants in 1964. There is some ambiguity in the coverage of these data. It is probable that plants with their own fleets will include boat maintenance and supervisory personnel, but not crews, as plant employees; employment figures for plants that buy their fish from independent fishermen would not, of course, include such personnel.

[c] Compiled from notes of interviews with 12 firms that dominate the industry; refers to 1966. Assumes that the fraction of total work force producing equipment for fishmeal industry is equal to the fraction of total sales going to fishmeal industry.

[d] Low figure from notes of interviews with four firms; high estimate uses labor-output ratio given by Instituto Nacional and Banco Industrial, *Yute*, pp. 72–78, for jute industry; estimates refer to 1965.

[e] From dependency percentages of Table 7.2, applied to total employment in the sector as given by the *Censo de Manufacturas 1963*.

[f] Same as n. (e), except using the employment statistics of the Banco Central, *Cuentas Nacionales* (1966), p. 38 for 1965.

[g] Assumes that labor-output ratios for boatbuilding and metal fabricating, calculated from 1963 census of manufactures, apply; low estimate uses only contracted portion of maintenance (per 1963 census); high estimate includes all maintenance expenditures from Table 7.1, which represents 1964.

men are counted in both the numerator and the denominator, the latter fraction rises to 7%. The contribution looks larger when compared with the smaller sample of the 1963 census of manufactures, which covers only firms of five or more employees, and may have less complete coverage in other respects: 12% without fishermen and including only manufacturing supply industries, and 19% with fishermen included.[3] Thus the fishmeal industry is responsible for a considerable portion of the demand for labor among the larger scale manufacturing industries in the economy, without being a major contributor to employment when viewed in the broader context of all nonagricultural industry.

These total employment figures do not go very far in determining the nature of fishmeal's demand for labor, nor do they say very much about external economies or diseconomies emanating from that demand. The most reliable and consistent set of data on employment by categories of labor skill is presented in the 1963 census of manufactures, a segment of which is reproduced in Table 9.2. The first three lines of that table give statistics from the more complete data of the 1961 census of population.

Fish processing is complicated enough to require at least one qualified engineer on the premises; he is typically the plant manager. Because it is an industry of small units, the demand of the fishmeal industry for professional engineers is likely to be comparatively large. Table 9.2 shows that 8.3% of those listed as professionals are employed in the fish reduction industry. But the absolute number is likely to be greater than the 210 listed, since some of the engineers may be proprietors or administrators, both of which are carried under a different heading, not shown separately in the table. The industry's use of technicians is less intense, representing only 4.4% of the total.

The fishmeal industry's demand for professional people is specialized toward mechanical, electrical, and chemical engineers for the most part. To put this requirement in its proper context, the 210 listed in the 1963 census might be compared with the average university enrollment in these three fields of 1310 for the years from 1960 to 1963.[4] If one-fourth of these enrollees graduated each year, then the fishmeal industry's total employment of engineers would approximate two-thirds of a year's graduating class. The demand looks even heavier if each plant needs, not just a graduate engineer, but

TABLE 9.2. Peruvian fishmeal and supply industries: Employment by skill, 1963

	All employees[a]	Nonproduction workers			Production workers			
		Total	Professional	Technical	Total	Skilled, including supervisors	Semi-skilled	Unskilled
1961 Census of population								
Country (economically active)[b]	3,120,800	502,920	87,790	24,320	2,591,760	91,450	404,910	940,980
Four sectors[c]	590,430	48,370	5,740	3,960	565,100	77,720	288,520	168,890
Manufacturing	410,890	30,870	2,430	2,500	380,070	65,420	204,650	104,720
1963 Census of manufactures								
Manufacturing[d]	164,930	31,918	2,537	3,984	130,805	29,594	43,088	58,123
Fishmeal processing	12,592	2,033	210	174	10,544	1,690	2,435	6,419
Machinery (nonelectrical)	4,433	817	89	165	3,562	1,198	1,060	1,304
Naval construction	2,177	358	36	40	1,813	658	643	512

Sources: 1961: Organization for Economic Cooperation and Development, *Desarrollo Económico y Social, Recursos Humanos y Educación* (Lima, 1965), pp. 3–47. 1963: Dirección Nacional, *Censo de Manufacturas, 1963*, pp. 66–69.

[a] Not all workers in this total are classified by skills in subsequent columns.

[b] Agricultural independents are included in the total for production workers, but are not classified according to skill; military and religious workers are included only under total employment.

[c] Mining, manufacturing, construction, and energy.

[d] This line differs from the one above because the 1963 census covers only firms with five or more employees and may otherwise be less complete than the 1961 census of population; note that, of the discrepancy in the total employed (245,960), 62% is due to the textile industry.

a man with some experience, capable of running a plant of 50 to 100 workers. Since enrollment in all engineering fields in 1955 was less than 40% of the figure for 1963, the relative demand by processing plants for this specialized resource is even greater. And if, to the figure of 210, there is added roughly 60 engineers in the marine and processing equipment industries serving fishmeal, the requirement begins to look sizable, even in a country where *ingeniero* is a much-sought title of respect.

However, the Peruvian education system has been equal to the task. Although no statistics on the subject exist and those obtained through interviews are not complete enough to report, the overwhelming impression is that the engineers in fishmeal, boat construction, and metal fabrication are Peruvian, with a scattering of foreigners, probably 10% or less. Many of the processing companies have hired new graduates, but one hears frequently of plant superintendents taken from other processing industries, notably sugar refining and chemicals, and even from mining. The industry has been able to hire these men while still paying salaries below the average for manufacturing industries, since sugar refining and chemicals pay even less to their professionals.[5] This, of course, raises the average price for engineering talent, but there are no data to document the extent to which added fishmeal demand has led to higher wages for professionals.

Fishmeal processors hire skilled production workers primarily as mechanics and electricians whose functions are maintenance and repair. The latter are especially important, since the malfunctioning of any piece of equipment is likely to shut down a third or half of the plant's capacity. Semiskilled workers mostly operate processing machinery, a trade they learn on the job and one that, in the absence of sophisticated control equipment, is critical to the quality of the meal produced. Despite the importance of both groups of workers to efficient fish reduction, the group of skilled, including supervisory, and semiskilled production workers attributed to fishmeal in Table 9.2 is not large, even when compared with the smaller sample of the 1963 census. While the processing industry's share of the skilled and semiskilled workers is 5.7%, it employed 11.0% of the unskilled workers listed in the 1963 census. If fishermen were included, the fishmeal industry's relative dependence on unskilled workers would be even greater, since 10 of a typical crew of 12 would be classified as unskilled.

The fishmeal industry has tended to be a net absorber of skilled labor from the rest of the economy, but trains its own semiskilled workers. According to 1963 census figures, the average plant employs about ten skilled workers; these include mechanics and electricians who work on processing equipment and, for those plants with their own boats, on the fleet. Because each plant employs, perhaps, only two or three men with the same skills, there is little opportunity for training on the job. Some firms do have an apprenticeship system for mechanics and electricians, but these are mainly the larger producers with large fleets. Mines, repair shops, and other manufacturing have apparently been sources of skilled manpower. Some of the foreign companies also brought in a few specialists from abroad. Several of the managers interviewed indicated that the metal fabricating industry has supplied more than processing equipment to fishmeal: skilled production workers in equipment manufacturing became maintenance mechanics on the same equipment, when it was installed in a reduction plant. However, the demand of the fishmeal industry for skilled labor did not create enough of a strain on other industry to be reflected in relative wages. Skilled workers in fishmeal received wages slightly below the average for all manufacturing in 1963, close to that for machinery manufacturing and significantly less than the average in naval construction.[6]

The situation is different with machine operators, who form the bulk of those classified as semiskilled. They are used in larger numbers by the plants and their work is more easily learned by observation. More important, the precise tasks involved are rather specific to the fishmeal industry. Typically, an unskilled worker will receive informal training and eventually start operating some equipment. This is really a process of making an industrial worker out of a man who just happens to be working in industry, and it is largely this kind of training that the fishmeal industry has undertaken. Until 1965, it is unlikely that the industry supplied many such industrialized workers to other industry, since it was still in the process of expansion. Even now, if it is releasing semiskilled workers, they would have to be retrained by another industry before being useful, although that should not be a difficult undertaking if the worker has learned the discipline of industrial work. It should be clear from the numbers involved that, in the absence of very high turnover, which was not indicated by interviews, the supply of industrialized labor from fishmeal is not likely to be a major factor in the development of other industry.

Although the fishmeal industry itself has been an absorber of skilled workers, the mechanical industries stimulated by it have probably been suppliers of skilled labor to the rest of the economy. The metal-working shipyards and the process equipment manufacturers have been forced to train most of their own workers. Table 9.2 shows the heavy dependence of these industries on labor skills: about two-thirds of their production force is classified as either skilled or semi-skilled. At times the shipyards have been able to find skilled labor on the market. In the 1950s, wood boats were being built by carpenters who left other work for more lucrative employment in the yards. A particularly interesting linkage developed between the private shipyards and the navy yard at Callao. During the 1950s, the navy had been encouraged by the government to build a 6000-ton tanker in order to stimulate subsidiary industry. The job was begun in 1956 and finished two years later; 500 workers, trained by the navy, and 25 skilled British craftsmen were employed on the job. After the tanker was finished, the yard cut back its work and released most of the workers previously engaged on the tanker. These men formed a core of trained metal workers from which the shipyards specializing in metal *bolicheras* undoubtedly drew during their expansion of the early 1960s. The navy yard was also the source of some engineers and highly skilled technicians, a few of them foreign.[7]

However, the 12 manufacturers of fishing boats and reduction equipment who were interviewed in 1967 employed close to 1000 engineers and skilled workers and probably an equal number of semi-skilled workers. Roughly half of these were engaged in production for the fishmeal industry. This figure is probably scaled down from the employment during 1962 and 1963, when investment in fishmeal was at its peak. It seems most unlikely that these industries could have satisfied their demand for labor skills by hiring from other sectors, and interviews confirmed that a substantial amount of training has been done. The reduction in activity has meant some supplying of skills to other industry, including the navy yard, which undertook its second large tanker in 1964. One respondent mentioned the proliferating automobile assembly plants as an important beneficiary of labor trained to supply the fishmeal industry.

The most notable effect of the fishmeal industry on the labor market has been its demand for unskilled workers. Between 7000 and 9000 unskilled workers were employed in the reduction plants in 1964 and another 11,000 served as crews in the *bolicheras*.[8] These figures understate the number of unskilled workers actually hired, since neither turnover nor training of the unskilled is considered. Turnover for the industry as a whole may not have been too important during its expansive phase, especially in the regions, other than Callao, where fishmeal is the dominant industry. If all the semiskilled workers started as unskilled workers, then the total number hired might be as high as 21,000 to 23,000. This is one-fifth of all manufacturing workers listed as unskilled by the 1961 census of population, although only 2% of those listed for all fields outside agriculture.[9]

The outstanding feature of the unskilled labor force that mined Peruvian guano in the nineteenth century was its composition of Chinese coolies and convicts; Peruvian labor was immobile, both geographically and occupationally.[10] Societal responses have changed greatly in a century. The unskilled force of fishermen and factory hands exploiting anchovy in the twentieth century has come from all over Peru and from several different occupations. The rapid growth of Chimbote has been cited frequently already, but must be mentioned once more to underline the extent to which fishmeal, which accounted for over half the population of the town in 1960, has depended on migratory labor. A study made in 1960, covering 2625 heads of family in Chimbote, showed that at least two-thirds of them had come from the sierra; some of those from the coast were probably migrants as well.[11] In 1964, a sample of 600 fishermen was surveyed in Chimbote. Sixty-five percent had been fishermen for five years or less and only 25% had been fishing all their working lives. The men were young and not uneducated: 55% were in their twenties, and 56% had five to six years of school, although only 3% had more education. Fifty-three percent of them came from the coast, which would be the expected origin of a group of fishermen, but only 5% of those were from Chimbote.[12]

If Chimbote is typical and roughly half of all fishermen and two-thirds of the unskilled workers of fishmeal plants have come from noncoastal areas, then the industry has been responsible for drawing between 10,000 and 14,000 workers from the mountains and jungle into reasonably full-time employment in the coastal monetary economy.[13] If each of these men brought a family of four,[14] then between 40,000 and 56,000 people have been involved in this migration. The situation in Chimbote is probably fairly typical of that for fishmeal towns other than Callao. In the Lima-Callao area, which produces less than a fifth of the fishmeal, the pattern of migration from the sierra directly into industry may be less marked,[15] but no specific information is available on fishmeal industry workers.

Since the fish processors and boat owners were prepared to utilize untrained workers from the large underemployed population of the sierra, it might be anticipated that the wages of such workers would be lower than those for the unskilled of other industries, especially if fishmeal entrepreneurs were more willing than others to use migrants. The 1963 census shows that unskilled workers in fishmeal are paid 8% less than the average of $583 per year for all manufacturing industries, which is not a very great difference.[16] Moreover, fishermen do considerably better than the average. The 1964 survey of Chimbote fishermen, which included some captains and motormen, found an average income of $1340 a year;[17] the author's calculations show wages ranging from $1050 to $1490 a year, depending on the catch.[18] So, in fact, fishmeal pays relatively handsomely for its unskilled labor, perhaps because a premium is required for the strenuous work at sea.

Capital

There is no lack of estimates on the capital stock of the industry; the problem comes in reconciling them all, since no two are consistent. Table 9.3 tabulates eight sets of figures on investment in boats and plants, ranging from a hypothetical "best practice" minimum of $66 million in processing plants alone (estimate 1) to a high estimate for active plants and boats of $311 million in 1964 prices ($129 million for plants alone). The assumptions underlying each estimate are explained in notes to the table.

Choosing among these incomparable estimates is not a matter of

TABLE 9.3. Peruvian fishmeal industry: Capital stock estimates, 1963–1966

Source of estimate	Capital-output ratio	Gross capital stock (million dollars)		
		Processing	Fishing	Industry
Estimates based on efficient plants[a]				
1. Minimum	.389	66	–	–
2. Maximum	.590	101	–	–
Estimates based on actual investment				
3. 1964 industry totals[b]				
Processing	.752	129	–	–
Fishing	1.061	–	182	311
4. 1963 industry totals[c]	1.025	129	–	–
Census results				
5. 1964[d]	–	114	(53)	(167)
6. 1965[e]	–	–	–	(192)
Cumulated investment[f]				
7. 1957–1964	–	139	86	225
8. 1957–1966	–	143	121	264

[a] Ratios from the regressions of Table 6.2 on the 36 most efficient plants, using 1964 fishmeal output and prices. Shows "best practice" minimum capital stock.

[b] Active plants and boats at constant 1964 prices (see p. 95 above) using 1964 fishmeal output and prices.

[c] Ratio from Table 6.3, that is, 1963 census of manufactures with capital valued in current prices (book values); uses 1963 output and prices from Tables 5.5 and 5.6. The apparent corroboration with investment in processing from the third estimate is spurious, since the latter is in constant 1964 prices and should reflect some additional investment in 1964.

[d] From unpublished survey data of the Oficina Sectorial; investment in current prices (book values); 119 firms, representing 86% of output, responded, and the results were scaled to represent full production; figures in parenthesis represent boats owned by processors only.

[e] Oficina Sectorial, "Estadistica Pesquera," p. 81, also reflects book values and includes boats owned by processors only.

[f] From investment series in Tables 7.3 and 7.4, that is, allowing for improved boat quality; no allowance for inactive plants.

truth, but of purpose. The best approximation of investment in constant prices is undoubtedly the cumulation of annual investment (estimates 7 and 8), which allows for quality changes in boats, although it ignores investment before 1957; it gives a value of $264 million for capital stock in 1966. The census result for 1965 (estimate 6) will be used in calculations requiring gross book value of fixed assets; this estimate is $192 million, but excludes boats owned by independent fishermen. The latter omission is not serious, since book value will only be needed in cases when the data available on capital sources refer primarily to processing companies, including their boats.

One way to measure the impact on Peruvian capital markets of the demand for this capital stock is to compare annual investment in fishmeal with gross investment for the economy, as presented in Table 7.7. From 1960 to 1963, fishmeal contributed an average of 9.5% to the demand for additional capital stock in the private sector; in 1963, 15% of investment was due to the industry. Certainly, then, fishmeal has had an appreciable effect on the demand for capital during those peak years. But in order to measure its impact on capital markets, it is necessary to switch from real to monetary variables and discuss the sources of funds for the industry.

A composite balance sheet for the industry can give an indication of the magnitude of the variables involved. Table 9.4 presents such a statement. The reader should note, however, that balance sheets are notoriously prone to juggling; as explained in the note to the table, this balance sheet is no exception. Only processing firms and their own fleets are covered.

The sources of funds indicated by liabilities need to be interpreted with an eye for conditions in Peruvian financial markets and in the fishmeal industry. First of all, commercial banks do not generally lend for more than a year, so all of their $28.6 million in loans to the fishmeal industry will be included under short-term liabilities (see Table 9.5). Yet there is every expectation on the part of both borrower and lender that these loans will be extended for an indefinite period, and in that sense they are long-term liabilities. This makes it difficult to arrive at a sensible estimate of the debt-equity ratio, which is a convenient way of judging the extent to which fixed and working capital needs have been financed by equity capital. Typically, these ratios include only long-term debt, but in Peru a major share of what appears as a short-term debt has long-term characteristics. (If none of the short-term debt were considered long term, then net working capital turns out to be negative in 1965.) With net worth at $59 million and long-term debt defined to include short-term debt from commercial banks, the debt-equity ratio is 1.7; if all or part of the asset, accumulated losses, is netted out of free reserves, the ratio approached 3.0.[19]

TABLE 9.4.   Peruvian fishmeal industry: Indicative balance
sheet, end 1965

		Million dollars
Assets		
Cash	5	
Accounts receivable	35	
Inventories	34	
Current assets		74
Fixed assets at cost	192	
Less accumulated depreciation	−48	144
Total		218
Other assets (accumulated losses)		23
Total assets		241
Liabilities		
Short-term liabilities		85
Long-term debt (greater than one year)		69
Other liabilities (unspecified)		28
Net worth		
Paid-in capital	43	
Free reserves	16	
Total		59
Total liabilities		241

Source: Oficina Sectorial, 1965 census of fishmeal operators, unpublished. The totals from 119 respondents were scaled to represent
the 150 firms active in 1965. The industry as defined here includes
all processors and their owned boats, but not the boats of independents. With two exceptions, all figures shown are the same as
those tabulated from the 119 completed questionnaires. First, fixed
assets at cost were made equal to the sum shown in Table 9.3 as
estimate 6, which was derived from a different item in the same
census and is corroborated very closely by independent sources. To
do this and maintain the balance, it was necessary to include the
unspecified item, "other assets," in gross fixed assets, and to reduce
"other liabilities" by $2 million. Second, the unspecified item,
"other liabilities," was reduced by another $4 million in order to
correct imbalances in the figures reported by the 119 firms.

TABLE 9.5. Peruvian fishmeal: Known sources of credit to processors, 1965 and 1966 (millions of dollars)

	Short-term	Long-term	Total
Total to be explained for 1965 (Table 9.4)	*85*	*69*	*154*
1965			
Commercial banks[a]	28.6	–	28.6
Industrial Bank of Peru[b]	–	15.1	15.1
Suppliers[a,b]	n. a.	n. a.	41.2
Total known, 1965	–	–	84.9
1966			
Commercial banks[a]	25.3	–	25.3
Industrial Bank of Peru[a]	–	33.0	33.0
Suppliers[c]	63.6	–	63.6
Total known, 1966	–	–	129.1

Sources: Commercial bank loans: Banco Central, *Boletín* 37 (March 1967), 34. Industrial Bank: Banco Industrial, *Memoria Anual—Año 1966* (Lima, 1967), p. 28. Suppliers' credits, 1965: "1104 Milliones a la Carga de Proveedores," *Pesca*, 11:13 (December 1965). Suppliers' credits, 1966: Oficina Sectorial, unpublished data.

[a] May include some loans to independent boat owners.
[b] Includes domestic suppliers only.
[c] Preliminary estimate with sample representing 37% of output; its allocation completely to short-term credit is doubtful.

These ratios are very high by Peruvian standards. A compilation of the debt-equity ratios for 13 large companies listed on the Lima Stock Exchange shows that for 1963 the highest ratio was 1.6; over half were below 1.0.[20] Since the definition of debt used in that study included short-term debt as well as reserves for taxes and payments under social laws, the comparable ratio for fishmeal from Table 9.4, ignoring accumulated losses, is 3.1, almost double the highest for a listed company.

The range of debt-equity ratios implies that between 60 and 75% of net fixed assets and net working capital has been financed by debt. It has not been possible to account for all the sources of this debt finance, but Table 9.5 lists the sources and amounts of which there is definite knowledge. As already noted, commercial banks were committed to the extent of $28.6 million at the end of 1965 and slightly less in 1966. This reported figure is almost certainly an underestimate of the actual commitment, since bank guarantees of loans from suppliers are not included. Another important and growing source of finance has been the Industrial Bank of Peru, a government development bank. Its commitment grew from $15.1 million at the end of 1965 to $33.0 million a year later, as it attempted to consolidate the debt of the industry and reduce its debt service burden.

About two other sources of credit, much less is known with any certainty. Probably the most important of all sources has been credit from suppliers, which may include 12- to 36-month loans for nets, boats, and reduction equipment, as well as the usual short-term trade credit. An estimate by *Pesca* placed the amount owed Peruvian suppliers by fishmeal firms at $41.2 million at the end of 1965;[21] preliminary results from the 1966 census of fishmeal plants put the figure at $63.6 million at the end of 1966. The Industrial Bank had guaranteed, on behalf of fishmeal firms who also had loans from the bank, $44.8 million of supplier credits at the end of 1966. Finally, no figures are available on loans from the finance companies which were organized by domestic and foreign banks to make loans at greater risk and longer term than the commercial banks are able to do. Although these companies have been active in the fishmeal industry, they do not publish the extent of their involvement. One rather off-the-cuff estimate put this figure at just under $20 million in 1963.[22] The precise figure cannot be verified, but the magnitude seems correct. The amount may, however, have fallen since 1963.

The fishmeal industry's heavy dependence on debt finance has had stimulating effects on the finance companies. There were six of these companies in 1967 and their growth roughly coincided with that of the fishmeal industry. Although this was largely coincidence, there seems little question that the profitable opportunities in fishmeal made the expansion of the finance companies easier than it might otherwise have been. One prominent company had 40% of its portfolio investment in fishmeal just after the investment boom and, although down to 25% in 1967, it had another 15% in the metal fabrication industry that fishmeal stimulated.

The nature of the production function for fishmeal has been an important factor in the dependence of these companies and of the commercial banks on clients in fishmeal. As one respondent explained it, both the banks and their finance companies were used to dealing with processing industries. The fish reduction process represents a fairly simple technology and falls well within the competence of the one industrial engineer ordinarily kept on the staff. Moreover, the smaller domestic companies in the industry have little access to foreign capital markets, and present a fairly inelastic demand for funds as long as the return on new assets exceeds the cost of borrowing. Copper mining, which has also undergone rapid growth during the period since 1955, lacks these linkages to local financial institutions. The large, foreign copper companies have easy access to international capital markets, and the technology is too specialized for the usual complement of technical staff carried by a commercial bank.

The 30-year-old Industrial Bank of Peru is an instrument of the state, although some shares are held by the public. It was not in any sense a result of growth in the fishing sector. However, the heavy debt of the industry, with its attendant dangers of insolvency and foreign domination of the country's biggest single foreign-exchange earner, propelled the bank into a major role as a provider of comparatively cheap credit. In the process of becoming the supplier of over half of the industry's long-term debt finance, the Industrial Bank committed over 30% of its portfolio to the fishing sector; during 1966, over half of all loans approved went to fishing, fish processing, and boat construction. In undertaking this task, the bank became an intermediary between the New York market and Peruvian fishmeal operators: in 1966, $24 million of the loans to the fishing sector were covered by borrowing from a group of United States banks specifically for the purpose of consolidating the debt of the fishmeal industry.[23]

Although foreign capital has been of critical importance to the growth of the fishmeal industry, it has not dominated this industry the way it did the guano industry a century earlier. In fact, the channels between foreign capital sources and final users have been largely indirect, leaving effective control of the industry in Peruvian hands. It is not known precisely to what extent the industry's debt of $154 million, which may account for up to three-quarters of its capital, has been contracted with foreign sources. The $24 million borrowed by the Industrial Bank is a clear case of foreign supply, which nonetheless left substantial control in Peruvian hands. The commercial banking system and the finance companies are interlaced with, and in several cases dominated by, foreign investors. Yet these intermediaries had also received $450 million in domestic savings at the end of 1965, in the form of time plus savings deposits, enough to cover 75% of all their loans; demand deposits more than cover the rest.[24] In light of these statistics, no prima facie case can be made for the domination of foreign capital through the banking system.

There is no official or otherwise reliable and consistent source of statistics on suppliers' credits, to which Table 9.5 attributes the largest contribution toward industry finance. The estimate of $63.6 million for 1966 is more complete than that for 1965, $41.2 million; the latter includes only domestic suppliers, although some of them might have been importers with support from their foreign suppliers. One rough measure of the finance supplied by foreign manufacturers is the difference of $22.4 million between these two estimates. An equally rough approximation for 1966 of $24 million can be derived from Table 7.1.[25] But the closeness of these two order of magnitude estimates may provide assurance where none is warranted.

Equity capital presents a better target for an informed guess at the share of foreign capital. In 1966, 35% of the output was produced by firms with some foreign participation.[26] If only firms known to be controlled by foreign capital are included, the fraction drops to one-fifth. Applying known and estimated percentage shares of foreign owners to company outputs, 26% of output was attributable to foreigners in 1966. Thus, if we assume a constant capital-output ratio across firms and similar debt-equity ratios between foreign and Peruvian companies, about one quarter of the equity capital has been supplied by foreign firms and individuals.[27] There is some shaky evidence that the fraction of foreign capital was only 13% in 1963 and 21% in 1965.[28] Peruvians fear that the fraction will continue growing, and markedly so, as overcapacity forces weakly financed Peruvian firms to leave the industry, while the strongly backed foreign firms hang on. The loans of the Industrial Bank are one attempt to counter this tendency, but the fear is real enough. Nevertheless, the lure of profits in a primary product export industry has moved sufficient Peruvian risk and debt capital to control the industry substantially during its period of rapid growth.

Much less needs to be said about the principal supply industries stimulated by fishmeal, since the investment in them is a small fraction of the investment in fishmeal itself. As a rough estimate, the four industries stimulated primarily by fishmeal (boats and reduction equipment, both including repair, netting, and jute sacks), require only 7% of the capital stock in the fishmeal industry to supply the fishmeal industry.[29] The low requirement is partly a result of dealing with the conservative investment assumptions of Table 7.1 (see n. 30); the requirement for suppliers at the peak of the investment boom in fishmeal might have been considerably higher. It is also a result of the small capital requirements of the metal fabricating and boatbuilding industries. Most of the investment in these industries finances inventories of goods in process, which are not covered by the capital-output measures employed.

Of 16 firms interviewed in the boat construction, equipment manufacturing, and netting and jute processing industries, 15 gave information on sales and 12 on fixed assets for 1966. Foreign capital controlled five of the firms and represented half of the equity capital of two others. Thirty-six percent of combined sales of $23 million to fishmeal companies could be traced to foreign investors, including those with fractional interests, and 35% of fixed assets totaling $12 million were owned by foreigners. Hence the share of foreign capital in these supply industries was greater than the one-fourth estimated for the fishmeal industry itself. However, foreign domination is not indicated, with one exception. Although netting manufacture is dominated by foreign capital and technical personnel, there are one or more strong Peruvian firms in each of the other industries. Because inventories of goods in process are the most important assets of these firms, there was probably considerable financing through trade credit and commercial banks. In this respect, the story may be much the same as in fishmeal: commercial banks channel Peruvian capital into the industry, while many suppliers offer credit backed by foreign banks.

Entrepreneurship

The supply of potential entrepreneurs in an economy is a fairly straightforward notion, but the demand curve for entrepreneurs involves some conceptual difficulties. The demand for entrepreneurs, like that for all factors of production, could in theory derive from a production function which allows explicitly for entrepreneurship as a factor, together with the profit-maximizing rule that entrepreneurs should be employed up to the point at which their marginal cost (necessary profit) equals their marginal revenue product.[30] However, when the demand for factors of production is discussed, usually the concept in the back of economists' minds is that entrepreneurs are the agents of demand, who employ or discharge and thus allocate resources according to rational rules of behavior. Who, then, employs the employers?

This question does not arise in a general equilibrium system, where the amounts of factors employed in producing each good are determined simultaneously with all prices and outputs. No one really employs anyone or anything else. Instead, factors maximizing their incomes seek out disequilibrium situations, until all opportunities are exploited, all marginal conditions fulfilled and equilibrium reached. However, in trying to understand the development of a single industry, partial equilibrium analysis is more useful. To handle the demand for entrepreneurs in that context, one can borrow from general equilibrium analysis the behavioral concept of factors seeking inframarginal situations. Then the demand for entrepreneurs is viewed as a set of conditions brought about by the insertion of a new production function into an economy. The only trouble is that the entrepreneurs themselves must discover these conditions and determine what the demand for their own services may be. There is a difference in degree and not kind between this situation and that in which a laborer faces an easily discovered demand curve established by entrepreneurs. In both cases there is an objective demand function, but the perceptions of the supplying agents will partly determine the equilibrium point. With entrepreneurs, the perception of the demand function is more difficult and more open to error, so a greater dependence is introduced between supply and the perceived demand curve.

With this qualification in mind, the economic conditions that established a demand curve for entrepreneurs in the Peruvian fishmeal industry can be discussed. The observable fact is that from 1964 to 1966 there were about 150 fishmeal plants in operation and about 125 firms running them, which roughly marks the intersection of the supply and demand curves for entrepreneurs. But, to what extent is this outcome the result of faulty perception of the demand curve by potential fishmeal entrepreneurs? The investigations of Chapter 6 into the long-run cost curve for the industry showed a permissive structure, with very close to constant costs at outputs above 20,000 metric tons per year. However, the average output of all plants is half that figure, so clearly many of them produce in the range of noticeably falling costs, where marginal cost could only equal price if losses were being incurred in the long run. Although the cost structure defines a demand curve imprecisely at best, it seems clear that the number of entrepreneurs actually supplied is above the wide band which might be called a demand curve.

Some of what appears to be excess supply could be explained by market imperfections that limit the supplies of capital and management available to entrepreneurs. If entrepreneurs facing these constraints could still earn profits at prevailing and expected prices, then their entry was rational; the demand curve for entrepreneurs must be adjusted upward to account for constraints on complementary factors. However, recent losses and plant closures indicate that misperceptions by the entrepreneurs have led to some excess supply of their services.

Where did these fishmeal entrepreneurs come from? The section on capital supply anticipated the answer: about two-thirds of the 1967 output came from plants run entirely by Peruvians and perhaps another 5 to 10% from plants controlled by Peruvians, although with a minority participation by foreign investors. Only 13 of the 125 fishmeal firms were controlled by foreigners, while another 8 had some foreign participation.[31] The data on the number of firms shows that there were well over 100 Peruvian entrepreneurs in fish processing.

A study made at the Frederico Villareal National University in Lima has attempted to delineate the characteristics of these Peruvian fishmeal entrepreneurs.[32] A group of 114 Peruvian entrepreneurs was selected and 38 responded. However, not all respondents were bona fide entrepreneurs, since in several instances associates were offered in place of an occupied or simply unwilling owner. Of the group interviewed, 71% were born in Peru and the others mostly in Italy and Japan. More interesting, 60% were the sons of Peruvian fathers and mothers. If the sample is representative, recent immigrant groups are not dominant in the industry, although they play a considerable role. Seventy-one percent were university graduates and one-quarter of the sample were engineers. Sixty-three percent were under 45 at the time of the survey and thus probably under 40 when they entered the industry.

One characteristic of interest overlooked by the study was the previous occupation of the entrepreneurs. From personal interviews and various articles appearing in *Pesca,* it has been possible to compile a very brief list of the prior occupations of 13 entrepreneurs, 11 of them Peruvians. Four were in other parts of the fishing sector before switching to fish reduction; two others were in mining and two in construction, three of these four having been engineers or executives; the rest included an accountant, salesman, importer, textile entrepreneur, and student engineer. Fishmeal appears to have attracted experienced entrepreneurs, as well as neophytes. It has, in short, been both a receiver and creator of entrepreneurship.

The main lure for these men was, of course, high profits. Entry was not difficult. It is clear from the composite balance sheet of Table 9.4 that the financial resources of the entrepreneurs were inadequate for the capital needs of the industry. But it is equally clear that credit was not difficult to find, and wide profit margins made it possible to cover the high fixed costs of a heavily leveraged capital structure. The technology was not terribly demanding. As one respondent pointed out, an inexperienced operator could start small and learn how to run his plant while still making profits. Moreover, the beginner had several pioneers to imitate, men who had been in other parts of the fishing sector prior to fishmeal and, in several instances, had entered the reduction business with foreign partners supplying some of the technical skills. Since one plant is much like another, if a neighbor was getting good results it was always possible to copy him. With large margins, fine differences did not matter; the emphasis was not on cost reduction but on capacity expansion. The risk-taker was more essential than the technical expert. An entrepreneur who could not find the capital or managers necessary to establish an optimum-sized plant could often build a smaller one and operate profitably. It was unnecessary to overcome an apparent tendency to keep close personal control over the firm or to go outside the family for equity capital or top management. Thus, although several larger Peruvian-owned firms are characterized by wider participation and some delegation of authority, the family-owned, one-man operation is the rule in the industry.

Foreign participants in, and observers of, the industry point out that the risk-taking entrepreneur who characterized the early Peruvian entrants is not so well suited to handle the current problems of the industry, centering around the need to reduce costs in the face of a recent profit squeeze. This is an impressionistic conclusion that cannot be tested precisely. However, nothing in the data on unit costs, which were discussed intensively in Chapter 6, points to this conclusion. The absence of sharp economies of scale for plants producing over 20,000 metric tons a year has been belabored enough. The statistical analysis of Chapter 6 showed that multiplant firms do not have lower costs than single-plant companies. Moreover, the foreign companies do not appear to enjoy notably lower costs than their Peruvian competitors. The real advantage of the foreigners is their access to capital markets, which may enable them to survive periods of losses and invest in labor-saving equipment, especially for materials handling.

Foreign Exchange

The identification of foreign exchange as a factor of production has become a common theme in the development literature, especially in discussions of the two-gap model of growth (see p. 21). In these models, when foreign exchange earnings are insufficient to purchase the necessary imports implied by a target rate of output growth, then larger export earnings contribute to output by permitting greater imports. However, if foreign exchange earnings are sufficient to purchase necessary imports, then added export earnings are apparently not required for output growth. This may have been the case in Peru during the early 1960s, when the country maintained a fixed exchange rate and accumulated reserves. But, in 1966, reserves began falling and there has been an almost continual foreign exchange crisis since 1967, indicating a return to the foreign exchange constraint. Moreover, as demonstrated in Chapter 4 (pp. 49–54), export growth has been a strong stimulus to savings in Peru; even when savings constrained output, increased export earnings contributed to growth. So it appears that the foreign exchange supplied by the fishmeal sector has been, and most probably will be, relevant to Peruvian development.

Peru's need for, and use of, foreign exchange was discussed in general terms in Chapter 4. The task here is to estimate the contribution of the fishmeal industry to the supply of foreign exchange. Because input data of the sort presented in this study are not readily available for other export industries in Peru, the first attempt at demonstrating the relative importance of fishmeal and oil exports has to be in terms of gross foreign exchange earnings. Table 9.6

TABLE 9.6. Peru: Gross earnings of foreign exchange, 1955–1966

Year	Fishmeal and oil (million dollars)	All exports (million dollars)	Ratio of fishmeal and oil to total (percent)
1955	1.4	270.9	0.5
1958	10.3	292.4	3.5
1960	42.4	433.1	9.8
1961	60.4	496.4	12.1
1962	111.5	540.0	20.6
1963	112.6	541.2	20.8
1964	157.5	667.0	23.6
1965	178.3	667.3	26.8
1966	196.5	764.3	25.7
1967	173.3[a]	757.0	22.9[a]

Sources: All exports: Banco Central, *Cuentas Nacionales* (1968), pp. 44–45. Fishmeal and oil exports from Table 5.5.

[a] Fishmeal only.

shows the share of fishmeal and oil in total export earnings for the period from 1955 to 1967. The rapid growth of fishmeal exports has already been documented extensively in Chapter 5 (pp. 77–89). By 1962, the industry was responsible for one-fifth of all export earnings, and the fraction has not been below that since; in 1965 and 1966 it was over one-fourth.

A better comparison would include long-term capital inflows, both the total for the economy and that due to investment in the fishing sector. Unfortunately, the latter figure is not available and not easily estimated, or even guessed at, for any single year. However, as a rough estimate, the cumulative total to 1965 may be about $63 million.[33] The net long-term private capital inflow to Peru for all sectors, summed over the six years from 1960 to 1965, is $74 million; with official long-term capital added, the total is $432 million. Fishmeal production has clearly been a significant attractor of foreign exchange on capital account. This aggregate estimate will, of course, mask annual differences. It seems likely that the net flow of foreign capital into the fishmeal industry was a large fraction of the total during 1960 to 1963, when fishmeal investment was growing toward its 1963 peak and linkages were just developing, while the heavy investment in copper had subsided.

The next step is to determine if fishmeal is a particularly heavy consumer of its export earnings. Some of the groundwork for this calculation has been laid in Table 7.1, the input-output table for fishmeal. It shows that, of $157.5 million of foreign exchange earned in the typical year 1964, $34.3 million was expended on foreign exchange due to first- and second-round imports. As noted in the discussion of Chapter 7 (pp. 126–127), third- and subsequent-round expenditures on foreign exchange cannot be estimated from the data available, but may approximate $10 million, giving a total on all rounds of expenditure of $44 million.

One of the important points of staple theory and, in fact, of all recent discussions of export economies, is that foreign exchange expenditure does not stop with raw materials and intermediate goods, but continues into the disposition of factor payments by the recipients. This was a central thesis of Levin's work on the guano economy and played an important role in the explanations of North and Baldwin for the failure of residentiary industry to develop in plantation and mining economies. Four forms of factor payments are relevant in this context: wages and salaries, interest, profits, and taxes. Depreciation is not germane, because the import content due to investment has been counted by inserting an investment function (the sixth column) into the partial Leontief matrix of Table 7.1.

The treatment of the consumption linkage in Chapter 8 (pp. 131–134) led to the conclusion that the evidence for special consumption effects due to fishmeal wage and salary payments is not strong. Estimates of the direct import content of consumption due to fishmeal wages has to derive from general studies of the economy. The marginal propensity to import out of private consumption expenditure was estimated to be 0.268.[34] This should probably be applied only to direct payments to workers, which may be taken as approximately 75% of total wages.[35] If we ignore taxes and savings, of the total labor share of \$51.3 million, \$10.3 million may be spent directly on imported goods. Lack of data prevents any estimate of subsequent leakages.

In dealing with interest and profits, the strong caveats noted in Table 6.1 should be recalled: the share of output due to interest has an arbitrary element because of uncertainties in the share of fishing expenditures covered by interest, and the only measure of profit is a residual that is more of an errors and omissions term. However, accepting these poor estimates as they stand, interest paid to foreign lenders may be approximately \$4.0 million,[36] and profit repatriation about \$1.5 million a year,[37] out of a total capital share of \$47.0 million (Table 7.1).

It is not immediately obvious that taxes, and hence government imports out of payments from fishmeal, ought to be included in these calculations. However, it is plausible that government spending decisions have been changed at the margin by tax payments from fishmeal, which accounted for about 3% of government revenue in 1965.[38] This is in accord with Wallich's observations of the sugar economy

TABLE 9.7. Peru: Estimated annual leakages of foreign exchange earned by fishmeal industry, 1964–1966 (million dollars).

	Estimated foreign exchange loss on		
Source of leakage	First round	Second round	Subsequent rounds
Imported inputs	11.3	23.0	9.9
Wages and salaries	–	10.3	n. a.
Interest	–	4.0[a]	n. a.
Profits	–	1.5	n. a.
Taxes	–	2.6	n. a.
Total	11.3	41.4	9.9

[a] Some of this actually is paid directly to foreign lenders and should be considered a first-round expenditure.

of Cuba[39] and in the spirit of the structural equation for government expenditure utilized in the national income determination model of Chapter 4 (Table 4.6). The government's marginal propensity to spend out of tax revenues from that equation is 0.673 and its marginal propensity to import from expenditures is estimated at 0.196.[40] Thus the fraction of marginal tax revenues going to imports is 0.132,[41] giving an "import content" of fishmeal tax payments equal to $2.6 million.

The total of these input and factor payments, which appear in the first and second rounds as foreign exchange expenditures, is $52.7 million, or one-third of gross foreign exchange earnings, which leaves net receipts of $104.8 million (see Summary Table 9.7). If the leakages in the third and subsequent rounds of expenditures for intermediate goods, $10 million, are added, the net receipts are $95 million, or 60% of gross earnings. This excludes leakages due to factor payments beyond the second round, but also omits net inflows of foreign capital to finance the industry. It is clear that the fishmeal industry has been a major provider of foreign exchange to the Peruvian economy.

10

Peruvian Fishmeal
as a Staple

It is time to fit the Peruvian fishmeal industry into the staple theory of economic development and to draw from this case some implications for economic development in the last third of the twentieth century. The first task is essentially to weave the strands of this study into a set of conclusions that will be as tidy as the necessarily discursive subject matter permits. The second is to generalize from the experience of fishmeal to the potential success of other economies depending upon other primary product exports for development.

Fishmeal and Other Staples

Fishmeal makes a good macroeconomic impression as a staple when compared with the prime example, Canadian wheat. In the ten years from 1900 to 1910, volume exports of Canadian food products other than livestock increased at a compound annual rate of 6.7%, while the value of these exports grew to 4.4% of GNP by 1910. Gross national product increased by 5.3% a year over the same period, and GNP per capita grew at the annual rate of 2.5%.[1] By comparison, from 1955 to 1964, when the fishmeal boom ended, volume exports of all Peruvian fish products grew at a compound rate of 48% a year, until they accounted for 4.7% of 1964 GNP. During that period, real GNP grew at 5.5% and GNP per capita at 2.6%, rates almost identical to those for Canada.[2]

Although the expansion of both staple industries depended on increased inputs of natural resources, North American wheat production required an extensive exploitation of new land, while Peruvian fishmeal output was increased by a more intensive exploitation of coastal waters. The heavy investment in overhead capital that characterized Canadian prairie development was unnecessary in Peru. Although some harbor development can be traced to a stimulus from fishmeal, the external benefits are expected to be somewhat confined and certainly not as dramatic as opening the prairie. In this respect, fishmeal resembles mining or petroleum. These extractive industries often lead to infrastructure that is either too specialized or too isolated to benefit manufacturing industries and agriculture. However, the fishing industry did have to spread along much of the coast to avoid overfishing any single zone and to reduce the risk of unpredictable shifts in the location of the natural resource. Thus, like Canadian wheat, fishmeal activity was not concentrated in one area, although it was largely confined to urban and semiurban locations.

Wheat and fishmeal shared attributes that created a strong attraction for domestic entrepreneurs. Fish processing, like wheat production, is not technologically demanding and can be carried on as a small-scale activity. A similar pattern may have been at work on the Canadian prairie and the Peruvian coast. A few pioneers began to farm or fish in response to favorable market or technological stimuli. These men were the innovators who exploited the opportunity and demonstrated the feasibility of utilizing the natural resource. A group of lesser entrepreneurs followed, mainly imitating the pioneers, but probably bringing some minor innovations of their own. Because the technology was uncomplicated and the producing units small, there were no substantial barriers to entry and the group of potential entrepreneurs was large. A fair expectation of profitable operation brought a great number of these men into the industry. Once involved, some of the followers may have developed into innovators or at least become experienced entrepreneurs, prepared to exploit the next opportunity. Of course, the type of entrepreneur involved in each industry may have been very different. Wheat required no processing before export, while fishmeal did. So Canadian and American entrepreneurs were farmers, while Peruvians have been industrialists and commercial fishermen. It is not clear if these differences are significant for further development, but it is a possibility.

The straightforward technology of fish reduction also attracted domestic banks, which were familiar with processing industries. Peruvian banks supplied about a fifth of the debt finance for fishmeal, not including their loans to domestic suppliers of the industry. Peruvian capital markets were stimulated and new institutions prospered as a consequence of fishmeal development. This pattern might have been at work in Canada and the United States, also. However, in other respects the supply of capital to fishmeal did not conform to old patterns. There was little chance for foreign investors to finance social overheads, as they did in the wheat economies, because fishmeal required little infrastructure. Neither did foreign capital finance the bulk of the extractive industry itself, as in copper mining. Only about 30% of all capital, debt, and equity has been supplied from overseas. (There is also some foreign capital in the port works induced partly by fishmeal, but it has been provided by the World Bank and not by private investors.)

The demand of fishmeal operators for labor has not been very different from that of other industries in Peru, nor has it been especially intense. The boats were manned and plants staffed heavily with unskilled, migratory labor, so that the principal effect on labor markets was the attraction of agricultural workers into industry and, to some extent, their training for industrial tasks. So, unlike the small-scale agricultural production that supplied Canadian wheat and Danish dairy exports, mass education was not essential for the labor force. In contrast to copper mining in Northern Rhodesia, there was not an especially large demand for skilled labor. Although some foreign skills were imported, the Peruvian labor market was able to satisfy the bulk of the need. Because the distribution and type of skills required for fish reduction were like those for other Peruvian industry, wages in fishmeal were not markedly higher than in other industries; in fact, they were below average. This contrasts with the capital-intensive copper enclave in Northern Rhodesia, which for a time rationed jobs instead of lowering wages, and set a high wage standard for organized workers in other industries. The result there was a substitution of capital for labor throughout the manufacturing sector of the economy.[3] It is true that fishermen receive wages substantially above the average for unskilled workers in Peru, and there may be some informal rationing of jobs as organized fishermen maintain and even increase piece rates. However, to some extent those willing to go to sea and undertake the hazards of small-scale fishing form a noncompetitive group, which may explain at least part of the salary differential.

Like wheat and dairy exports, fishmeal growth did stimulate domestic supply industries. Fishmeal is capital-intensive, but composed of small units. It consequently provided a large demand for small units of fishing and processing capacity, and its comparatively uncomplicated technology encouraged a positive response from Peruvian manufacturing. As in fishing and processing themselves, it was possible for the capital goods industry to start small and learn rapidly, training skilled labor in the process. Fishmeal firms tended to be small, but the demand for many pieces of equipment might as well have come from a few large producers who expanded their capacity by the multiplication of small units. However, it is likely such an industry would have been dominated by foreign firms which, because of familiarity and habit, might have directed their purchases overseas and, by the influence of size, been able to obtain preferential treatment for imported capital goods. In Peruvian copper mining, for example, large foreign firms import mining equipment under concessions from the government, thereby stifling potential linkages. Thus this is a case in which the large number of small firms, although not necessary for linkage development, was helpful.

It should be obvious from what has been said that the fishmeal industry did not form an enclave within the Peruvian economy, as guano had done in the nineteenth century. Domestic factors responded to its stimulus, both in the industry itself and by creating or expanding supply industries. Close to two-thirds of its foreign exchange earnings were retained in Peru, with only a little assistance from taxes. Moreover, fishmeal production did not noticeably sharpen the dualism that pervades the Peruvian economy, and even alleviated the condition in some respects. Processing spread along the coast, creating small industrial centers and giving new importance to ports away from Lima and Callao. Migrants were attracted from the mountains and jungle to work in boats and plants, marginally reducing underemployment and improving land-labor ratios in the agricultural regions. The jute industry expanded largely because of fishmeal demand, employing jungle farmers to produce one of that region's few viable cash crops. Of course, the wage payments of the fishmeal industry to skilled workers and salaried personnel, as well as its profits, may have contributed to the skewed income distribution that characterizes the economy. However, fishmeal's effect compares favorably with that of mining, which usually employs very few unskilled workers and stimulates considerably less domestic industry.

It is implicit in the foregoing that fishmeal growth did increase the capacity of the Peruvian economy to transform in the future. Some semiskilled labor was trained by the processors, although probably not in important amounts. It seems likely that fishmeal has been a training ground for entrepreneurs, whose availability should stimulate the development of other industries. The investment boom of 1958–1963 created a capital goods industry, part of which is now capable of supplying a wide range of industries in Peru and developing export markets. Moreover, boat building and equipment manufacturing firms have been training labor in skills needed critically elsewhere in the economy, and some of these external economies are already being felt. Peru is not yet a developed country and no single staple industry can be expected to lead a country all the way through diversification and industrialization. The lesson from Canadian history is that a series of vigorous staples is required before the capacity to transform is great enough to avoid the instabilities of an export economy. Peru has had other staples and will need more, but fishmeal has certainly been an outstanding contributor to the country's industrial development.

Implications for Development

The history of fishmeal in Peru counteracts the skepticism of writers like Nurkse, Prebisch, and Levin on the possibilities for primary export-led growth. Under the right circumstances, given industries with compatible production functions and societies that encourage or at least permit strong responses, primary product exports can still be a leading sector in economic development. But how special are the circumstances? It will not be possible to replicate the fishmeal industry on a large scale in many developing countries. Unlike the world market for petroleum in recent years, that for fishmeal is not large enough to sustain great increments to supply at profitable prices, even if the resources for fishmeal were widely available. However, there are other export industries based on raw materials that have characteristics

similar to fish reduction. The task at hand is to isolate the characteristics that were essential to the transmittal of a stimulus from the
fishing sector to the rest of the Peruvian economy and then to see
if other export industries share these traits.

The catalogue of production function attributes that encouraged
linkages from Peruvian fishmeal must by now be familiar to the
reader. Based on the experience with fishmeal, the maximum response
is likely to be elicited by a capital-intensive industry composed of
many small units, which refines raw materials using a technology
that is uncompilcated or at least familiar. The specification of small
factories does not require diseconomies of scale, although they would
help. Rather, it requires that there not be sharply decreasing costs.
Then imperfections in the markets for capital and management are
more likely to result in small units, since the relative cost disadvantage
is not great and profitable operation may be possible.

The reasons for these desirable characteristics have been discussed
already, but a few further comments are pertinent. First of all, it
is not essential that the activity be industrial. As the North American
wheat economies have shown, linkages can develop from agricultural
units to manufacturing. In that case, since factor payments to labor,
land, and capital accrue mostly to farm families, consumption linkages
are likely to be stronger than for capital-intensive industry. Similarly,
although the specification of capital intensity does work to encourage
linkages to domestic capital goods industries, there is a trade-off between the stimuli to producers of investment goods and consumer
goods. High labor intensity is more likely to promote the latter at
the expense of the former. As long as both linkages could work, it
may not be very important which is favored by the staple industry.
Furthermore, if the labor-intensive process is also skill-intensive, then
the external economies of training will be strong. This effect was
weak in fishmeal itself, but important in the industries it stimulated.
Geographically dispersed production may also enhance the stimulative
effects of the export industry. Fishmeal production was spread along
the coast, which helped alleviate the geographic aspects of dualism
to some extent. However, the most important external economy consequent upon dispersal is the provision of infrastructure in support
of the export industry, a linkage that was not especially forceful in
Peru. In short, it is not essential that the Peruvian model be followed

precisely. Export-stimulated development can take place under other conditions, although small-scale production and simple technology remain compelling attributes.[4]

It would require a complete and separate study to develop any comprehensive, authoritative list of primary product export industries which might fit the specifications for staple-led growth. The brief discussion here can only be indicative. Staley and Morse give four categories of resource-processing industry that are likely to be composed of small units:

1. Weight-reducing or preservative processes based on widely scattered resources, of which rice cleaning and polishing, pork curing, dairy production, vegetable oil extraction, and sawmilling are prominent examples.
2. Semiprocessing industries that open up new territories, such as sugar in India and Mexico, milk in Peru and fruit elsewhere.
3. Multicrop processors, located in nodal towns, such as fruit and vegetable canning, fish preservation, and the extraction of cottonseed and groundnut oil.
4. By-product utilization, including bagasse hardboard, molasses products, and by-products of meat.[5]

The first and third of these categories are more likely to produce substantial export industries than the other two, primarily because they depend on broader resource bases and less specialized situations. Fishmeal falls into the first group, which includes such other familiar staples as pork and dairy products (Denmark), palm oil (Nigeria), and rice (southeast Asia).[6]

The success of fishmeal as a staple strongly suggests two other possibilities: fish flour for human consumption and the preservation of seafood in several forms. The use of fish flour simply reduces further the protein chain from the sea to man. When exploited as guano, the protein travels from plankton to fish to birds to fertilizer to plants to grazing animals to humans; as fishmeal, the birds, fertilizer, and plants are eliminated and chickens and hogs substituted for grazers; with fish flour, the animals are also eliminated. (The next step in reducing the chain will be to eliminate the fish also, using sea vegetation directly as human food.) Although problems of quality control will be greater and the equipment perhaps a bit more sophisticated, fundamentally the reduction of fish for human consumption resembles that for animal consumption. Although the market is inchoate now, it promises to be a growing one, and several underdeveloped countries have the resources to supply it. Peru is beginning to produce flour already, but the industry necessarily competes with established fish processors. The canning and freezing of fish for export should also have the properties conducive to linkage formation and may afford growing markets for some developing countries. In both these cases, and in many of the others mentioned in this section, the extent of the resource is a problem. Peru has been exploiting a particularly abundant fishery, and many of the linkages developed because of sheer size. A few canning and freezing plants along the coast will not induce supply industries to locate in the producing country, nor will they stimulate factor responses of important magnitudes.

Meat, dairy, vegetable oil, and grain products remain export possibilities with desirable characteristics. Other agricultural products, traditionally grown as plantation crops in colonial areas, are being adapted to smallholder systems, which have favorable properties for staple-led growth. Tea in Kenya, coffee in several countries, cotton in Sudan and Uganda, sisal in East Africa, and fruits (particularly bananas and pineapples) in Latin America and Africa are examples that come to mind. Not all of these exports involve processing; in other cases, either the plants are subject to scale economies or the resource base is not extensive enough to require many factories. However, there may be strong consumption linkages from the raw material suppliers themselves, as happened with North American wheat.

Kenya tea is an excellent example. In that country, smallholders have been encouraged to add tea to their mix of cash crops by a government program that includes processing factories, access roads, and loans to growers. By the middle 1970s there are expected to be 30,000 growers with 28,000 acres under full production, supplying 20 factories that will produce 26 million pounds of tea a year. There are too few factories, constructed over too long a period, to encourage local manufacturing of processing equipment. However, the concomitant road improvement is expected to stimulate production of other crops in the tea areas and will have broad external economies in other respects. Most important, tea production is intensive in proprietor-laborers, who have the potential to develop into entrepreneurs.

Tea and the other cash crops grown on African farms in Kenya are in fact producing a growing group of entrepreneurs capable of branching out into small-scale, local industry in the agricultural areas. Moreover, since the return on land and capital will, after loans are repaid, accrue to the farmer and his family, consumption linkages are probably strong. There may also be linkages to industries producing agricultural implements and, eventually, more sophisticated farm equipment. The latter effect will be enhanced by the diversified crop mix of many farmers who grow tea.[7] Several other former plantation crops, which require centralized processing in relatively large units or no processing at all, should have similar linkage effects.

Intensive studies of other potential and actual staples need to be made before drawing definite conclusions. But it appears that the Peruvian experience with fishmeal, although it has special characteristics, can be repeated elsewhere. Peru's recent history shows that opportunities for export-led growth should be sought and the strategy emphasized in development planning. Conditions seem promising enough in mid-twentieth century to justify the effort.

Notes

1. Introduction

1. National income data taken from, and growth rates calculated from, Banco Central de Reserva del Peru, *Cuentas Nacionales del Perú, 1950–1967*, (Lima, 1968).

2. Banco Central, *Cuentas Nacionales* (1968), pp. 44–45.

3. "Anchovy" is a close, but not exact, translation of the Spanish name, *anchoveta,* for the species, whose Latin name is *Engraulis ringens.*

4. The sources of statistics on the fishmeal industry are noted in Chap. 5.

2. The Staple Theory of Export-led Growth

1. For a concise summary of Innis's work, see R. E. Caves and R. H. Holton, *The Canadian Economy,* Chap. 2.

2. For the first of several expositions, see R. E. Baldwin, "Patterns of Development in Newly Settled Regions," *Manchester School of Economic and Social Studies,* 24: 161–179 (1956).

3. See, for example, D. C. North, "Agriculture in Regional Economic Growth," *Journal of Farm Economics,* 49: 943–951 (1959).

4. Caves and Holton, *The Canadian Economy,* pp. 31–33.

5. The following discussion owes much to the synthesis of theories by M. H. Watkins, "A Staple Theory of Economic Growth," *Canadian Journal of Economics and Political Science,* 29: 141–158 (1963). C. P. Kindleberger, *Foreign Trade and the National Economy,* pp. 196–205, provides many brief but concrete illustrations of the mechanisms discussed below.

6. A. O. Hirschman, *The Strategy of Economic Development,* Chap. 6.

7. Ibid., pp. 116–117.

8. R. E. Baldwin, *Economic Development and Export Growth: A Study of Northern Rhodesia, 1920–1960,* pp. 68–69.

9. D. C. North, "Location Theory and Regional Economic Growth," *Journal of Political Economy,* 63: 252 (1955). The term "residentiary industry" en-

compasses the production of both consumer and producer goods for sale in the home market.

10. Baldwin, *Economic Development and Export Growth,* p. 66.

11. R. E. Baldwin, "Patterns of Development in Newly Settled Regions," *Manchester School of Economic and Social Studies,* 24: 169–176 (1956).

12. North, "Agriculture in Regional Economic Growth," p. 947.

13. Baldwin, *Economic Development and Export Growth,* pp. 66–67.

14. D. C. North, *The Economic Growth of the United States, 1790–1860,* pp. 4–5.

15. Caves and Holton, *The Canadian Economy,* Chaps. 1, 2; the following discussion of Canadian staples, unless noted, is based on their Chap. 2.

16. Calculated from data in 1900 prices given by M. C. Urquhart and K. A. H. Buckley, eds., *Historical Statistics of Canada,* pp. 174–175.

17. Ibid., p. 532; Caves and Holton, *The Canadian Economy,* p. 43.

18. Caves and Holton, *The Canadian Economy,* pp. 34, 43–44.

19. Calculated from data in 1935–1939 prices given by O. J. Firestone, *Canada's Economic Development 1867–1953,* p. 66, and from Urquhart and Buckley, *Historical Statistics of Canada,* p. 14. The use of 1935–1939 price weights probably biases the growth rate downward, since the prices, and therefore the weights, of goods whose output grew most rapidly over 1900 to 1910 were probably comparatively lower in 1935–1939 than in 1900–1910.

20. G. W. Bertram, "Economic Growth in Canadian Industry, 1870–1915: The Staple Model and the Take-off Hypothesis," *Canadian Journal of Economic and Political Science,* 29: 174–175 (1963).

21. Caves and Holton, *The Canadian Economy,* pp. 18–21.

22. E. J. Chambers and D. F. Gordon, "Primary Products and Economic Growth: An Empirical Measurement," *Journal of Political Economy,* 74: 315–332 (August 1966).

23. North, *Economic Growth of the United States.*

24. Calculated from R. F. Martin, *National Income in the United States, 1799–1938,* p. 6; United States Bureau of the Census, *Historical Statistics of the United States, Colonial Times to 1957* (Washington, D.C., 1960), pp. 537–541, for the United States; and from Urquhart and Buckley, *Historical Statistics of Canada,* pp. 141, 174–175, for Canada.

25. Calculated from North, *Economic Growth of the United States,* pp. 233, 239.

26. Calculated from data in 1926 prices given by Martin, *National Income in the United States,* p. 6, and from the United States Bureau of the Census, *Historical Statistics of the United States,* p. 25. Here, again, the use of later-period price weights may cause a downward bias in the growth rate.

27. Calculated from North, *Economic Growth of the United States,* pp. 233, 239.

28. Ibid., pp. 125–133.

29. Calculated from ibid., pp. 250, 262.

30. R. W. Fogel estimates that in 1890 about 3% of national income was

saved by lower costs due to rail transport; see "Railroads as an Analogy of the Space Effort: Some Economic Aspects," in B. Mazlish, ed., *The Railroad and the Space Program*, p. 101. A. Fishlow, using a different concept of cost reduction, puts the savings at 4% of GNP in 1859, but at 10% or more in 1890; see *American Railroads and the Transformation of the Ante-Bellum Economy*, pp. 52–62.

31. North, *Economic Growth of the United States*, pp. 153–155.

32. A. J. Youngson, *Possibilities of Economic Progress*, Chap. X, on which the following discussion is based.

33. Calculated from ibid., p. 223.

34. Calculated from data in 1929 prices given by ibid., pp. 191, 223. Again, the use of late-period price weights probably causes an understatement of the growth rate.

35. Baldwin, *Economic Development and Export Growth*.

36. Ibid., pp. 30, 33, 35–36; growth rates calculated from data in 1949 prices. The use of monetary domestic product probably overstates the growth rate, because part of the increase may be matched by a decline in the subsistence (nonmarket) sector.

37. Ibid., pp. 105–107.

38. Ibid., Chap. 7.

39. Hirschman, *Strategy of Economic Development*, pp. 116–117.

40. Baldwin, *Economic Development and Export Growth*, pp. 187, 218, 221.

41. C. W. Reynolds, "Development Problems of an Export Economy: The Case of Chile and Copper," in Mamalakis and Reynolds, *Essays on the Chilean Economy*, especially pp. 329–331.

42. L. C. A. Knowles and C. M. Knowles, *The Economic Development of the British Empire*, III, p. 210; Baldwin, *Economic Development and Export Growth*, p. 105.

43. D. A. Farnie, "The Mineral Revolution of South Africa," *South African Journal of Economics*, 24: 125–134 (1956).

44. The main lines of this contrast are indicated in R. E. Caves, " 'Vent for Surplus' Models of Trade and Growth," in R. E. Baldwin, et al., *Trade, Growth and the Balance of Payments*, pp. 102–103. The standard review of the vast literature on neoclassical growth models is F. H. Hahn and R. C. O. Matthews, "The Theory of Economic Growth: A Survey," *Economic Journal*, 74: 779–902 (1964), especially Parts I and II.

45. R. R. Nelson, "Aggregate Production Functions," *American Economic Review*, 54: 575–607 (1964).

46. E. F. Denison, *The Sources of Economic Growth in the United States*, discusses these and other contributing factors.

47. See, for example, H. G. Johnson, *Money, Trade and Economic Growth*, Chap. 4; R. Findlay and H. Grubert, "Factor Intensities, Technological Progress and the Terms of Trade," *Oxford Economic Papers*, 11: 111–121 (1959); J. Bhagwati, "Growth, Terms of Trade and Comparative Advantage," *Economia Internazionale*, 12: 393–414 (1959).

48. H. Oniki and H. Uzawa, "Patterns of Trade and Investment in a Dynamic Model of International Trade," *Review of Economic Studies*, 32: 15–38 (January 1965); P. K. Bardhan, "Equilibrium Growth in the International Economy," *Quarterly Journal of Economics*, 74: 455–464 (August 1965).

49. These points are discussed by K. Berrill, "International Trade and the Rate of Economic Growth," *Economic History Review (Series 2)*, 12: 351, 359 (1960); and D. Seers, "An Approach to the Short-Period Analysis of Primary Producing Economies," *Oxford Economic Papers*, 11: 3–9 (1959).

50. The best-known of a long list of such models was presented by H. B. Chenery and A. M. Strout, "Foreign Assistance and Economic Development," *American Economic Review*, 56: 679–733 (September 1966). An earlier version was given by R. I. McKinnon, "Foreign Exchange Restraints in Economic Development," *Economic Journal*, 74: 388–409 (1964).

51. Moreover, the realism of a linear model is dubious, especially in the long run. Chenery and Strout themselves allow for some substitution of imports for investment. See "Foreign Assistance," pp. 679–698. R. R. Nelson, "The Effective Exchange Rate, Employment and Growth in a Foreign Exchange Constrained Economy," unpublished RAND paper, RM-5680-AID (July 1968), has emphasized the possibilities of substitution between domestic resources and imports. Whenever such substitution is possible, export growth can potentially contribute to growth of output.

52. H. Myint, "The 'Classical Theory' of International Trade and the Underdeveloped Countries," *Economic Journal*, 68: 317–337 (1959).

53. Caves, " 'Vent for Surplus' Models of Trade and Growth," in Baldwin, et al., *Trade, Growth and the Balance of Payments*, p. 109.

54. G. L. Hicks and G. McNicoll, "Foreign Trade and the Growth of the Dual Economy: A Study of the Philippines, 1950–66," National Planning Association, draft final report (Washington, October 1968).

55. W. W. Rostow, *Stages of Economic Growth*, pp. 38, 55–57.

56. Fogel, "Railroads as an Analogy of the Space Effort," in Mazlish, *The Railroad and the Space Program*, pp. 98–104.

57. Fishlow, *American Railroads*, Chaps. 2, 3, 4.

58. Bertram, "Economic Growth in Canadian Industry," pp. 165–166, 170, 174–175, 183–184.

3. Barriers to Export-led Growth

1. R. Nurkse, *Equilibrium Growth in the World Economy*, Chaps. 10, 11.

2. Ibid., pp. 294–295.

3. A. H. Imlah, *Economic Elements in the Pax Britannica*.

4. Growth rates calculated from United Nations, *Yearbook of International Trade Statistics, 1966*, pp. 12–13, 32–34.

5. B. C. Swerling, "Some Interrelationships between Agricultural Trade and Economic Development," *Kyklos*, 14: 375–376 (1961); A. K. Cairncross, *Factors in Economic Development*, p. 216.

6. H. Myint, *The Economics of Developing Countries,* pp. 151–152.
7. United Nations (R. Prebisch), *The Economic Development of Latin America and Its Principal Problems,* pp. 8–14. See also H. W. Singer, "The Distribution of Gains between Investing and Borrowing Countries," *American Economic Review Papers and Proceedings* 40: 473–485 (1950); and G. M. Meier, *The International Economics of Development,* pp. 56–59, whose summary of the entire terms of trade discussion, Chap. 3, is excellent.
8. C. P. Kindleberger, *The Terms of Trade,* p. 234.
9. Ibid., pp. 17–20, 336–337.
10. Ibid., pp. 18–20.
11. Meier, *International Economics of Development,* pp. 60–61, 64–65.
12. Kindleberger, *Terms of Trade,* pp. 247, 253–257.
13. Singer, "The Distribution of Gains," pp. 473–485, made much of the enclave and undynamic nature of export industries.
14. J. Levin, *The Export Economies.*
15. Ibid., pp. 109, 115–123, 116–117, 180–184.
16. For one description of a dual economy, see B. Higgins, "The 'Dualistic Theory' in Underdeveloped Areas," *Economic Development and Cultural Change,* 4: 99–115 (1956). The factor intensity aspect is formalized in neoclassical terms by R. S. Eckaus, "The Factor Proportions Problem in Underdeveloped Areas," *American Economic Review,* 45: 539–565 (1955).
17. D. C. McClelland, *The Achieving Society,* and E. E. Hagen, *On the Theory of Social Change.*
18. McClelland has recently changed his view. D. C. McClelland and D. G. Winter, *Motivating Economic Achievement,* present evidence that individuals can be taught the attributes of achievement motivation in a few weeks, at low cost, with consequent measurable improvement in their performance as entrepreneurs. This puts McClelland closer to the optimism of the sociological school.
19. J. H. Kunkel, "Values and Behavior in Economic Development," *Economic Development and Cultural Change,* 13: 257–277 (April 1965).
20. The opposing points of view outlined above have been succinctly presented by J. R. Harris, "Industrial Entrepreneurship in Nigeria," Ph.D. dissertation, Massachusetts Institute of Technology, 1967, Chap. 2, pp. 26–39.
21. Ibid., Chap. 2, pp. 1–26. This approach is also implicit in G. F. Papanek, "The Development of Entrepreneurship," *American Economic Review Papers and Proceedings,* 52: 46–58 (1962).
22. McClelland, *Achieving Society,* pp. 430–437.
23. B. F. Hoselitz, *Sociological Aspects of Economic Growth,* pp. 72–73.
24. This constellation of policy implications is represented by Nurkse, *Equilibrium Growth,* pp. 257, 318–324; R. Prebisch. "Commercial Policy in the Underdeveloped Countries," *American Economic Review Papers and Proceedings,* 49: 251–261, 264–266 (1959); and G. Myrdal, *An International Economy,* p. 229.
25. Hirschman, *Strategy of Economic Development,* pp. 120–125.

26. H. B. Chenery, S. Shishido, and T. Watanabe, "The Pattern of Japanese Growth," *Econometrica,* 30: 118 (1962); and C. W. Reynolds, "Changing Trade Patterns and Trade Policy in Mexico: Some Lessons for Developing Countries," unpublished Research Memorandum No. 17 of the Center for Development Economics, Williams College, October 1967.

27. H. J. Bruton, "The Import Substitution Strategy of Economic Development: A Survey of Findings," unpublished Research Memorandum No. 27 of the Center for Development Economics, Williams College, April 1969. Earlier statements of the problem appear in the United Nations (R. Prebisch), *Towards a Dynamic Development Policy for Latin America,* pp. 69–72, and G. M. Meier, "Export Stimulation, Import Substitution and Latin American Development," *Social and Economic Studies,* 10: 42–62 (1961).

28. A. O. Hirschman, "The Political Economy of Import-Substituting Industrialization in Latin America," *Quarterly Journal of Economics,* 82: 1–32 (February 1968), has discussed this feature of import substitution-led growth, emphasizing the sociological and political conditions that may lead to it.

29. Nurkse, *Equilibrium Growth,* p. 257.

4. Export-led Growth in Peru

1. All conversions have been made at 26.82 soles per dollar, the rate from 1961 to 1967. The sol was freed and devalued in September 1967.

2. Banco Central, *Cuentas Nacionales* (1968).

3. Ibid., pp. 11, 28.

4. Instituto Nacional de Planificación, *La Evolución de la Economía en el Período 1950–1964: Comercio Exterior,* II, p. 98.

5. Calculated from Banco Central, *Cuentas Nacionales* (1968), p. 28.

6. Servicio del Empleo y Recursos Humanos, *Población del Perú,* p. 20.

7. Instituto Nacional de Planificación, *La Evolución de la Economía en el Período 1950–1964: Analisis y Comentarios,* I, Chap. 3, p. 23.

8. Banco Central, *Cuentas Nacionales* (1968), pp. 16, 24, 30. Note that, when shares are measured in current prices, the decline of agriculture's share is more marked and the group of service industries shows a substantially increased share of national income.

9. E. Thorbecke, *Determination of Aggregate and Sectoral Growth Rates for Peru, 1960–1970,* pp. 14–15.

10. A. Lamfalussy, *The United Kingdom and the Six,* p. 47.

11. The countries are the six of the European Economic Community plus Sweden, United Kingdom, United States, and Japan; the commodities are sugar, coffee, cotton, wool, fishmeal, fish oil, iron, copper, lead, zinc, silver, and crude petroleum.

12. W. B. Brown, "Government Measures Affecting Exports in Peru, 1945–62: A Study of Policy and its Making," unpublished dissertation, Tufts University, 1966.

13. Brown, "Measures Affecting Exports," pp. 68–69, 152–159. Exchange rates

are from International Monetary Fund, *International Financial Statistics,* various. In 1960 the two-market system was abolished and by 1962 par value had been established with the IMF at 26.82 soles, where it remained until the crisis of 1967, when the Central Bank's decimated reserve position forced it to abandon support of the sol.

14. Ibid., pp. 192, 225–230.

15. For a good graphical presentation of this kind of model, see G. Ackley, *Macroeconomic Theory,* Chap. 14; his treatment is, however, short-term Keynesian and excludes any foreign sector.

16. E. Thorbecke and A. Condos, "Macroeconomic Growth and Development Models of the Peruvian Economy," in Adelman and Thorbecke, *The Theory and Design of Economic Development,* pp. 181–208. The basic features of their model closely resemble the description of the Cuban economy given by H. C. Wallich in *Monetary Problems of an Export Economy,* pp. 197–206. He observed that, in underdeveloped, export-oriented economies, exports are the primary determinant of investment and hence of national income. Imports and taxes depend on national income, and government expenditure depends on taxes, since there is little fiscal control to allow surpluses and the capital markets are too rudimentary to permit deficits. Thus all the major aggregate demand variables are ultimately determined by the level of exports.

17. For a country like Peru, the dependence of investment on lagged exports is not entirely devoid of meaning. Since virtually all investment goods are imported, to the extent that lagged exports (and terms of trade) indicate the availability of foreign exchange, they also indicate the availability of imported goods. However, capital goods imports make up only about 35% of total imports, allowing considerable room for the total to vary without a marked effect on capital goods imports. Moreover, foreign capital has also been an important source of foreign exchange.

18. Calculated from Banco Central, *Cuentas Nacionales* (1966), p. 30; (1968), p. 22.

19. United Nations Conference on Trade and Development Secretariat (UNCTAD), "Trade Projections for Peru," *Trade Prospects and Capital Needs of Developing Countries,* pp. 544–589. The model builder was Julián Gómez.

20. UNCTAD, *Trade Prospects,* pp. 550–551. The two regressions in question are:

$$V = 1390 + .327CI_n - 179D, R^2 = .98 \tag{1}$$

and

$$I_p = 153 + .645X_{-1} + .935TTE_{-1}, R^2 = .88 \tag{2}$$

where V is output; CI_n is cumulated net investment; D is a dummy variable representing the recession years, 1957–1959; I_p is real private investment; X is export volume; and TTE is the "terms of trade effect," representing the increased purchasing power of exports due to changes in the terms of trade. All coefficients are highly significant.

21. UNCTAD, *Trade Prospects*, pp. 548–549. The two relevant regressions are:

$$W = 367 + .818Y - .759 \ (X^*/P_m), \ R^2 = .99 \tag{1}$$

and

$$C_p = 100 + 1.080W_d + 0.533NW_d, \ R^2 = .99 \tag{2}$$

where W, W_d, and NW_d are real wage, disposable wage, and disposable non-wage incomes, respectively; Y is real national income; X^* is export earnings; P_m is the import price index; and C_p is real private consumption. All coefficients except the constant in Eq. 2 are significant at the 0.05 level.

22. In the early 1960s, import duties actually collected represented about 12% of the value of imports, according to data from the Banco Central, *Cuentas Nacionales* (1966, 1968). A study by the Economic Commission for Latin America showed that, during the late 1950s, of 11 Latin American countries, only Mexico and Uruguay had substantially lower average tariffs than Peru, whether weighted averages or arithmetic means were used. Most of the other countries had much higher average tariffs, especially in the important category of "current consumer manufactures." Also, Mexico's low tariffs are deceptive, since import licensing is the preferred instrument of commercial policy. See S. Macario, "Protectionism and Industrialization in Latin America," in Economic Commission for Latin America, *Economic Bulletin for Latin America*, 9: 68–71 (March 1964). On export duties, see p. 48.

23. Calculated from Banco Central, *Cuentas Nacionales* (1966), pp. 54–55, and (1968), p. 46.

24. Enclave economies may have some demonstration effects if the labor force is migratory. In parts of Africa, for example, laborers work in mines or industry for a period of years and typically return to their farms, probably with an enhanced motivation to produce for the market economy. See, for example, W. Elkan, *Migrants and Proletarians*.

25. R. Vandendreis, "Foreign Trade and the Economic Development of Peru," Ph.D. dissertation, Iowa State University, 1967, Chap. 4.

26. Ibid., Chap. 4, pp. 16–21.

5. The Fishmeal Industry in Peru

1. A metric ton is 1000 kilograms or 2205 pounds. Unless otherwise specified, "ton" always refers to metric tons.

2. Figures for fishmeal are from Table 5.1; others are from the Food and Agriculture Organization (FAO) *Trade Yearbook 1967*.

3. Consorcio Pesquero del Perú, *Peruvian Fishmeal*, pp. 22–33.

4. This example is from G. R. Allen, "The World Outlook for Fishmeal," in FAO, *Future Developments in the Production and Utilization of Fishmeal*, II, pp. 4–7.

5. Ibid., pp. 5–8.

6. Ibid., pp. 12, 35. It is interesting to note that, at prices high enough to allow the use of fishmeal only for its unidentified growth factor, fishmeal

is a complement of, and not a substitute for, vegetable protein sources like soybean meal. It remains a substitute for meat meal, which has some (inferior) growth qualities. This situation probably did prevail before 1954, when fishmeal was in short supply.

7. The following variables were used in the regressions: E = world exports, thousand metric tons, from Table 5.4; P = unit value of fishmeal (fob) relative to the annual average price of soy meal in the Chicago market, from Table 5.4 and *Commodity Yearbook 1968*, p. 308; I = combined index of production for pork, poultry meat, and eggs, each product with equal weights, from Table 5.2; and t = time in years measured from 1957. The results, with standard errors in parentheses and coefficients insignificant at the 0.10 level indicated with an asterisk, were:

$$\log E = 7.80 - 0.489 \log P + 4.62 \log I_{-1}, \qquad R^2 = 0.973 \qquad (1)$$
$$ (.101) \quad (.220) \qquad\quad (.382)$$

$$\log E = 6.57 - 0.593 \log P + 0.158t, \qquad R^2 = 0.973 \qquad (2)$$
$$ (.170) \quad (.219) \qquad\quad (.013)$$

$$\log E = 7.21 - 0.526 \log P + 2.43* \log I_{-1} + 0.0763*t, \qquad R^2 = 0.978 \quad (3)$$
$$ (.535) \quad (.218) \qquad\quad (1.97) \qquad\qquad (.0673)$$

$$\log E = 7.66 - 0.483 \log P + 5.09 \log I, \qquad R^2 = 0.970 \qquad (4)$$
$$ (.111) \quad (.229) \qquad\quad (.479)$$

All Durbin-Watson statistics were satisfactory. Elasticities using fishmeal export unit values alone were slightly lower.

8. D. A. Robinson, *Peru in Four Dimensions*, pp. 233–236; R. J. Owens, *Peru*, p. 1; A. Elijalde Z., *La Industria Pesquera*, pp. 13–20.

9. J. Lora, *Crecimiento de la Flota Pesquera Industrial al 31 de Diciembre de 1963*, p. 23; "Se Construyen Bolicheras de Gran Capacidad," *Pesca*, 14:16 (April 1967); *Pesca*, 18:9 (May 1969).

10. This type of fishing has been described by J. Hedges, "Drama of the Catch," *Andean Airmail and Peruvian Times*, Special Issue, October 28, 1963, p. 34.

11. The limit varies slightly each year, depending on the status of the anchovy stock. Prohibitions on fishing during February or March are primarily to protect young fish, allowing them to grow before capture. The author is indebted to Professor Milner B. Schaefer, Director of the Institute of Marine Resources, University of California at San Diego, for information about recent developments in the study and control of the anchovy fishery.

12. Instituto del Mar del Perú, *Efectos de la Pesca en el Stock de Anchoveta*, Informe No. 7, pp. 4–5, 7; and correspondence with Professor Schaefer. See also, Instituto del Mar, *La Pesquería de la Anchoveta*, Informe No. 14.

13. For a complete economic analysis of the overfishing problem, see H. S. Gordon, "The Economic Theory of Common Property Resources: The Fishery," *Journal of Political Economy*, 62:130–131 (1954); A. D. Scott, "The Fishery: The Objectives of Sole Ownership," *Journal of Political Economy*, 63:122–131 (1955); A. D. Scott, "Food and the World Fisheries Situation," in M. Clawson, ed., *Natural Resources and International Development*, pp.

142–145; and R. Turvey, "Optimization and Suboptimization in Fishery Regulation," *American Economic Review*, 54:64–78 (1964).

14. The description of the production process is based partly on personal observation, but leans heavily on Consorcio Pesquero, *Peruvian Fishmeal*, pp. 8–19; and Sharples del Pacífico, S. A., *Elaboración de Harina de Pescado para Alimento de Animales*, pp. 3–23.

15. Sharples, *Elaboración*, p. 13.

16. Data on plants in operation from *Pesca, Anuario 1965–66*, p. 118.

17. Unpublished data from Oficina Sectorial de Planificación Pesquera, 1967.

18. Unless, of course, there are scale economies in fishing. These would favor purchasing supplies from large independents, unless the processing firm were large enough to achieve such economies in supplying its own needs. However, independent fishing has been carried out with extremely limited capital and there have apparently not been any independent fleet operators large enough to achieve important scale economies if indeed they exist.

19. Based on data in *Pesca*, 18:28–29 (February 1969); 14:24–25 (February 1967); 7:31 (October 1963); and 2:75 (June 1961).

20. Sociedad Nacional de Pesquería, *Harina de Pescado*, pp. 2–7; "Qué es la FEO?" *Pesca*, 8:9–11 (June 1964).

21. Sociedad Nacional, *Estatuos* (Lima, August 1964), p. 6.

22. *Pesca*, 12:14–16 (May 1966).

23. "1960 El Año de la Salvación," *Pesca*, 2:8 (January 1961); and information supplied by the Consorcio Pesquero and the Sociedad Nacional.

24. "Breve Historia de la Pesquería Peruana," *Pesca Anuario 1964–65*, p. 19; C. Uriarte, "La Evolución de la Industria Pesquera en el Perú," *Pesca*, 1:10 (October 1960); and personal interviews.

25. "Pescando en un Mar de Deudas," *Pesca*, 6:17 (June 1963), speaks of costs around $60 per ton before 1960.

26. "Año de la Salvación," *Pesca*, p. 9; and Table 5.5.

27. FAO, *Future Developments in Fishmeal*, I, pp. 13–15.

28. Sociedad Nacional, *La Crisis de Pesquería*, p. 2.

29. Luis Banchero was quoted as saying, "The only limitation that I am disposed to accept is one that may come from a technical-biological study. I would accept control only for conservation purposes, but not for the convenience of the international markets." (Translation by the author.) "El Magnate de la Pesca Peruana," *Pesca*, 1:23 (October 1960).

30. "El Exportador mas Grande del Mundo," *Pesca*, 2:11 (February 1961).

31. The 1961 figure is from Dirección Nacional de Estadistica y Censos, *Censos Poblados;* the others were communicated in conversation with an official of Chimbote and cannot be verified by published material.

32. I. Tilic, *Material Estadistico sobre la Industria Peruana de Harina de Pescado;* and *Pesca, Anuario 1965–66*, p. 117.

33. "1200 Barcos Nuevos," *Pesca*, 6:35–46 (April 1963).

34. "Requiem para los Astilleros," *Pesca*, 8:57 (January 1964); and "Se Construyen Bolicheras de Gran Capacidad," *Pesca*, 14:16–18 (April 1967).

35. "Pescando en un Mar de Deudas," *Pesca,* 6:20–21 (June 1963).

36. FAO, *Yearbook of Fishery Statistics 1965,* p. 27.

37. Instituto del Mar, *Stock de Anchoveta.*

38. The figure of 7000 tons per hour is based on press capacity. Since some plants undoubtedly have bottlenecks at other points in the reduction process, this is an overestimate of actual capacity.

39. Sociedad Nacional, *Crisis de Pesquería,* pp. 5–6.

40. Caves and Holton, *The Canadian Economy,* pp. 31–33.

6. The Production Function for Fishmeal

1. For sources, see Table 6.1.

2. I. Tilic, *Costos y Beneficios en la Industria de la Pesca Anchoveta.* The segregation of interest from profits is not required for many applications of economic theory in which the share of capital is the only relevant quantity. However, the analysis of factor payments in Chap. 9 will make use of this further breakdown.

3. Gross value added is the sum of taxes, interest, depreciation, wages and benefits, and the residual.

4. The prices for plants and boats were estimated by an involved process that will be described in context in Chap. 7; those for fishmeal and oil come from Table 5.5.

5. The selection process was done primarily for work on industry cost functions and is explained in detail in that section of this chapter.

6. Assumed to be $1,340 per year; see Chap. 9, p. 147.

7. The regressions used a Cobb-Douglas production function of the form, $Q = aM^bL^cK^du,$ where Q is the gross output; M, raw materials; L, labor; K, capital stock, measured in the three ways listed in Table 6.2; and u is the random disturbance term. A typical regression, using the 36 most efficient firms discussed above, gave the result:

$$\log Q = -1.804 + .896 \ \log M + .061 \ \log L + .062 \ \log K$$
$$(.304) \quad (.049) \qquad (.052) \qquad (.050)$$

with $R^2 = .983$. Standard deviations are in parentheses. When the labor and capital terms were dropped, the R^2 was still 0.980.

8. All average costs were calculated and plotted vs. output. To select the most efficient plants, output was divided into four ranges: 0 to 5000 metric tons of fishmeal per year; 5000 to 10,000 tons; 10,000 to 25,000 tons; and over 25,000, up to 52,000 tons for the largest plant in Peru. In each range, the one-third of the plants with lowest average costs was selected, a decision rule that yielded a sample of 25 plants. A second sample was constructed using three output ranges: 0 to 10,000 tons; 10,000 to 25,000 tons; and over 25,000 tons. In the first range, the rule was to select the plant with the lowest average cost for each interval of 1000 tons of output; in the second range, the plant with lowest average cost in each interval of 3000 tons was selected;

in the third range, the intervals grew to 5000 tons, from each of which one plant was chosen. This process gave a second sample of 18 plants, only two of which had not been chosen previously. The statistical results using this second sample were similar to those found using the first. To simplify the presentation, only the results from the first sample are reported below.

9. According to the list of the 27 largest producers in 1966, appearing in *Pesca,* 14:24–25 (February 1967).

10. See W. J. Dixon and F. J. Massey, Jr., *Introduction to Statistical Analysis,* pp. 124–127.

11. The test used involves an assumption of normality that may have been violated. To overcome that defect, a less powerful, nonparametric test on the signs of the differences of average costs was tried. It gave the same result, that is, it accepted the hypothesis of no difference between average costs for the two groups.

7. Backward Linkages

1. No recent, complete Leontief table was available for this analysis.

2. The "second round of expenditure" refers to inputs purchased by industries that also produce inputs used in fishmeal production. In the familiar Leontief notation, gross output is given by

$$X = AX + (C + I + G + E) \tag{1}$$

where X is the $(n \times 1)$ matrix of gross output for all sectors of the economy; A is the $(n \times n)$ matrix of Leontief coefficients, so that AX is the $(n \times 1)$ matrix of production of intermediate goods; $C, I, G,$ and E are $(n \times 1)$ matrices of final output, for consumption, investment, government expenditure, and exports, respectively. Imports are assumed to be included as part of X. Solving for X and, for convenience, considering only goods produced as a consequence of production for exports, we obtain

$$X = (I^* - A)^{-1}E \tag{2}$$

where I^* is the identity matrix. The Leontief inverse, $(I^* - A)^{-1}$, can be replaced by a series expansion, so that

$$X = E + AE + A^2E + A^3E + \cdots \tag{3}$$

The first-order term, AE, represents direct inputs into the export sector, while the second-order term, A^2E, represents inputs into industries supplying the export sector, or "second-round" expenditures. The series of Eq. 3 will converge for any Leontief matrix that is the result of a correct observation of an economy. See R. Dorfman, P. A. Samuelson, and R. M. Solow, *Linear Programming and Economic Analysis,* p. 253.

3. Although the discussion of backward linkages will consider the first- and second-round inputs due to continuing investment in plant, equipment, and boats by fishmeal operators, it is not legitimate to include the implied capital-output ratios as part of the Leontief coefficient, $A,$ in the development of

n.2 Capital stock inputs are required for future, not present, production; the Leontief system to describe the situation must be dynamic. As Dorfman, Samuelson, and Solow, *Linear Programming,* pp. 285–300, demonstrate, the solution of the resulting set of difference equations need not be convergent, and the system cannot determine the allocation of resources without the addition of some choice criteria, such as the objective (social welfare) function used in linear programming. This does not invalidate the discussion in this chapter, however, which is only trying to determine the inputs required to produce fishmeal, including the *observed* bill of investment goods purchased by fishmeal producers each year. If one knows, or assumes he knows, the quantities of capital goods actually purchased, then the problem of finding how an economy should allocate its resources to allow for investment does not arise.

4. Lora, *Crecimiento de la Flota Pesquera Industrial,* p. 8.

5. The lowest figure was calculated from the 1963 census of manufactures, while estimates of from 50 to 70% came from interviews with various shipyard managers. Because the latter were consistently above the 1963 census figure, and because the census leaves over 30% of output value unitemized and therefore unexplained, the higher range of estimates seems more dependable.

6. The weighted average includes the following elements: 770 tons of netting imported at an average of $2.66 per pound (including duty) in 1966, and 730 tons produced domestically (to make up the estimated market of 1500 tons) and sold for $2.31 per pound.

7. Table 7.1 implies that 47% of the market is supplied by domestic manufacturers, since the difference between the estimated long-run market of 1500 tons a year and 1966 imports of 770 tons was attributed to local production.

8. Since there was some attempt to measure changes in boat quality when estimating investment in fleets, the relation between fleet and plant investment is biased upward.

9. The 1964 figure is a necessary fabrication. All the statistics in this section, except where otherwise noted, come from interviews with the firms involved. Data were solicited for two years, 1963 and 1966. Unfortunately, sales information for the firm that had been the dominant factor in the industry was not available for 1963. Its 1964 data together with that for 1963 for the other firms, has been used; the result is called 1964 sales. Sales in 1963 were swelled by the investment boom that ended late in the year, and the dominant firm probably had a larger drop in sales for 1964 than the others. Of the other two large firms in the group of six, one was growing over the period and the other declining; the changes should approximately cancel each other, making the 1964 estimate a reasonable one.

10. This firm failed after the author had left Peru and it was impossible to study the consequences. It should have had a beneficial effect on the market for skilled labor, however; on this, see Chap. 9.

11. This qualifies but does not destroy the Baldwin-Reynolds thesis that demand for mining equipment does not induce linkages due to economies of scale in mining. The Peruvian producers in question supplied only the small mines in what was a highly cyclical operation. (The fishmeal boom

caught them in a depressed period.) Large mining companies did import most of their equipment under special concessions.

12. The upper limit estimate is not so unreasonable as it might seem. The company known to do the greatest share of its business with other suppliers also has the smallest fishmeal business in the group, while one of the other two probably sells only to processors.

13. Oficina Sectorial, unpublished data.

14. This figure was found using an estimate of 22.8 bags per ton of fishmeal given by the Sociedad Nacional, *Crisis de Pesquería,* p. 5, together with production for 1966, given in Table 5.6 as 1.47 million metric tons.

15. Instituto Nacional de Promoción Industrial and Banco Industrial del Perú, *La Industria del Yute en el Perú: Situación Actual y Potencial,* Part 1, pp. 10, 27–28; also, personal interviews. These figures are consistent with those in the Leontief function of Table 6.1.

16. Instituto Nacional, *Industria del Yute,* p. 17.

17. Ibid., pp. 6–7.

18. International Labor Office, *Yearbook of Labor Statistics, 1966,* pp. 525, 534, 536, 538.

19. Assume, to use what may be reasonable figures for the post-1963 period, that purchasers of Peruvian boats can obtain credit for three years at 12%, while importers can offer them seven years at 8%. If these loans are amortized, then the purchaser of a domestic craft with $150,000 of credit pays $33,700 a year more over the first three years than does the buyer of an imported boat with the same amount of credit, but on the easier terms specified. In years four to ten, however, the importer pays out $28,000 a year and the local buyer pays nothing. Using the Peruvian market rate of 12%, the present value of that seven-year stream of positive and negative net payments is $18,500, indicating an advantage of only 12% on the boat price for foreign manufacturers and Peruvian importers. However, it is quite likely that the time horizon of a boat purchaser is much shorter than seven years. If it were as short as three years, then he only looks at the disadvantages of higher payments on the local loan in the early years; at 12%, the present value of those differences is $80,000, which is 54% of the value of the loan. These circumstances could explain a 60% tariff.

20. Banco Central, *Cuentas Nacionales* (1968), p. 12.

21. Let S' represent the value of domestic goods purchased to produce S, S'' the value of domestic goods purchased to produce S', and so on indefinitely. Then, using the notation above,

$$S' = dS, \ S'' = d(dS) = d^2S, \ S''' = d^3S, \ \cdots$$

and

$$
\begin{aligned}
M' &= m(S + S' + S'' + S''' + \cdots) \\
&= mS(1 + d + d^2 + d^3 + \cdots) \\
&= \frac{mS}{(1 - d)}
\end{aligned}
$$

where M' is all imports on the second and subsequent rounds, but excluding first-round, direct imports. Since second-round imports are already known the magnitude desired is

$$M'' = M' - mS = \frac{mdS}{(1-d)}$$

With the values given above, this quantity is $9.9 million.

22. If the fraction, d, of output value represented by domestic inputs were as high as 0.5, which unrealistically implies a fractional value added in each industry of just 0.185 (since $m' = 0.315$), then the proportion of fishmeal-related final goods that is spent on imports would still be only 28%

23. Estimated from Banco Central, *Cuentas Nacionales*.

24. It might be noted that the estimate from Table 7.1 of gross fixed investment in fishmeal totaling $30.4 million a year is higher than that for 1964 through 1966 in Table 7.7. However, the latter excludes nets and renewal, explicitly included in Table 7.1, and the investment series is in 1963 prices, while the investment column of the input-output table most clearly approximates 1966 prices. Making these allowances, we find that the two tables do not give very different estimates for the years after 1963.

8. Other Linkages

1. Hirschman, *Strategy of Economic Development*, pp. 101–102, 116–117.

2. Banco Industrial and Instituto Nacional, *Situación de la Industria Manufacturera en 1965*, p. 88.

3. Allowing for the use of fishmeal in Peru up to the limit of its amino acid contribution, we find that this would account for only 7.5% of livestock rations (see Figure 2). Outlays on rations, in turn, comprise perhaps 45% of the total cost of chicken production, based on cost estimates for fryers in the United States by E. L. Baum and H. G. Walkup, "Economic Considerations in Fryer Production in the Pacific Northwest," *Journal of Farm Economics*, 33:98–100 (1951). So fishmeal cannot be responsible for more than 3.4% of the total cost. Assume the cost saving on fishmeal newly produced in Peru were equal to the difference between the unit value of world exports for 1958 and Peruvian unit value for 1963 and 1964 (Tables 5.4 and 5.5), which is $35 per metric ton, plus the saving on transportation costs of roughly $25 (cif to the United States from Peru). Then the reduction in the cost of meal would be 38%. Applied to the maximum fraction of fishmeal in total cost, the reduction due to fishmeal production in Peru would be 1.3%.

4. A range calculated from ibid., p. 99, based on alternative assumptions as to the make-up of fixed assets.

5. See the discussion on the supply industries in Chap. 7, pp. 110–122.

6. Calculated from data in Sociedad Nacional, *Crisis de Pesquería*, pp. 5, 10.

7. Banco Central, *Cuentas Nacionales* (1968), p. 14.

8. This figure is probably low for the jute bag and nylon net manufacturers, but high for boat construction, paper, and petroleum products.

9. E. Tolentino A., "Estudio de 600 Pescadores de Anchoveta en el Puerto de Chimbote," Ph.D. dissertation, Escuela de Servicio Social del Perú, 1964, pp. 48–49; parts of the study appeared as "Complejo Socio-económico del Pescador," *Pesca*, 12 (June 1966).

10. Dirección Nacional, *Censo de Manufacturas 1963*, pp. 3–5.

11. Hirschman, *Strategy of Economic Development*, pp. 86–89.

12. Corporación Nacional de Fertilizantes, *Boletín*, 4:24 (January–April 1966), and *Memoria 1965*, p. 47.

13. Reported in "Mito del Guano," *Mundo Pesquero*, 3:33 (August 1966); assumes anchovy-fishmeal ratios of 5.7:1 and uses 1964 prices for guano, fishmeal, and fish oil.

9. Factor Markets

1. Levin, *Export Economies*, p. 47.

2. Banco Central, *Cuentas Nacionales*, p. 38.

3. Dirección Nacional, *Censo de Manufacturas 1963*, p. 66. This estimate takes only 12,690 for processing, the figure given by the 1963 census, but uses the same figures for satellite industry employment and fishing as before.

4. Organization for Economic Cooperation and Development, *Desarrollo Económico y Social, Recursos Humanos y Educación*, Chap. 2, p. 31.

5. The comparison for professionals is: all industry, $3500 a year; fishmeal, $2900; sugar refining, $2700; and chemicals, $2800. Calculated from Dirección Nacional, *Censo de Manufacturas 1963*, pp. 66–69, 104–107; figures refer to 1963.

6. The figures for 1963 are: all industry, $1150; fishmeal, $1090; nonelectrical machinery, $1120; naval construction, $1270. Calculated from ibid., pp. 66–69, 104–107.

7. The only supply industry depending heavily on foreign technicians and skilled supervisory personnel has been net manufacturing.

8. These rounded figures are from the same sources as, and are consistent with, the upper and lower limits of fishmeal employment given in Table 9.1. Of the average crew of 12 employed in a *bolichera,* the captain and the motorman are considered to have some skills and the rest are unskilled.

9. As total employment in manufacturing grew by only 17% from 1961 to 1966 (Banco Central, *Cuentas Nacionales*, 1968, p. 30), the comparison for later years would not be very different.

10. Levin, *Export Economies*, pp. 86–88.

11. C. A. Solis, "Fuentes de Migración al Puerto Industrial de Chimbote, 1960," in H. F. Dobyns and M. C. Vasquez, eds., *Migración y Integración en el Perú*, pp. 79–80.

12. Tolentino, "Estudio de 600 Pescadores," pp. 33–52.

13. The lower limit excludes 3000 semiskilled workers who might have been hired as unskilled workers; the upper limit includes them.

14. Although Solis, "Fuentes de Migración," takes the average family size in Chimbote to be five, this would probably yield too high an estimate, considering that the migrants were young and many left their families at home. Matos ("Consideraciones General Acerca del Proceso Migratorio en la Ciudad de Chimbote," in Dobyns and Vasquez, *Migración y Integración,* pp. 74–75) found 1152 heads of household in a survey of 6431, indicating a family of about six, but also finds that two of the five dependents were born in Chimbote. The latter yields the estimate of four used above.

15. G. Briones and J. Mejía V., *El Obrero Industrial,* pp. 12–32, present some data leading to this tentative conclusion.

16. Dirección Nacional, *Censo de Manufacturas 1963,* pp. 66–69, 104–107.

17. Tolentino, "Estudio de 600 Pescadores," p. 42.

18. With the upper limit of fishermen from Table 9.1, the unskilled crew's share of 60 soles per ton that prevailed before 1967, and the catch of 6.24 million metric tons for 1963, the annual income for a fisherman is $1050; with the 1964 catch of 8.86 million tons, the average income is $1490. Of the total of 80 soles, the captain typically retained 20; the motorman is paid a separate wage. These figures exclude meals served during the voyage, worth about 3.5 soles per ton for the unskilled crew, which would raise the average annual income to $1110 for 1963 and $1580 for 1964.

19. Accumulated losses are carried on the asset side, rather than as a subtraction from net worth. If they refer to losses during start-up and for a short period thereafter, they may legitimately be included as part of the cost of fixed capital. But it is possible that this point has been stretched in the balance sheets of fishmeal firms in order to avoid small or negative net worth.

20. Deltec Peruana, S. A., "Capital Markets of South America: Peru," unpublished study prepared for the Interamerican Development Bank (September 1966), Chap. 10, p. 4.

21. "1104 Milliones, a la Carga de Proveedores," *Pesca,* 11:13 (December 1965).

22. "Mar de Deudas," *Pesca,* 6:21 (June 1963).

23. Banco Industrial, *Memoria Anual, Año 1966,* pp. 11–12, 21–23, 28.

24. Banco Central, *Boletín* 37: 33–34 (March 1967).

25. Credits are given principally on boats, processing equipment, and netting. Direct imports of these items (using the higher estimate of equipment imports) plus a third of the import content of boats (to represent the major items, such as motors, on which foreign credit might be given) is equal to 38% of the total consumption of the same items by the fishmeal industry. Applying that percentage to total suppliers' credit for 1966 gives an estimate of $24 million.

26. Based on a list of firms with foreign participation appearing in "Inversiones Extranjeras son Necesarios," *Pesca,* 14:25 (May 1967), together with unpublished data supplied by the National Fishing Society.

27. Although the author has no supporting data, it seems likely that foreign firms are more conservative financially than Peruvian ones and probably have lower debt-equity ratios. If so, then the fraction of equity capital supplied from overseas is greater than 26%.

28. "Inversiones," *Pesca*, p. 20.

29. An approximation of the fixed assets required can be obtained using the fishmeal capital-output ratio of 1.81 (see Chap. 6, p. 95), the input-output information of Table 7.1, and supply industry capital-output ratios calculated from the 1963 census of manufactures. These latter are 3.6 for textiles (the assumed figure for netting and jute sacks), 1.6 for nonelectrical machinery (plant equipment), and 1.8 for transportation equipment (boats). Capital is defined as fixed assets at original cost. Calculated from Dirección Nacional, *Censo de Manufacturas 1963*, pp. 194–197, 262–269.

30. Such a concept has been employed by Harris, "Entrepreneurship in Nigeria," Chap. 2, pp. 1–13.

31. *Pesca*, 14:24–25 (February 1967), and "Inversiones," p. 25; and Sociedad Nacional, unpublished data on output by plants for 1966.

32. M. Max Neff, et al., *Concentración del Poder Económico y Motivación Empresarial: El Caso del Sector Pesquero*, pp. 91–120.

33. The total was estimated as follows:

1. Applying the 26% of 1966 output attributed to foreign shares of processing companies (p. 154) to the equity capital for 1965 as given in Table 9.4, we find that $15 million of equity capital is due to foreign sources.
2. Of the $33 million listed in Table 9.5 as loans from the Industrial Bank, $24 million resulted from a loan from a group of North American banks (Banco Industrial, *Memoria Anual 1966*, pp. 11–12).
3. The share of suppliers' credits of $63.6 million (Table 9.5) that came from foreign manufacturers has been roughly estimated as 38% (n. 25) or $24 million.

The sum of these elements is $63 million.

34. Estimated by two-stage least squares using the national income determination model of Chap. 4 (Table 4.6) and various linear import functions with private consumption, private investment, government consumption, and government investment as the explanatory variables in different configurations (forcing relative price changes, most of which are probably due to changes in aggregate demand, to be reflected in the marginal propensities to import). The six equations estimated gave excellent fits (R^2 above 0.99 in each case) and highly significant coefficients for the marginal propensity to import from consumption expenditures. Those ranged from 0.208 to 0.293; the average was 0.268.

35. Calculated from data in Sociedad Nacional, *Crisis de Pesquería;* the balance is for social welfare payments.

36. The interest was estimated as follows:

1. Total interest payments implied by the known sources of finance, given in Table 9.5 for 1966, come to $15.7 million on the assumption that the Industrial Bank and suppliers' loans bear 12% interest rates and the commercial bank loans carry 16%. (The interest bill thus calculated is 9.1% of gross output given in Table 7.1, against the coefficient of 9.3% in that table.)

2. The Industrial Bank's loans are backed by $24 million of funds borrowed from North American banks, which carry interest rates averaging 6.5%; it is assumed that, in the first instance at least, commercial bank loans involved no interest payments to foreign entities and profit repatriation by foreign-owned banks can be ignored; it is further assumed that on the 38% of supplier credits attributed to foreign sources above, 10% is the interest rate actually received by those sources, the balance of 2% being retained by local importers or agents. These calculations give interest payments to foreign lenders of $4.0 million.

37. The simplest estimate of profit share due to foreign companies is the 26% share of equity estimated above, applied to the residual, which yields a figure of $3.8 million. However, some allowance must be made for profits taxes of about 36%, which are almost certainly not included as expenditures elsewhere, since the tax item in Tables 6.1 and 7.1 is of the right magnitude to account for export taxes on fishmeal only. However, Peru's Industrial Promotion Law exonerates from taxes between 30 and 50% of profits reinvested in the fishmeal or other industry (Deltec, "Capital Markets of South America, Chap. 4, pp. 3–4). Assuming that foreign companies take advantage of this law and reinvest 40% of their profits in Peru, they can repatriate 60% of profits less profits taxes of 36%. The indicated outflow is $1.5 million. If foreign firms have below-average debt-equity ratios, this is an underestimate of the annual repatriation of profits.

38. The taxes were found as follows: Table 7.1 gives direct tax payments of $13.2 million and these are assumed to include only export taxes; the upper estimate of import duties is $3.4 million; profits taxes are taken at 36% and applied to the residual of $14.6 million after deducting 40% of the residual to account for tax-free reinvestment of profits under the Industrial Promotion Law. The total is then $19.8 million. Information on the profit tax rate and allowable tax-free reinvestment comes from Deltec, "Capital Markets of South America," Chap. 4, pp. 3–4; however, the profit base itself and the application of the tax law to it are conjectural.

39. Wallich, *Monetary Problems,* pp. 197–206.

40. The linear import functions mentioned in n. 34 in connection with the marginal propensity to import contained the information needed to determine the government's propensity to import. However, the estimate is highly sensitive to simple changes in the specification of the model. Since the marginal propensity to import from government expenditure was not significantly different from zero, it was taken to be zero. Estimates without that variable showed

a marginal propensity to import from government investment of slightly over one, which is not realistic. Assuming the propensity to be one (an upper limit and probably a considerable overestimate), and taking the 1950–1965 average fraction of investment in total government outlays, the marginal propensity to import for government expenditure is 0.196.

41. Equal to 0.673 × 0.196.

10. Peruvian Fishmeal as a Staple

1. Urquhart and Buckley, *Historical Statistics of Canada,* pp. 141, 174–175; Firestone, *Canada's Economic Development, 1867–1953,* p. 66.

2. Banco Central, *Cuentas Nacionales* (1968), pp. 11, 44.

3. Baldwin, *Economic Development and Export Growth,* pp. 84–85, 105–107.

4. There is one important alternative model: the large-scale extractive industry that is heavily taxed to finance a development program. In this case, the stimulus is indirect.

5. E. Staley and R. Morse, *Modern Small Industry for Developing Countries,* p. 148.

6. Danish exports were covered in Chap. 2; Staley and Morse, *Modern Small Industry,* pp. 149–150, discuss palm oil; Levin, *Export Economies,* Chap. 5, discusses Burmese rice.

7. The author was involved in Kenya's smallholder tea project as a planning officer for the Government of Kenya from 1962 to 1964. See Government of Kenya, *Development Plan, 1966–1970,* pp. 178–179; and Kenya Ministry of Agriculture, *African Land Development in Kenya 1946–1962.*

Bibliography

A. Export-led Growth (general treatises and country studies)

Baldwin, Robert E. *Economic Development and Export Growth: A Study of Northern Rhodesia, 1920–1960.* Los Angeles: University of California Press, 1966.

———. "Patterns of Development in Newly Settled Regions," *Manchester School of Economic and Social Studies,* 24:161–179 (1956).

Bardhan, Pranab K. "Equilibrium Growth in the International Economy," *Quarterly Journal of Economics,* 74:455–464 (August 1965).

Berrill, Kenneth. "International Trade and the Rate of Economic Growth," *Economic History Review* (Series 2), 12:351–359 (1960).

Bertram, Gordon W. "Economic Growth in Canadian Industry, 1870–1915: The Staple Model and the Take-off Hypothesis," *Canadian Journal of Economics and Political Science,* 29:159–184 (1963).

Bhagwati, Jagdish. "Growth, Terms of Trade and Comparative Advantage," *Economia Internazionale,* 12:393–414 (1959).

Bruton, Henry J. "The Import Substitution Strategy of Economic Development," unpublished Research Memorandum No. 27 of the Center for Development Economics, Williams College, April 1969.

Cairncross, Alexander K. *Factors in Economic Development.* London: George Allen and Unwin, 1962.

Caves, Richard E. " 'Vent for Surplus' Models of Trade and Growth," in Robert E. Baldwin, et al. *Trade, Growth and the Balance of Payments.* Chicago: Rand McNally and Company, 1965.

Caves, Richard E., and Richard H. Holton. *The Canadian Economy.* Cambridge, Mass.: Harvard University Press, 1959.

Chambers, Edward J., and Donald F. Gordon. "Primary Products and Economic Growth: An Empirical Measurement," *Journal of Political Economy,* 74:315–332 (August 1966).

Chenery, Hollis B., Shuntaro Shishido, and Tsunehiko Watanabe. "The Patterns of Japanese Growth," *Econometrica,* 30:98–139 (1962).

Chenery, Hollis B., and Alan M. Strout. "Foreign Assistance and Economic Development," *American Economic Review,* 56:679–733 (September 1966).

Denison, Edward F. *The Sources of Economic Growth in the United States.* New York: Committee for Economic Development, 1962.

Eckaus, Richard S. "The Factor Proportions Problem in Underdeveloped Areas," *American Economic Review,* 45:539–565 (1955).

Elkan, Walter. *Migrants and Proletarians.* London: Oxford University Press, 1960.

Farnie, D. A. "The Mineral Revolution in South Africa," *South African Journal of Economics,* 24:125–134 (1956).

Findlay, Ronald, and Harry Grubert. "Factor Intensities, Technological Progress and the Terms of Trade," *Oxford Economic Papers,* 11:111–121 (1959).

Firestone, O. John. *Canada's Economic Development, 1867–1953.* London: Bowes and Bowes, 1958.

Fishlow, Albert. *American Railroads and the Transformation of the Ante-Bellum Economy.* Cambridge, Mass.: Harvard University Press, 1965.

Fogel, Robert W. "Railroads as an Analogy of the Space Effort: Some Economic Aspects," in Bruce Mazlish, ed., *Space Program: An Exploration in Historical Analogy.* Cambridge, Mass.: M.I.T. Press, 1965.

Government of Kenya. *Development Plan, 1966–1970.* Nairobi, 1966.

Hagen, Everett E. *On the Theory of Social Change.* Homewood, Ill.: Dorsey Press, 1962.

Hahn, Frank H., and Robert C. O. Matthews. "The Theory of Economic Growth: A Survey," *Economic Journal,* 74:779–902 (1964).

Harris, John R. "Industrial Entrepreneurship in Nigeria," Ph.D. dissertation, Northwestern University, 1967.

Hicks, George L., and Geoffry McNicoll. "Foreign Trade and the Growth of the Dual Economy: A Study of the Philippines, 1950–1966," Washington: National Planning Association draft final report, October 1968.

Higgins, Benjamin. "The 'Dualistic Theory' in Underdeveloped Areas," *Economic Development and Cultural Change,* 4:99–115 (1956).

Hirschman, Albert O. *The Strategy of Economic Development.* New Haven, Conn.: Yale University Press, 1958.

Hoselitz, Bert F. *Sociological Aspects of Economic Growth.* Glencoe, Ill.: Free Press, 1960.

Imlah, Albert H. *Economic Elements in the Pax Britannica.* Cambridge, Mass.: Harvard University Press, 1958.

Johnson, Harry G. *Money, Trade and Economic Growth.* Cambridge, Mass.: Harvard University Press, 1962.

Kenya Ministry of Agriculture. *African Land Development in Kenya, 1946–1962.* Nairobi, 1962.

Kindleberger, Charles P. *Foreign Trade and the National Economy.* New Haven, Conn.: Yale University Press, 1962.

———. *The Terms of Trade: A European Case Study.* New York: John Wiley & Sons, 1956.

Knowles, Lillian C. A., and Charles M. Knowles. *The Economic Development of the British Overseas Empire,* Vol. 3. London: George Rutledge and Sons, 1936.

Kunkel, John H. "Values and Behavior in Economic Development," *Economic Development and Cultural Change,* 13:257–277 (April 1965).

Lamfalussy, Alexander. *The United Kingdom and the Six.* London: Macmillan and Company, 1963.

Levin, Jonathan V. *The Export Economies.* Cambridge, Mass.: Harvard University Press, 1960.

McClelland, David C. *The Achieving Society.* Princeton, N.J.: D. Van Nostrand Company, 1961.

—— and David G. Winter. *Motivating Economic Achievement.* New York: Free Press, 1969.

McKinnon, Ronald I. "Foreign Exchange Restraints in Economic Development," *Economic Journal,* 74:388–409 (1964).

Martin, Robert F. *National Income in the United States, 1799–1938.* New York: National Industrial Conference Board, 1939.

Meier, Gerald M. "Export Stimulation, Import Substitution and Latin American Development," *Social and Economic Studies,* 10:42–62 (1961).

——. *The International Economics of Development.* New York: Harper and Row, 1968.

Myint, Hla. "The 'Classical Theory' of International Trade and the Underdeveloped Countries," *Economic Journal,* 68:317–337 (1959).

——. *The Economics of Developing Countries.* London: Hutchinson and Company, 1964.

Myrdal, Gunnar. *An International Economy.* New York: Harper and Row, 1956.

Nelson, Richard R. "Aggregate Production Functions," *American Economic Review,* 54:575–607 (1964).

——. "The Effective Exchange Rate, Employment and Growth in a Foreign Exchange Constrained Economy," unpublished RAND paper, Research Memorandum 5680 AID (July 1968).

North, Douglass C. "Agriculture in Regional Economic Growth," *Journal of Farm Economics,* 41:943–951 (1959).

——. *The Economic Growth of the United States, 1790 to 1860.* Englewood Cliffs, N.J.: Prentice-Hall, 1961.

——. "Location Theory and Regional Economic Growth," *Journal of Political Economy,* 63:243–258 (1955).

Nurkse, Ragnar. *Equilibrium Growth in the World Economy.* Cambridge, Mass.: Harvard University Press, 1961.

Oniki, H., and Hirofumi Uzawa. "Patterns of Trade and Investment in a Dynamic Model of International Trade," *Review of Economic Studies,* 32:15–38 (1965).

Papanek, Gustav F. "The Development of Entrepreneurship," *American Economic Review Papers and Proceedings,* 52:46–58 (1962).

Prebisch, Raul. "Commercial Policy in the Underdeveloped Countries," *American Economic Review Papers and Proceedings,* 49:251–273 (1959)

Reynolds, Clark W. "Changing Trade Patterns and Trade Policy in Mexico: Some Lessons from Developing Countries," unpublished Research Memorandum No. 17 of the Center for Development Economics, Williams College, October 1967.

———. "Development Problems of an Export Economy: The Case of Chile and Copper," in Mamalakis, Markos, and Reynolds. *Essays on the Chilean Economy.* Homewood, Ill.: Richard D. Irwin, 1965.

Rostow, Walt W. *The Stages of Economic Growth.* Cambridge, England: Cambridge University Press, 1960.

Seers, Dudley. "An Approach to the Short-Period Analysis of Primary-Producing Economies," *Oxford Economic Papers,* 11:1–35 (1959).

Singer, Hans W. "The Distribution of the Gains between Investing and Borrowing Countries," *American Economic Review, Papers and Proceedings,* 11:473–485 (1950); reprinted in Singer. *International Development: Growth and Change.* New York: McGraw-Hill, 1964.

Staley, Eugene, and Richard Morse. *Modern Small Industry for Developing Countries.* New York: McGraw-Hill, 1965.

Swerling, Boris C. "Some Interrelationships between Agricultural Trade and Economic Development," *Kyklos,* 14:364–391 (1961).

United Nations (Raul Prebisch). *The Economic Development of Latin America and Its Principal Problems.* Lake Success, N.Y., 1950.

———. *Towards a Dynamic Development Policy for Latin America.* New York, 1963.

Wallich, Henry C. *Monetary Problems of an Export Economy.* Cambridge, Mass.: Harvard University Press, 1950.

Watkins, Melville H. "A Staple Theory of Economic Growth," *Canadian Journal of Economics and Political Science,* 29:141–158 (1963).

Youngson, Alexander J. *Possibilities of Economic Progress.* Cambridge, England: Cambridge University Press, 1959.

B. Methodology (sources of some analytic methods used in the study)

Ackley, Gardner. *Macroeconomic Theory.* New York: Macmillan Co., 1961.

Dixon, Wilfrid J., and Frank J. Massey, Jr. *Introduction to Statistical Analysis,* 2nd ed. New York: McGraw-Hill, 1957.

Dorfman, Robert, Paul A. Samuelson, and Robert M. Solow. *Linear Programming and Economic Analysis.* New York: McGraw-Hill, 1958.

C. Statistics (standard sources used in the study)

Commodity Research Bureau. *Commodity Yearbook.* New York, 1960–1968.

Food and Agriculture Organization. *Production Yearbook.* Rome, 1958–1968.

———. *Trade Yearbook 1967.* Rome, 1968.

———. *Yearbook of Fishery Statistics.* Rome, 1960–1968.

International Labor Office. *Yearbook of Labor Statistics, 1966.* Geneva, 1966.
International Monetary Fund. *International Financial Statistics.* Washington, 1960–1969.
United Nations. *Commodity Trade Statistics,* Series D, Vols. 5 and 17, January to December, 1955 and 1967. New York, 1956 and 1968.
———. *Yearbook of International Trade Statistics, 1966.* New York, 1968.
United States Agency for International Development. *Gross National Product: Growth Rates and Trend Data.* Washington, April 25, 1969.
United States Bureau of the Census. *Historical Statistics of the United States, Colonial Times to 1957.* Washington, 1960.
Urquhart, Malcom C., and Kenneth A. H. Buckley, eds. *Historical Statistics of Canada.* Cambridge, England: Cambridge University Press, 1965.

D. Peru (general economic and social conditions; includes statistical sources)

Banco Central de Reserva del Perú. *Boletín* (37–424), March 1967.
———. *Cuentas Nacionales del Perú, 1950–1965.* Lima, 1966.
———. *Cuentas Nacionales del Perú, 1950–1967.* Lima, 1968.
Banco Industrial del Perú. *Memoria Anual, Año 1966.* Lima, 1967.
——— and Instituto Nacional de Promoción Industrial. *Situación en la Industria Manufacturera en 1965.* Lima, 1966.
Briones, Guillermo, and Jose Mejía Valera. *El Obrero Industrial.* Lima: Instituto de Investigaciones Sociologicas de la Universidad Nacional Mayor de San Marcos, 1964.
Brown, Wilson B. "Governmental Measures Affecting Exports in Peru, 1945–1962: A Study in Policy and Its Making," Ph.D. dissertation, Fletcher School of Law and Diplomacy, Tufts University, 1966.
Deltec Peruana, S. A. "The Capital Markets of South America: Peru," unpublished study prepared for the Interamerican Development Bank, Lima, September 1966.
Dirección Nacional de Estadistica y Censos. *Censos Poblados,* Vol. 1: *Censo de 1961.* Lima, June 1966.
———. *Primer Censo Nacional Económico 1963: Directorio de Censo de Manufacturas.* Lima, 1966.
———. *Primer Censo Económico, 1963: Censo de Manufacturas.* Lima, 1966.
Instituto Nacional de Planificación del Perú. *La Evolución de la Economía en el Período 1950–1964,* Vol. 1: *Análisis y Comentarios.* Lima, May 1966.
———. *La Evolución de la Economía en el Período 1950–1964,* Vol. 2: *Comercio Exterior.* Lima, May 1966.
———. *Plan Desarollo Económico y Social, 1967–1970,* Vol. 4: *Inventorio General de Proyectos.* Lima, 1966.
Instituto Nacional de Promoción Industrial and Banco Industrial del Perú. *La Industria del Yute en el Perú: Situación Actual y Potencial.* Lima, 1965.

————. *Situación de la Industria Peruana en 1964*. Lima, 1965.

Macario, Santiago. "Protectionism and Industrialization in Latin America," in Economic Commission for Latin America. *Economic Bulletin for Latin America*, 9:61–102 (March 1964).

Matos Mar, José. "Consideraciones General Acerca del Proceso Migratorio en la Ciudad de Chimbote," in H. F. Dobyns and M. C. Vasquez, eds., *Migración y Integración en el Perú*. Lima: Editorial Estudios Andinos, 1963.

Ministerio de Hacienda y Comercio. *Arancel de Aduanas: Importación*. Lima, 1964.

Organization for Economic Cooperation and Development. *Desarrollo Económico y Social, Recursos Humanos y Educación*. Lima: Instituto Nacional de Planificación, 1965.

Owens, R. J. *Peru*. London: Oxford University Press, 1963.

Robinson, David A. *Peru in Four Dimensions*. Lima: American Studies Press, 1964.

Servicio del Empleo y Recursos Humanos. *Población del Perú*, Documento de Trabajo No. R. H. 2-1. Lima, 1965.

Soberman, Robert M. *Transport Technology for Developing Regions*. Cambridge, Mass.: M.I.T. Press, 1966.

Solis, Cesar A. "Fuentes de Migración al Puerto Industrial de Chimbote, 1960," in H. F. Dobyns and M. C. Vasquez, eds., *Migración y Integración en el Perú*. Lima: Editorial Estudios Andinos, 1963.

Superintendencia General de Aduanas del Perú. *Estadistica del Comercio Exterior*. Lima, 1950–1967.

Thorbecke, Erik. *Determination of Aggregate and Sectoral Growth Rates in Peru, 1960–1970*, Monograph No. 1, International Studies in Economics. Ames, Iowa: Iowa State University, January 1966.

Thorbecke, Erik, and Apostolos Condos. "Macroeconomic Growth and Development Models of the Peruvian Economy," in Irma Adelman and Thorbecke, eds., *The Theory and Design of Economic Development*. Baltimore: Johns Hopkins Press, 1966.

United Nations Conference on Trade and Development. "Trade Projections for Peru," in *Trade Prospects and Capital Needs of Developing Countries*. New York, 1968.

Vandendreis, Rene. "Foreign Trade and the Economic Development of Peru," Ph.D. dissertation, Iowa State University, 1967.

E. Fishmeal Industry (primarily relating to Peru but including general works)

Baum, Emanuel L., and H. G. Walkup. "Economic Considerations in Fryer Production in the Pacific Northwest," *Journal of Farm Economics*, 33:90–107 (1951).

"Breve Historia de la Pesquería Peruana," *Pesca Anuario 1964–1965* (1965).

Consorcio Pesquero del Perú, S. A. *Peruvian Fishmeal*. Lima, May 1965.

Corporación Nacional de Fertilizantes. *Boletín* No. 14 (January–April 1966). Lima, 1966.

————. *Memoria 1965*. Lima, 1966.

Elijalde Zea, Alfonso. *La Industria Pesquera*. Banco Central del Perú, Actividades Productivas del Perú, Vol. 5. Lima, 1966.

"El Exportador mas Grande del Mundo," *Pesca*, 2:9–11 (February 1961).

Food and Agriculture Organization. *Future Developments in the Production and Utilization of Fishmeal*. Rome, 1961.

Gordon, H. Scott. "The Economic Theory of a Common Property Resource: The Fishery," *Journal of Political Economy*, 62:124–142 (1954).

Hedges, John. "Drama of the Catch." *Andean Airmail and Peruvian Times*, Special Issue (October 28, 1963).

Instituto del Mar del Perú. *Efectos de la Pesca en el Stock de Anchoveta*, Informe No. 7. Callao, 1965.

————. *La Pesquería de la Anchoveta*, Informe No. 14. Callao, December 1966.

"Inversiones Extranjeras son Necesarios," *Pesca* 14:20–23 (May 1967).

Lora, Juan. *Crecimiento de la Flota Pesquera Industrial al 31 de Diciembre de 1963*. Instituto del Mar del Perú, Informe No. 2. Callao, 1965.

"El Magnate de la Pesca Peruana," *Pesca*, 1:23–26 (October 1960).

Max Neff, Manfred, et al. *Concentración del Poder Económico y Motivación Empresarial: El Caso del Sector Pesquero*. Lima: Universidad Nacional "Frederico Villarreal," 1965.

"Mito del Guano," *Mundo Pesquero*, 3:27–35 (August 1966).

Oficina Sectorial de Planificación Pesquera. "Estadistica Pesquera 1964 y 1965," mimeo. Lima, 1966.

"Perú Exportará Embarcaciones Pesqueras al Brazil," *Pesca*, 14:24 (January 1967).

Pesca. 12 (May 1966); 14 (February 1967) and 18 (February–May 1969).

Pesca Anuario 1965–66 (1966).

"Pescando en un Mar de Deudas," *Pesca*, 6:15–23 (June 1963).

"Qué es la FEO?" *Pesca*, 8:9–11 (June 1964).

"Requiem para los Astilleros," *Pesca*, 8:55–58 (January 1964).

Scott, Anthony D. "The Fishery: The Objectives of Sole Ownership," *Journal of Political Economy*, 63:116–124 (1955).

————. "Food and the World Fisheries Situation," in Marion Clawson, ed., *Natural Resources and International Development*. Washington: Resources for the Future, 1964.

"Se Construyen Bolicheras de Gran Capacidad," *Pesca*, 14:14–18 (April 1967).

Sharples del Pacífico, S. A. *Elaboración de Harina de Pescado para Alimento de Animales*. Lima, June 1965.

Sociedad Nacional de Pesquería. *La Crisis de Pesquería: Altos Costos*. Lima, February 1967.

————. *Harina de Pescado: Regimenes de Exportación*, Publicación No. 18. Lima, February 1967.

Tilic, Ivo. *Costos y Beneficios en la Industria de la Pesca Anchoveta.* Instituto de Investigación de los Recursos Marinos, Informe No. 21. Callao, 1963.

———. *Material Estadistico sobre la Industria Peruana de Harina de Pescado.* Instituto de Investigación de los Recursos Marinos, Informe No. 14. Callao, 1963.

Tolentino Alquilar, Elva. "Estudio de 600 Pescadores de Anchoveta en el Puerto de Chimbote," Ph.D. dissertation, Escuela de Servicio Social del Perú, 1964. Part published as "Complejo Socio-Económico del Pescador," *Pesca,* 12:18–26 (June 1966).

Turvey, Ralph. "Optimization and Suboptimization in Fishery Regulation," *American Economic Review,* 54:64–78 (1964).

Uriarte, Carlos. "La Evolución de la Industria Pesquera en el Perú," *Pesca,* 1:10–11 (October 1960).

"1,104 Milliones, a la Carga de Proveedores," *Pesca,* 11:12–16 (December 1965).

"1200 Barcos Nuevos," *Pesca,* 6:26–46 (April 1963).

"1960, El Año de la Salvación," *Pesca,* 2:7–9 (January 1961).

Index

Africa, 7, 17, 134

Agriculture, 41, 43; plantation, 7, 43; Canadian prairie, 11–12; Danish, 16; subsistence, 43–44; Peruvian, 43–44, 58; major commodities in world trade, 60

Allen, G. R., 63, 64

Aluminum, 26

Amazon basin, 41

Anchovy, 1–2, 31, 46, 137; fishing and fish reduction processes, 60–73, 82, 83, exploitation of, 66–69, 87, 89

Andes, 41

Angola, 75

Apprenticeship system, 144

Argentina, 3

Asia, 21; Southeast, 170

Australia, 3

Automobile assembly plants, 146

Backhaul, 8, 16

Backward linkages, 108–128; input-output table, 108–110; supply industries, 110–111; shipyards, 111–116; netting, 116–117; plants and equipment, 117–120; paper and jute sacks, 120–122; nature of the stimulus, 122–123; competiveness of suppliers, 123–126; macroeconomic assessment, 126–128

Bacon, 15–16

Baldwin, Robert E., 6, 7, 13, 17, 18, 31, 32, 131, 134, 161

Bananas, 60, 171

Banchero Rossi, Luis, 74, 83, 86

Banks, *see* Financial institutions

Bardhan, Pranab K., 20

Bertram, Gordon W., 23

Bhagwati, Jagdish, 20

Bolicheras, 80, 94, 122, 129, 145; described, 66–68; fleets of anchovy producers, 73; and Peruvian boat-building boom, 86–87; gross investment in, 111–114; crews of, 146. *See also* Fishing boats

Bonita (tuna), 81–82

Britain, 15, 29; trade, 25–26

Brown, Wilson, 48

Bruton, Henry, 37

California, 82

Callao, 2, 71, 72, 145, 167; incomes, 132; import traffic, 135; fishmeal labor, 147

Canada, 6, 9–13, 16, 22, 24, 89; production function of wheat, 9–12; railroad mileage, 9–10; capacity for economy to transform itself, 10–11; character of inhabitants and social institutions, 11; applications of staple theory, 16

Canning, 77, 83, 89–90

Capital: factor of production, 20, 22, 30, 108; foreign, 31, 123, 152–155, 161; in fishmeal, 102, 107, 147–155; overhead, 108, 134–136; and the entrepreneur, 158–159; inflow, 160–161

Capital equipment, 2, 84

Capital intensity, 6, 16; of Peruvian industry, 97–98

Capital-intensive industries, 32, 59, 169; production, 16, 21; techniques, 37; mining, 48, 131